ICQ For Dum[...]

Communication Icons

Icon	You Have Been Sent...
	An invitation to engage in a chat
	A message from another ICQ member
	A Web page address
	A message from ICQ or a notice that someone wants to put your name on his or her Contact List
	A system announcement that someone has put your name on their Contact List
	An e-mail message from someone outside the ICQ network
	Names from someone's Contact List
	A request from someone to send you a file
	A recorded message or sound file
	A greeting card
	A request for your phone number
	A request for a game or chat on a telephony application
	A notice that e-mail has arrived for you at your Internet service provider

Making New Friends in ICQ

- ✔ **Chat Request page:** Find someone to chat with on the Chat Request page. You can also put out a request to chat with others. See Chapter 5.
- ✔ **Chat room:** Find and join a chat room. ICQ members can also create chat rooms of their own. See Chapter 5.
- ✔ **Interest group:** Find and join an interest group, a page on the ICQ Web site where the names of people who share common interests are listed. See Chapter 7.
- ✔ **Message Board:** Go to the Message Board, read messages, reply to messages, and post messages of your own for others to read and reply to. See Chapter 7.
- ✔ **Random chats:** Find someone at random who is plugged into ICQ and engage him or her in a chat. While you're at it, make yourself available for chats. See Chapter 2.
- ✔ **User list:** Find a user list, a list of ICQ members who share the same interests. User lists are not kept on the ICQ Web site, but are maintained by ICQ members on their Web sites. See Chapter 7.
- ✔ **White Pages:** Search for ICQ members who are interested in the same things you are interested in, live in your town, have the same occupation as you, or are affiliated with the same institutions you are. See Chapter 7.

...For Dummies®: Bestselling Book Series for Beginners

ICQ For Dummies®

BESTSELLING BOOK SERIES

Cheat Sheet

Searching the Internet from ICQ

- ✔ Enter a keyword in the Enter Search Keyword box (you'll find it in the middle of the ICQ window) and click the GO button.

- ✔ Click the Float/Minimize Web Search Panel button in the ICQ window to open the ICQ iT! toolbar. Then choose how to search and what to search for from the Search Group menu, choose a search engine from the Search Engine menu, enter keywords for the search, and click the GO! button.

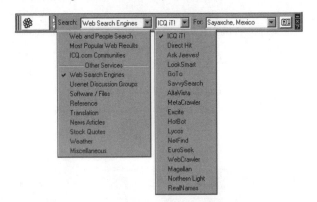

Changing Your Online Status

Status Menu Option	What It Tells Others
Available/Connect	You are available for chatting, receiving messages, and receiving other kinds of communications.
Free For Chat	You want to chat very much and you will accept requests to chat automatically.
Away	You are gone from your computer momentarily.
N/A (Extended Away)	You are gone from ICQ for an extended period of time.
Occupied (Urgent Msgs)	You are busy doing something else, but others can send you messages and mark them as Urgent so that you will be alerted when the urgent message arrives.
DND (Do not Disturb)	You do not want to be disturbed but you want others to know that you are online.
Privacy (Invisible)	You do not want others to know you are online. People who have added your name to their Contact Lists think that you are offline.
Offline/Disconnect	You want to disconnect from the ICQ network but retain your connection to the Internet.

...For Dummies®: Bestselling Book Series for Beginners

ICQ

FOR

DUMMIES®

by Peter Weverka
and
Michael Taylor

IDG Books Worldwide, Inc.
An International Data Group Company

Foster City, CA ◆ Chicago, IL ◆ Indianapolis, IN ◆ New York, NY

ICQ For Dummies®

Published by
IDG Books Worldwide, Inc.
An International Data Group Company
919 E. Hillsdale Blvd.
Suite 400
Foster City, CA 94404
www.idgbooks.com (IDG Books Worldwide Web site)
www.dummies.com (Dummies Press Web site)

Library of Congress Catalog Card No.: 99-64907

ISBN: 0-7645-0586-6

Printed in the United States of America

10 9 8 7 6 5 4 3 2 1

1B/RQ/QY/ZZ/IN

Distributed in the United States by IDG Books Worldwide, Inc.

Distributed by CDG Books Canada Inc. for Canada; by Transworld Publishers Limited in the United Kingdom; by IDG Norge Books for Norway; by IDG Sweden Books for Sweden; by IDG Books Australia Publishing Corporation Pty. Ltd. for Australia and New Zealand; by TransQuest Publishers Pte Ltd. for Singapore, Malaysia, Thailand, Indonesia, and Hong Kong; by Gotop Information Inc. for Taiwan; by ICG Muse, Inc. for Japan; by Norma Comunicaciones S.A. for Colombia; by Intersoft for South Africa; by Eyrolles for France; by International Thomson Publishing for Germany, Austria and Switzerland; by Distribuidora Cuspide for Argentina; by LR International for Brazil; by Galileo Libros for Chile; by Ediciones ZETA S.C.R. Ltda. for Peru; by WS Computer Publishing Corporation, Inc., for the Philippines; by Contemporanea de Ediciones for Venezuela; by Express Computer Distributors for the Caribbean and West Indies; by Micronesia Media Distributor, Inc. for Micronesia; by Grupo Editorial Norma S.A. for Guatemala; by Chips Computadoras S.A. de C.V. for Mexico; by Editorial Norma de Panama S.A. for Panama; by American Bookshops for Finland. Authorized Sales Agent: Anthony Rudkin Associates for the Middle East and North Africa.

For general information on IDG Books Worldwide's books in the U.S., please call our Consumer Customer Service department at 800-762-2974. For reseller information, including discounts and premium sales, please call our Reseller Customer Service department at 800-434-3422.

For information on where to purchase IDG Books Worldwide's books outside the U.S., please contact our International Sales department at 317-596-5530 or fax 317-596-5692.

For consumer information on foreign language translations, please contact our Customer Service department at 1-800-434-3422, fax 317-596-5692, or e-mail rights@idgbooks.com.

For information on licensing foreign or domestic rights, please phone +1-650-655-3109.

For sales inquiries and special prices for bulk quantities, please contact our Sales department at 650-655-3200 or write to the address above.

For information on using IDG Books Worldwide's books in the classroom or for ordering examination copies, please contact our Educational Sales department at 800-434-2086 or fax 317-596-5499.

For press review copies, author interviews, or other publicity information, please contact our Public Relations department at 650-655-3000 or fax 650-655-3299.

For authorization to photocopy items for corporate, personal, or educational use, please contact Copyright Clearance Center, 222 Rosewood Drive, Danvers, MA 01923, or fax 978-750-4470.

is a registered trademark or trademark under exclusive license to IDG Books Worldwide, Inc. from International Data Group, Inc. in the United States and/or other countries.

About the Authors

Peter Weverka is the best-selling author of several ...*For Dummies* books, including *Word 2000 For Dummies Quick Reference* and *Money 99 For Dummies*, as well as 15 other computer books. Before writing computer books, Peter edited them — he edited 80 books in all on topics ranging from the Internet to desktop publishing to word processing. His books have been translated into 16 languages and sold half a million copies. Peter's humorous articles and stories — none related to computers — have appeared in *Harper's, SPY,* and other magazines for grown-ups.

Michael Taylor, a computer consultant and ICQ member since 1997, is an expert on Internet messaging and interactive media. He has done extensive work with the messaging engines (that's the software that makes messages and chats fly across the Internet), including the Mirabilis engine, the one that makes ICQ chats and messages fly so quickly. Michael is one of those pioneer types who is helping make the Internet a communications medium, not just a way to trade e-mail gossip.

ABOUT IDG BOOKS WORLDWIDE

Welcome to the world of IDG Books Worldwide.

IDG Books Worldwide, Inc., is a subsidiary of International Data Group, the world's largest publisher of computer-related information and the leading global provider of information services on information technology. IDG was founded more than 30 years ago by Patrick J. McGovern and now employs more than 9,000 people worldwide. IDG publishes more than 290 computer publications in over 75 countries. More than 90 million people read one or more IDG publications each month.

Launched in 1990, IDG Books Worldwide is today the #1 publisher of best-selling computer books in the United States. We are proud to have received eight awards from the Computer Press Association in recognition of editorial excellence and three from Computer Currents' First Annual Readers' Choice Awards. Our best-selling *...For Dummies®* series has more than 50 million copies in print with translations in 31 languages. IDG Books Worldwide, through a joint venture with IDG's Hi-Tech Beijing, became the first U.S. publisher to publish a computer book in the People's Republic of China. In record time, IDG Books Worldwide has become the first choice for millions of readers around the world who want to learn how to better manage their businesses.

Our mission is simple: Every one of our books is designed to bring extra value and skill-building instructions to the reader. Our books are written by experts who understand and care about our readers. The knowledge base of our editorial staff comes from years of experience in publishing, education, and journalism — experience we use to produce books to carry us into the new millennium. In short, we care about books, so we attract the best people. We devote special attention to details such as audience, interior design, use of icons, and illustrations. And because we use an efficient process of authoring, editing, and desktop publishing our books electronically, we can spend more time ensuring superior content and less time on the technicalities of making books.

You can count on our commitment to deliver high-quality books at competitive prices on topics you want to read about. At IDG Books Worldwide, we continue in the IDG tradition of delivering quality for more than 30 years. You'll find no better book on a subject than one from IDG Books Worldwide.

John Kilcullen
Chairman and CEO
IDG Books Worldwide, Inc.

Steven Berkowitz
President and Publisher
IDG Books Worldwide, Inc.

Eighth Annual
Computer Press
Awards ≥ 1992

Ninth Annual
Computer Press
Awards ≥ 1993

Tenth Annual
Computer Press
Awards ≥ 1994

Eleventh Annual
Computer Press
Awards ≥ 1995

IDG is the world's leading IT media, research and exposition company. Founded in 1964, IDG had 1997 revenues of $2.05 billion and has more than 9,000 employees worldwide. IDG offers the widest range of media options that reach IT buyers in 75 countries representing 95% of worldwide IT spending. IDG's diverse product and services portfolio spans six key areas including print publishing, online publishing, expositions and conferences, market research, education and training, and global marketing services. More than 90 million people read one or more of IDG's 290 magazines and newspapers, including IDG's leading global brands — Computerworld, PC World, Network World, Macworld and the Channel World family of publications. IDG Books Worldwide is one of the fastest-growing computer book publishers in the world, with more than 700 titles in 36 languages. The "...For Dummies®" series alone has more than 50 million copies in print. IDG offers online users the largest network of technology-specific Web sites around the world through IDG.net (http://www.idg.net), which comprises more than 225 targeted Web sites in 55 countries worldwide. International Data Corporation (IDC) is the world's largest provider of information technology data, analysis and consulting, with research centers in over 41 countries and more than 400 research analysts worldwide. IDG World Expo is a leading producer of more than 168 globally branded conferences and expositions in 35 countries including E3 (Electronic Entertainment Expo), Macworld Expo, ComNet, Windows World Expo, ICE (Internet Commerce Expo), Agenda, DEMO, and Spotlight. IDG's training subsidiary, ExecuTrain, is the world's largest computer training company, with more than 230 locations worldwide and 785 training courses. IDG Marketing Services helps industry-leading IT companies build international brand recognition by developing global integrated marketing programs via IDG's print, online and exposition products worldwide. Further information about the company can be found at www.idg.com.   1/24/99

Dedications

To 12 Adler Place, *in vino veritas*.

— P.W.

To my beautiful wife Jeri, and my wonderful kids Joshua, Lucy, and Holden.

— M.W.T.

Authors' Acknowledgments

This book owes a lot to many hard-working people at IDG Books Worldwide, Inc. We would especially like to thank acquisitions editor Sherri Morningstar for giving us the opportunity to write this book and for suggesting how to make this book a better one. Sherri has always been a pleasure to work with, and we were kind of sad to learn that she now acquires programming books (!) instead of books like the one you are holding in your hands. We will miss Sherri.

Colleen Esterline wore two hats as she worked on our book. As copy editor, she wielded the editorial scalpel with great skill; as project editor, she made sure all manuscripts landed in the right place. We are very grateful to Colleen.

Technical editor Jimmi Johnson from the Creativity Center dogged our every step to make sure that all the instructions in this book are indeed correct, and we thank him for his work. We would also like to thank Sherry Massey for her index.

These people at the offices of IDG in Indianapolis also gave their all to this book, and we want to acknowledge all of them: Laura Carpenter, Mary Corder, Steve Hayes, Carmen Krikorian, Beth Parlon, Nancy Price, Megan Roney, Marianne Santy, Brent Savage, Jacque Schneider, Janet Seib, Rebecca Senninger, Regina Snyder, Rob Springer, Michael A. Sullivan, Suzanne Thomas, and Brian Torwelle.

We would also like to thank the many friends we made on the ICQ network for telling us why they like ICQ and how to get the most out of the program.

Finally, Peter would like to thank his family — Sofia, Henry, and Addie — for their forbearance while he wrote the book. Michael would like to thank his family for putting up with the late nights.

Publisher's Acknowledgments

We're proud of this book; please register your comments through our IDG Books Worldwide Online Registration Form located at http://my2cents.dummies.com.

Some of the people who helped bring this book to market include the following:

Acquisitions, Editorial, and Media Development

Project Editor: Colleen Williams Esterline

Acquisitions Editors: Steven Hayes, Sherri Morningstar

Technical Editor: Jimmi Johnson

Media Development Coordinator: Megan Roney

Associate Permissions Editor: Carmen Krikorian

Media Development Manager: Heather Heath Dismore

Editorial Assistant: Beth Parlon

Production

Project Coordinator: Regina Snyder

Layout and Graphics: Amy Adrian, Angela F. Hunckler, Theodore T. Sendak Jr., Dave McKelvey, Douglas L. Rollison, Brent Savage, Janet Seib, Jacque Schneider, Michael A. Sullivan, Brian Torwelle

Proofreaders: Joanne Keaton, Nancy Price, Nancy Reinhardt, Marianne Santy, Rebecca Senninger

indexer: Sherry Massey

Special Help
Suzanne Thomas

General and Administrative

IDG Books Worldwide, Inc.: John Kilcullen, CEO; Steven Berkowitz, President and Publisher

IDG Books Technology Publishing Group: Richard Swadley, Senior Vice President and Publisher; Walter Bruce III, Vice President and Associate Publisher; Steven Sayre, Associate Publisher; Joseph Wikert, Associate Publisher; Mary Bednarek, Branded Product Development Director; Mary Corder, Editorial Director

IDG Books Consumer Publishing Group: Roland Elgey, Senior Vice President and Publisher; Kathleen A. Welton, Vice President and Publisher; Kevin Thornton, Acquisitions Manager; Kristin A. Cocks, Editorial Director

IDG Books Internet Publishing Group: Brenda McLaughlin, Senior Vice President and Publisher; Diane Graves Steele, Vice President and Associate Publisher; Sofia Marchant, Online Marketing Manager

IDG Books Production for Dummies Press: Michael R. Britton, Vice President of Production; Debbie Stailey, Associate Director of Production; Cindy L. Phipps, Manager of Project Coordination, Production Proofreading, and Indexing; Shelley Lea, Supervisor of Graphics and Design; Debbie J. Gates, Production Systems Specialist; Robert Springer, Supervisor of Proofreading; Laura Carpenter, Production Control Manager; Tony Augsburger, Supervisor of Reprints and Bluelines

◆

The publisher would like to give special thanks to Patrick J. McGovern, without whom this book would not have been possible.

◆

Contents at a Glance

Cartoons at a Glance

By Rich Tennant

"QUICK KIDS! YOUR MOTHER'S FLAMING SOMEONE ON THE INTERNET!"

page 173

"Face it Vinnie— you're gonna have a hard time getting people to subscribe online with a credit card to a newsletter called 'Felons Interactive.'"

page 223

"He should be all right now. I made him spend two and a half hours on a prisoners' chat line."

page 283

Did I mention there's a balloon folding chat line on ICQ?

page 49

"Mona, this is no way to deal with your chat-line addiction."

page 311

IT WAS ACTUALLY ON THE WEB ONE NIGHT THAT CAPT. AHAB CAUGHT UP WITH HIS OBSESSION.

WHALE CHAT
White? Really? Where can we meet?

page 5

Fax: 978-546-7747 • E-mail: the5wave@tiac.net

Table of Contents

Introduction

*I*CQ is gigantic. You'll soon discover that if you spend any time in ICQ. Click a menu command and ICQ might hurl you to a far corner of its Website. Click a hyperlink and suddenly you find yourself at the Message Board or some other tantalizing place you didn't know about. Wherever you go in ICQ, intriguing possibilities await. How can you take advantage of all the superb features that ICQ has to offer?

This book is your guide to getting the most out of ICQ. When you get lost in the ICQ maze, when you want to try something you're unsure of, when you tell yourself *there has to be a better way,* open this book, and we'll tell you what it is and how to do it.

Everybody uses ICQ to chat and exchange messages. We'll show you how to do the conventional stuff. And we'll also tell you about the 101 other ICQ features. For example, we'll show you how to find people in the ICQ community who share your interests, exchange files and other items with ICQ members, and search the Internet from ICQ. We'll show you how to maintain your privacy and still reach into every corner of ICQ.

This book takes you on the grand tour of ICQ. More importantly, it explains how you can take advantage of every amenity that ICQ has to offer.

About This Book

This book is for everybody who wants to get the most out of ICQ. It is for everybody who has ever stumbled onto foreign ground in ICQ and been intrigued by what they found.

ICQ is an adventure. You never know what you'll find, and getting lost is easy. This book is for ICQ adventurers. It demonstrates how to get there, what to do when you get there, and how to use ICQ features to the hilt.

How This Book Is Organized

To find what you're looking for in this book, your best bet is to go to the index and table of contents. Other than that, we've organized this book into six parts, and you're invited to browse in one part or another until you find what you are looking for. Here is a bare-bones outline of what you'll find in the six parts of this book:

- **Part I: Getting Started with ICQ:** Finding your way around the ICQ program, downloading ICQ from the Internet, registering with ICQ, random chatting, and handling the ICQ window.

- **Part II: Making Friends in the ICQ Community:** Engaging in chats, locating chat rooms, adding names to and managing the Contact List, sending all manner of stuff — files, messages, and more — across ICQ, finding like-minded people, and publicizing yourself.

- **Part III: ICQ and the Internet:** Sending and receiving Web page addresses, surfing the Internet with ICQ iT!, creating an ICQ homepage, and navigating the PeopleSpace directory.

- **Part IV: Getting More out of ICQ:** Customizing ICQ, maintaining your privacy and security, managing the Message Archive, and using telephony applications to video-conference with ICQ.

- **Part V: The Parts of Tens:** Ten cool things to do in ICQ, ten tips for searching the Internet, ten techniques for maintaining your privacy, and ten common ICQ hoaxes.

- **Part VI: Appendixes:** At the end of this book are instructions for getting help with ICQ and backing up your Contact List and bookmarks. And you will also find a chat acronym dictionary, smiley lookup reference, and glossary of ICQ terms.

Foolish Assumptions

Excuse us, reader, but we made one or two assumptions about you. Hope you don't mind. We assumed that

- You have an account with an Internet service provider (ISP). Sure, you can chat and send e-mail messages with ICQ, but ICQ doesn't take the place of an ISP. You need an account with an ISP to connect to the Internet and do all the things you want to do in ICQ.

- You have a browser software program. You need a browser such as Internet Explorer or Netscape Navigator to run ICQ. A browser is a program that connects to and displays Web pages on the computer screen.

✔ Your computer has about 10MB of free disk space. You need that space for the ICQ software.

✔ You look both ways before you cross the street.

A Word about Advanced and Simple Mode

As the start of Chapter 3 explains, ICQ offers two modes, Simple and Advanced. More commands and menus are available in Advanced mode. Rather than tell you time and time again to switch to Advanced mode, we assume throughout this book that you are working in Advanced mode. Not that getting there is very difficult — all you have to do is click the To Advanced Mode button in the middle of the ICQ window.

If we describe a command or menu selection in this book and you don't see it in the ICQ window, you are in Simple mode, not Advanced mode. Click the To Advanced Mode button to switch to Advanced mode and follow the instructions in this book.

Conventions Used in This Book

We want you to understand all the instructions in this book, and in that spirit we've adopted a few conventions.

Where we tell you to click a button, often a picture of the button appears in the left-hand margin. For example, the button you see here is the ICQ button. When we tell you to "click the ICQ button to open the pop-up menu," you see the ICQ button to the left so that you know exactly which button to click.

To show you how to give commands, we use the ➪ symbol. For example, you can click the ICQ button and choose Find/Add Users➪White Pages to search the ICQ membership directory. The ➪ is just a shorthand method of saying "Choose Find/Add Users and then choose White Pages from the submenu that appears."

Occasionally, characters in menu command names and option names in dialog boxes are underlined. Underlined letters are called *hot keys*. You can press hot keys to give commands and select options. Where a letter is underlined in a command name or in a dialog box, it is underlined in the step-by-step instructions in this book as well.

Where you see boldface letters in this book, it means to type the letters. For example, "Type **Let's make friends** in the text box" means to do exactly that: Type **Let's make friends**.

Icons Used in This Book

To help you get the most out of this book, we've placed icons here and there. Here's what the icons mean:

Next to the Tip icon, you can find tricks of the trade to make your visit to ICQ Land more enjoyable.

Where you see the Warning icon, tread softly and carefully. It means that you are about to do something you may regret later.

We are in favor of taking shortcuts. We take shortcuts whenever we can. When we describe a shortcut in ICQ, we mark it with the Shortcut icon.

When we explain a juicy little fact that needs remembering, we mark it with a Remember icon. When you see this icon, prick up your ears. You will find out something that you have to remember throughout your adventures in ICQ.

When we are forced to describe high-tech stuff, a Technical Stuff icon appears in the margin. Good news: Only a half-dozen Technical Stuff icons are found in this entire book (we don't like reading about technical stuff any more than you do).

Of course, there is a lot of cool stuff in ICQ. You knew that already. When we describe something that we think is especially cool, we mark it with the Cool Stuff icon.

Part I

Getting Started
with ICQ

The 5th Wave   By Rich Tennant

IT WAS ACTUALLY ON THE WEB ONE NIGHT THAT
CAPT. AHAB CAUGHT UP WITH HIS OBSESSION.

WHALE CHAT

White? Really?
Where can we
meet?

In this part . . .

Hello, this is your captain speaking. Thank you for flying ICQ. In the next three chapters, you can take off, soar above the clouds, discover what ICQ is, register with ICQ, and get going with the program.

Please observe the "Fasten your seat belts" sign. And if I ask you to hold your breath and flap your arms to help the plane stay aloft, please do so promptly.

Chapter 1

New Kid on the Block

. . . .

In This Chapter

▶ Seeing the ICQ "big picture"

▶ Finding your way around the ICQ window

. . . .

*I*CQ ("I Seek You") reflects the spirit of the people who made it and use it. It wasn't built from the top down like a commercial software program. When the makers of ICQ came up with a new idea for their program, they simply attached it. When enough members asked for a new feature, the makers of ICQ built it onto the software. Consequently, ICQ resembles one of those European castles that was built over the course of a century or two. You never know what you will find in the next room — and getting lost is easy.

This brief chapter is for people who are new to ICQ. Read on to find out how ICQ works and get the lay of the land. This chapter explains the major components of ICQ and describes all the things you can do with the program.

What Is "I Seek You" Anyway?

ICQ is a way for people to chat and send messages over the Internet — it is that and about a hundred other things. During the writing of this book, we interviewed about four-dozen ICQ members to find out how they use the program and what they like about it. We discovered a nationwide company that does all its e-mailing in ICQ. We found another firm that uses ICQ to conduct its weekly staff meetings. We found, believe it or not, a prayer group that meets on ICQ. And we found a lot of people who use ICQ for recreational purposes to meet and enjoy the company of others.

Besides being a way to communicate with others, ICQ is a way to meet people. You can go to chat rooms or write an invitation to chat on the Chat Request page (see Chapter 5). You can to go to the White Pages, user lists, interest groups, or the Message Board to find like-minded people (see Chapter 7). You can search by topic for people who share your interests in the PeopleSpace Directory (see Chapter 12).

Why is ICQ free?

Sooner or later, every ICQ member asks, "Why is ICQ free?" The program works well. It does so much. How can the thing be free when other Internet programs that don't work near as well (no names, please) charge so much?

That's a darn good question. And as Chapter 20 points out, it is also the subject of a lot of hand-wringing and message exchanging in ICQ.

ICQ, Inc., the company that owns and manages ICQ (America Online is the parent company),

states that it has no intention of charging for the program. We suspect, however, that banner ads will someday appear on the ICQ homepage and perhaps on other pages. What's more, we suspect that the ICQ iT! Website (www.icqit.com), the starting point for searching the Internet with the ICQ search engine, will also present banner ads and other money-making clutter.

This latest edition of ICQ also lets you search the Internet directly from the ICQ window (see Chapter 10) and create a homepage, a sort of mini-Web page that others can visit while you are online (see Chapter 11).

Whether you are online or not, anybody, ICQ members and nonmembers alike, can go to your Personal Communications Center and drop you a note (see Chapter 9). The Personal Communications Center is a page on the Internet. Every ICQ member gets one. When you register with ICQ, you also get the much-coveted "Web presence" that everybody is supposed to have these days.

ICQ keeps a record of all the communications you exchange with others — chats, files, messages, Web page addresses, photos, voice recordings, and more — in the Message Archive (see Chapter 15). You can dig into the Message Archive to find artifacts of your past. You can also use the Message Archive to write reminder notes to yourself.

ICQ also offers special features for video-conferencing and game playing (see Chapter 16). By means of ICQ, you can find and engage others in conferences or games.

However, ICQ was and always will be chiefly a way of sending stuff over the Internet. What kind of stuff? Chats, messages, e-mail messages, files, photos, voice messages, phone numbers, and Web page addresses (see Chapters 4, 5, 8, 9, and 10).

A Quick Geography Lesson

ICQ can be a bit overwhelming at first, especially if you try to acquaint your-self with the program by visiting the ICQ homepage shown in Figure 1-1. The ICQ homepage is surely the most complicated Web page ever devised by man or beast. The number of hyperlinks per square inch (the hps ratio, a term we just devised but you're free to use) is nothing short of phenomenal. People have been known to disappear in the ICQ homepage and never be heard from again.

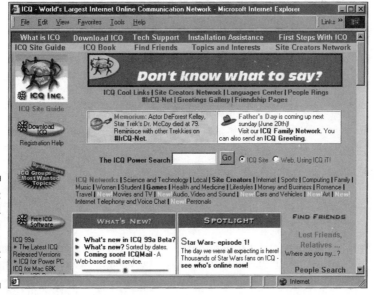

Figure 1-1:
The ICQ homepage — it's a jungle out there!

In fact, we've heard stories of people trying to use ICQ from the homepage and giving up on the program. Make sure you don't become one of those people! And to make sure you don't become one, always use ICQ by way of the ICQ window shown in Figure 1-2.

Sure, you can click hyperlinks on the homepage to use ICQ, but you need a prodigious memory to remember what all the hyperlinks are and where they take you. The better way is to click buttons and choose menu options on the ICQ window.

For the purposes of this book, we ignore the ICQ homepage. All the directions we give start from the ICQ window. We just think it's far easier to get from place to place from the ICQ window than it is to get from place to place by clicking homepage hyperlinks. What's more, you can go everywhere you need to go in ICQ by starting in the ICQ window.

Contact List

Click a name and choose
a command to communicate
with someone.

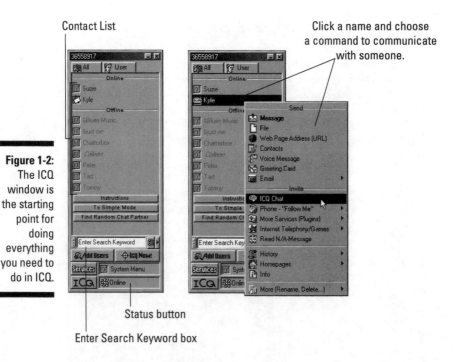

Figure 1-2:
The ICQ
window is
the starting
point for
doing
everything
you need to
do in ICQ.

Status button

Enter Search Keyword box

The Status button

At the bottom of the ICQ window are buttons for doing this, that, and the
other thing. When and why to click the buttons is explained throughout this
book. For now, we want you to commit one button to memory — the Status
button. As Figure 1-2 shows, the Status button is the button in the lower-right
corner of the ICQ window. We want you to commit it to memory because,
unlike the other buttons, it changes names depending on which Status option
you choose from the Status menu, the pop-up menu that appears when you
click the Status button.

The Contact List

In the middle of the ICQ window is the Contact List (if you just started with
ICQ, you don't have a list yet). Names of friends you made in ICQ are kept on
the Contact List. By clicking a name on the list and choosing an option from
the pop-up menu, you can engage someone in a chat or do any number of
things (refer to Figure 1-2). Chapter 6 explains how to put names on the list
and manage the list.

The Enter Search Keyword box

Near the bottom of the ICQ window is the Enter Search Keyword box. All you have to do to search the Internet is enter a keyword in the box and click the GO button. Chapter 10 explains how to search the Internet starting from the ICQ window.

Lower-right corner of the screen

Besides the ICQ window, ICQ appropriates one more part of the screen — the lower-right corner. When you are online and connected to ICQ (see Chapter 3), a green flower appears in the lower-right corner. What's more, different icons appear there as different kinds of communications arrive. For example, you can tell when someone wants to chat with you because the Chat icon starts flashing in the lower-right corner of the screen where the flower button normally is. Double-click the Chat icon to open the Incoming Chat Request dialog box and see who wants to talk.

A Word about Your Privacy

The subject of how to maintain your privacy and still be an active member of the ICQ community is taken up in Chapters 14 and 19. However, maintaining your privacy is important, so we think you should know one or two things about it before you register with ICQ.

First, the information you give out when you register is made public instantly. Anyone can go to the White Pages (see Chapter 7) and "read all about you," as newspaper vendors say. Therefore, you should be careful from the start what you say about yourself when you register. We don't recommend giving phone numbers and home addresses, for example, to ICQ when you register.

Chapter 2

Registering Yourself with ICQ

● ●

In This Chapter

▶ Obtaining the ICQ software

▶ Registering to chat on ICQ

▶ Registering an alter ego

▶ Searching at random for a chat partner

▶ Making yourself available for random chats

▶ Unregistering from ICQ

● ●

*T*his chapter explains how to take your first steps in ICQ. Come to think of it, you take a giant leap in this chapter. Here you find out how to get up and running in ICQ and how to begin chatting with someone else.

It goes without saying, but you have to download the ICQ software and register with ICQ before you can start gabbing. This chapter explains how to obtain the ICQ software and how to register. In case you want to register under more than one name or register on your home computer and your office computer, this chapter explains how to register more than once. You will also find instructions for "unregistering" on the chance that ICQ isn't your cup of tea after all.

Loading the ICQ Software onto Your Computer

If you search for ICQ software at the local computer store, you will search in vain because the only way to obtain the ICQ software is to go online. ICQ's Website at www.icq.com offers the software for free. To obtain the software, you visit the ICQ Website, click a couple of buttons, and twiddle your thumbs while the software is copied from the ICQ Website to your computer. After you load the software, you can register and begin chatting.

By the way, ICQ isn't an Internet service provider (ISP). In order to run ICQ, you must have set up an account with an ISP such as America Online or EarthLink. ICQ offers many services that ISPs also offer — you can send and receive e-mail messages and files, for example — but you must have signed up with an ISP before you can run ICQ.

Loading the software and registering with ICQ takes about 20 to 30 minutes, depending on the speed of your Internet connection. You need about 10MB of free disk space to load the software. Follow these steps to go online, obtain the ICQ software, and copy it to your computer:

1. **Close all programs (except your Web browser), if any are running.**

2. **Start your Web browser if you have not already done so.**

   In case you didn't know already, a *browser* is a computer program that reads and displays Web pages.

3. **Go to the following Website address:** `www.icq.com`.

   To go to a Website address, type the address in the Address bar of your Web browser and press the Enter key.

   When you arrive at `www.icq.com`, the ICQ homepage, look for a hyperlink that says "Download ICQ."

4. **Click the Download ICQ hyperlink.**

   Soon you arrive at a Web page with instructions for downloading the ICQ software to your computer. ICQ offers programs designed for Windows, the Macintosh, and other platforms. Look for a link that describes the ICQ program that will work on your computer.

5. **Click the appropriate hyperlink to start downloading the ICQ software.**

   You go to another Web page with instructions and notices about down-loading the software. Read them carefully.

6. **Click the Download hyperlink.**

   You might have a little trouble finding the hyperlink. But keep looking — it's there. In a moment, you see the File Download dialog box.

7. **Make sure the <u>S</u>ave This Program to Disk option button in the File Download dialog box is selected, and then click OK.**

8. **In the Save As dialog box, choose a folder for storing the ICQ file you're about to download, and then click the <u>S</u>ave button.**

   To choose a folder, click the down arrow to open the Save In drop-down menu (you will find it near the top of the dialog box), choose (C:) from the drop-down menu, and then double-click folders until you arrive at the one in which you want to store the ICQ file. Later, you have to go to the folder you select, so choose carefully. Choose a folder whose name you will remember later.

Downloading can take some time, depending on the speed of your Internet connection. The ICQ file is approximately 4MB in size.

9. **Click OK in the Download Complete dialog box when the file has finished downloading.**

10. **Close your Web browser, but don't disconnect from the Internet. (If a dialog box asks if you want to disconnect, click the No button).**

You can't register unless you're still connected to the Internet. Make sure you're still connected to the Internet before you complete the following steps. If you're connected by a modem and you're in Windows, you can tell if you're still connected by looking for the Internet net icon — two tiny computer monitors — in the lower-right corner of the screen next to the clock.

11. **Open Windows Explorer or My Computer and find the file you just downloaded. The file is called icq99a.exe.**

If you can't find the file, click the Start button and choose Find⇨Files or Folders. Then, in the Find dialog box, enter **icq99a.exe** and click the Find Now button. The Find dialog box tells you where the file is located.

12. **Double-click the icon to the left of the icq99a.exe file.**

By double-clicking, you activate the file and start to load ICQ on your computer.

13. **Read the notice, click the Continue button, read the User Agreement, and click the I Agree button.**

14. **Click the Next button in the Welcome screen.**

15. **In the Select Destination Directory dialog box, click Next to store the ICQ program in the C:\Program Files folder on your computer.**

16. **Click the Next button to put the ICQ program on the Windows Start menu.**

This dialog box wants to know if you want to start ICQ by clicking the Start button on the Taskbar.

17. **Click Next in the following dialog box to put the ICQ menu commands in the ICQ program group.**

This way, you can start ICQ by clicking the Start button and then clicking Programs on the Start menu.

18. **In the following dialog box, which concerns languages, make sure the second option button, I'm Using an English Operating System, is selected, and then click the Next button.**

Wait while the program files are copied to your computer. Eventually, you see the first ICQ Registration Wizard dialog box, which asks whether you're a new user. Read on to find out how to register with ICQ. And make sure that your connection to the Internet is still going strong. You can't register unless you're still connected to the Internet.

Registering the First Time

After you download the ICQ software from the Website to your computer, your next step is to register. By registering, you enter your name and your particulars on the ICQ computers. In other words, you join the ICQ cult — er, the ICQ community. Only community members can chat with one another and invite others to chat.

Follow these steps to register with ICQ for the first time:

1. **In the Registration Wizard dialog box, click the New ICQ radio button and then click Next.**

2. **Under Connection Type in the following dialog box, click the second radio button, Modem User, and then click Next.**

   I don't give instructions to local area network (LAN) users for registering with ICQ. If your computer is connected to a LAN, click the LAN User option button and promptly seek the assistance of the network administrator. Network administrators get paid to help with tasks such as the one you are undertaking. Crack the whip and ask the network administrator to help you with that proxy and firewall business if you're connecting to the Internet through a network.

3. **In the second Registration Wizard dialog box, shown in Figure 2-1, enter a nickname, your name, your last name, and your e-mail address. Click the Don't Publish My Email Address check box if you want to keep other ICQ members from knowing how to reach you by e-mail. Click Next to go to the following dialog box.**

   The information you enter in the second dialog box will be known to other ICQ members. The most important piece of information you enter here is a nickname. That is the name you will be known by on ICQ.

Figure 2-1:
List your nickname and name. Other ICQ members will know you by the names you enter here.

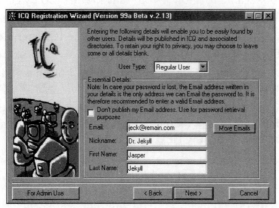

You can enter as much or as little information as you please. Leave all the boxes blank if you want, but remember that describing yourself thoroughly helps other ICQ members whose interests and backgrounds are similar to yours find you.

Be sure to enter an e-mail address, whether you want it to be public knowledge or not. As long as you list an e-mail address, you can recover your password if you lose it. Clicking the Don't Publish My Email Address check box keeps your e-mail address from being made public to ICQ members. You can also click the More Emails button to list more than one e-mail address.

4. **In the next Registration Wizard dialog box, shown at the top of Figure 2-2, describe yourself by clicking buttons and entering information about yourself in the dialog boxes that appear. Click the Next button when you're done.**

Figure 2-2: The information you enter in the Registration Wizard dialog box (top) is entered in the White Pages (bottom) and will help like-minded ICQ members find and engage you in chats.

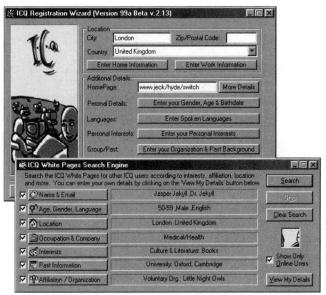

The information you enter in the dialog box will be entered in the White Pages, a directory that ICQ members can search to find people who share their interests (refer to Figure 2-2). Chapter 7 explains how to search the White Pages for kindred souls. For now, you need to know that the information you enter will help others find you and that you can always go back and change the information you enter, as explained in "Because, like, people change: Seeing and changing your description," the next sidebar in this chapter.

All information you enter in the Registration Wizard dialog box will be made available to ICQ members. We suggest not entering your telephone number or street address. You can always give this information to others after you get to know them. In fact, as Chapter 9 explains, ICQ offers a special command for sending your telephone number to someone else.

5. **Fill in the next dialog box, which asks a question about your occupation and where you use ICQ, and click Next.**

   As the dialog box says, the information you enter will help "improve the ICQ experience." By that, ICQ means that the information you enter will help ICQ tailor the program to meet your needs.

6. **Enter and confirm your password, choose a privacy level, and click a check box to say whether you want others to know when you go online; then click OK.**

   This dialog box comes in three parts:

   - **Password Protection:** Everyone must enter a password, actually enter it twice: once in the Password and once in the Confirm Password text box. If you uncheck the Auto Save Password check box, you have to enter your password whenever you connect to ICQ. Uncheck the Auto Save Password check box if you share your computer with others and you want to prevent them from chatting with your ICQ account (Chapter 14 explains passwords in detail).

     Write down your password in a secret place where no one will find or recognize it. Even if you "Auto Save" your password, you need it if you decide to unregister ICQ. (As long as you know your ICQ number and you submit your e-mail address when you register, which you had the opportunity to do in Step 3, you can get your password back if you forget it by going to the Web address. From there, you can submit a request for your password.)

   - **Privacy Level:** The Privacy Level options are for deciding whether others need permission to put your name on their Contact Lists. As Chapter 6 explains, you can put the names of people you want to chat with on the Contact List. The list, which appears prominently in the ICQ window, tells you who is and who isn't online. When someone on your Contact List is online, you know right away and you can invite them for a chat.

     If you select the My Authorization Is Required radio button, others need your permission to put your name on their Contact Lists. In effect, choosing My Authorization Is Required tells ICQ that you want to decide who does and doesn't know when you're online (Chapter 6 explains the Contact List in detail).

   - **Other Options:** Don't bother checking either of these check boxes. The first has to do with letting others know whether you're online. As Chapter 3 explains, you can go online without other ICQ members knowing it by choosing "Invisible" status. However, if you check the first check box, anyone who finds you in the White Pages or your Personal Communications Center will know you're online even if you want to be invisible. Likewise, a visitor to your homepage will know whether you're online even if you choose to be invisible.

The second check box tells ICQ not to let others know your IP address. You may as well check the Do Not Publish IP Address check box. As Chapter 14 points out, keeping others from knowing your IP address helps prevent your computer from being hacked.

7. **Write down your ICQ number and click the Next button.**

   The next dialog box lists your ICQ number. Write it down beside your password. Come to think of it, write down your password backward so that only you can read it. At last count, 30 million people had registered to use ICQ. No doubt one of them at least shares your nickname, even if it's Ragtop or Geekman. However, nobody else has your ICQ number. You can use it to identify yourself to other ICQ members.

8. **For now, click the Next button in the dialog box that asks for your outgoing e-mail server.**

   By entering a mail transfer protocol in this dialog box, you can be alerted when mail arrives at your private e-mail account. However, this subject is taken up again in Chapter 8. Don't worry about it for now.

9. **Click the Done button.**

   You're done — and not a moment too soon. Congratulations! You're a registered member of the ICQ community.

The ICQ window appears on your desktop. Notice the number that ICQ assigned you at the top of the window.

By the way, you can register yourself more than once with ICQ. Not that we're encouraging you to take on multiple personalities, but ICQ does permit Dr. Jekyll, for example, to also register under the name Hyde. The next section in this chapter explains how to register a second time and how to register your ICQ membership on a second computer. If you're anxious to start chatting, skip ahead to "Finding, or Being, a Random Chat Partner." That section explains the easiest way to find someone to gab with.

Because, like, people change: Seeing and changing your description

"Hey, people change," as they used to say in California in the 1970s. In that much-maligned but thoroughly enjoyable decade (at least in our opinion), you could show up, for example, at the dentist's office to discover that your staid, conservative dentist had adopted disco garb, died his hair blond, and frozen his hair into a perm. In today's more timid times, the freedom to completely overhaul yourself is only found online. What happens if your interests or affiliations change? For that matter, suppose you change addresses? How do you update your personal information in the ICQ White Pages?

To see or change your description, including your name and nickname, follow these steps:

1. **Click the ICQ button in the ICQ window. You will find this button in the lower-left corner of the window.**

2. **Choose Add/Change Current UserÍView/ Change My Details.**

   You see the ICQ Global Directory dialog box. On the nine tabs in this dialog box is the most up-to-date information on ICQ's computers — information about you.

3. **Visit each tab and describe yourself anew.**

4. **Click the Save button.**

5. **Click the Done button.**

By the way, clicking the Retrieve button in the ICQ Global Directory dialog box fetches information from ICQ's computers and puts that information in the dialog box. Click the Retrieve button if you try to describe yourself, make a hash of the job, and want to start all over with the information that ICQ has on file.

Registering More than Once with ICQ

Two people who share the same computer can each register with ICQ. Each
person can have his or her own ICQ membership and membership number.
And if you want to chat on ICQ at work or take the program on the road, you
can register your membership on your office computer or laptop computer.
In other words, you can register your membership in ICQ on a second computer and be able to chat from there as well.

Read on to find out how to register a second person or personality and how
to register so that you can chat on ICQ from more than one computer.

Registering your alter ego

ICQ permits more than one person to register from the same computer. For
example, three members of the same family who share a computer can each
register as ICQ members. We suspect, however, that most people register a
second time not to register a second person, but to register a second personality. The Internet is a masquerade. Shy Walter Mitty turns into the second
coming of Napoleon when he enters a chat room. Dr. Jekyll registers with ICQ
as Mr. Hyde.

Whatever your reason for registering from the same computer under a
second name, follow these steps to do so:

1. **Click the ICQ button in the ICQ window.**

2. **On the pop-up menu, choose Add/Change Current User⇨Register A
   New User (ICQ#).**

   A message box advises you that the same person should not register
   under more than one ICQ number. Why? Because others won't know
   which number to contact when they want to chat or send messages.
   Hmmmm. The fact is others will think you're someone else entirely.

3. **Click OK in the message box.**

   You see the first Registration Wizard dialog box. Does this dialog box
   look familiar? It ought to because this is the same dialog box you saw
   the first time you registered. To register, keep filling in the dialog boxes
   and clicking the Next button. If you need a little handholding, turn back
   a few pages to the previous section in this chapter and start reading at
   Step 2 under "Registering the First Time."

Switching from one alter ego to another

If you registered under more than one name, or if more than one person who shares your computer is registered with ICQ, you have to know how to tell ICQ which name to go online with. When you start ICQ, you enter under the name of the person who was online last time around. Follow these steps to step into a phone booth and switch, for example, from Clark Kent to Superman:

1. **Click the ICQ button.**

2. **Choose Add/Change Current User.**

   You see a submenu with three sets of options, as shown in Figure 2-3.

Figure 2-3:
Going online
under a
different
name.

3. **Under My Computer, choose Change the Active User.**

4. **Select the name of the person whose name you want to go online with.**

   A checkmark appears beside the name of the person who is online at present.

5. **Click Yes in the Confirm Change User (ICQ#) message box.**

Registering on a second computer

Feeling muzzled because ICQ is loaded on your home computer and you can't chat at the office or on the road? You needn't feel muzzled, because you can register on a second or third computer as well.

To register on a second computer, you download the ICQ software to the second computer (see "Loading the ICQ Software onto Your Computer" at the start of this chapter) and then re-register under the same name and number you are currently registered under. To register on a second computer, you need to know your ICQ number and password.

Follow these steps to re-register on a second computer:

1. **Click the ICQ button in the ICQ window.**

2. **Choose Add/Change Current User⇨Add Another Registered User.**

   You see the first Registration Wizard dialog box.

3. **Choose the <u>M</u>odem User or <u>L</u>AN User option, depending on how you are connected to the Internet, and then click Next.**

   Most likely, <u>M</u>odem User is the right choice, but if you're connected to the Internet through a network, select <u>L</u>AN User and get the help of the network administrator to register with ICQ.

4. **In the next dialog box, describe your work situation and where you use ICQ by making choices from the drop-down menus, and then click the Next button.**

5. **Enter your ICQ number and password in the next dialog box, as shown in Figure 2-4, and then click the Next button.**

   Uncheck the <u>S</u>ave Password dialog box if you share your computer with others and you want to keep them from using ICQ with your membership. If the password isn't saved, you have to enter the password whenever you connect to ICQ. Chapter 14 describes passwords in detail.

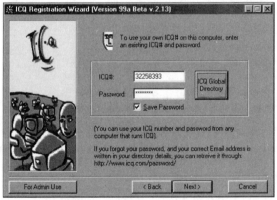

Figure 2-4:
You have to know your ICQ number and password to register on a second machine.

6. **Click the Next button when the dialog box tells you that you have been successfully re-registered.**

   If all goes as planned, the ICQ number listed in the dialog box is identical to the one you entered in Step 5.

7. **Click the Next button in the dialog box that asks for your outgoing e-mail server.**

   Chapter 8 explains how you can configure ICQ to alert you when you receive e-mail messages at your ISP mailbox. You needn't bother with that complex subject right now.

8. **Click the Done button in the final dialog box.**

Finding, or Being, a Random Chat Partner

Throughout this book we describe numerous ways to find and chat with ICQ members whose interests are similar to yours. One of the fastest ways to find someone to chat with, however, is to look at random. In the middle of the ICQ window is the Find Random Chat Partner button. Click the button to run a random search for others who are online and are eager to chat with strangers.

Well, the search doesn't have to be made entirely at random. You can lay down a few rules concerning who you want to chat with and what topics you want to discuss. While you're at it, you can also make yourself available to others who are looking for someone to chat with. Better keep reading.

Looking at random for a chat

Follow these steps to look at random for someone to chat with:

1. **Click the Find Random Chat Part Partner button in the ICQ window.**

   The Random dialog box appears, as shown in Figure 2-5. In the figure, a chat partner has been found, and information about the chatter appears in the dialog box (the next few steps show how to find a chat partner).

2. **From the Group drop-down list, choose a subject for a chat or an age group.**

   When others make themselves available for random chatting, they can choose a subject or pick an age group to chat with (the next section in this chapter explains how). By choosing an option from the Group list, you target random chatters who have described themselves a certain way or proudly declared which age category they belong to.

Figure 2-5:
Click the
Find a
Random
Chat Partner
button to
search for
someone to
chat with.

3. **Click the Find a Random Chat Partner button.**

   Soon, with any luck, the name of a prospective chatter appears. As shown in Figure 2-5, the chatter's age and other information sometimes appears as well in the Random dialog box. How much information appears depends on how thoroughly the chatter filled out the Details tab of the Random dialog box (refer to the next section in this chapter).

4. **Click either the Request Chat button to invite the other party for a chat or the Send Message button to send the other party a message.**

   Sorry to send you scurrying to another place in this book, but Chapter 4 explains how to start chatting with someone and Chapter 8 describes how to send someone a message. Why not click the Request Chat button and wing it? Chatting is easier than you think.

Making yourself available for random chats

The flip side of searching at random for someone to chat with is offering yourself for random chats. Go ahead; give it a try. You never know who will come knocking at your door. Follow these steps to make yourself available for chats and describe yourself to prospective chatters:

1. **Click the Find Random Chat Partner button in the ICQ window.**

   You see the Finding tab of the Random dialog box (refer to Figure 2-5).

2. **Click the Details tab.**

   As shown in Figure 2-6, the Details tab offers a chance for you to present yourself to others. When your name comes up in a random search, others see the information you enter on the Details tab. To see how the information entered on the Details tab compares to what others see when a name comes up in a random search, compare Figure 2-5 to Figure 2-6.

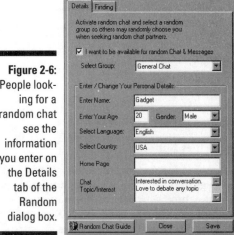

Figure 2-6: People looking for a random chat see the information you enter on the Details tab of the Random dialog box.

3. **Click the I Want to Be Available for Random Chat & Messages check box.**

4. **In the Select Group drop-down menu, choose an age category or subject if you want to be sought out by others searching in the category or subject you chose.**

   People in search of random chatters can select these categories. By choosing a Group option, you make yourself available to people searching for a particular group.

5. **Describe yourself by entering information in the Details tab.**

   The information that appears on the Details tab comes from the White Pages and is very likely accurate. You entered this information on ICQ's computers when you registered or updated the information in the Global Directory.

   However, you can enter new information on the Details tab to make yourself more presentable. In fact, you can make yourself into an entirely new person. Whatever you enter in the Details tab appears on the Finding tab when someone finds you in a random search (refer to Figure 2-5). You can exaggerate all you want on the Details tab, but a

---

Getting the scoop on a random chatter

The information you see on the Finding tab isn't necessarily accurate, but you can find out more about someone who wants to chat with you by clicking the chatter's name in the ICQ window and choosing Info from the pop-up menu. Choosing Info brings up a dialog box called User Info On. Click the various tabs in the dialog box to investigate the chatter. The information in the User Info On dialog box comes straight from the White Pages, the dossier that ICQ keeps on all members. Therefore, the information in the User Info On dialog box is more accurate than what you see on the Finding tab of the Random dialog box (refer to Figure 2-5).

---

savvy ICQ member can always get the goods on you by clicking your name in the ICQ window and choosing Info. See the sidebar "Getting the scoop on a random chatter."

Enter the subjects you want to discuss in the Chat Topic/Interest box. For that matter, if a subject is taboo, say as much. That way, you won't be bothered by people who want to discuss matters you don't want to discuss.

6. **Click the Save button if you entered new information about yourself on the Details tab.**

7. **Click the Close button.**

By the way, you can't make yourself available for random chats unless your online status is Available. Click the Status button in the lower-right corner of the ICQ window and choose Available/Connect to offer yourself to random chatters.

You know you've received a chat request when a bubble caption appears on the ICQ window beside the name of the person who wants to chat. A message icon appears if someone has found you in a random search and sent a message. Click the bubble caption or message icon in the ICQ window and choose Receive from the pop-up menu to reply to a chat request or message. Chapter 4 explains chatting; Chapter 8 describes receiving and sending messages.

Unregistering Your Membership in ICQ

Suppose you decide to withdraw your membership from ICQ? For that matter, suppose you registered a second time under a different name and now you want to withdraw your second name? Unregister when you want to quit ICQ, quit using one of the names you registered under, or stop using ICQ on a second machine such as a laptop or office computer. The next few sections tell you how to go about all this.

Unregistering a membership in ICQ

Follow these steps to unregister a membership in ICQ and expunge it forever:

1. **Click the ICQ button at the bottom of the ICQ window.**

2. **Choose Add/Change Current User➪Unregister Existing User.**

   You see the Unregister Existing User dialog box, shown on the left side of Figure 2-7.

Figure 2-7:
Unregis-
tering once
and for all
from ICQ.

3. **If necessary, open the ICQ# drop-down menu and choose the name of the person you want to unregister, if you are registered under more than one name.**

4. **Enter your password in the Password text box and click the Next button.**

   If you've forgotten your password, you can go to the www.icq.com/password Website and ask ICQ to send it to you.

5. **In the second Unregister Existing User dialog box, also shown in Figure 2-7, click the Yes, Please Remove Me radio button and click Next.**

6. **Click Yes in the message box that warns you that your ICQ membership will be "permanently terminated."**

   Permanently terminated? Could it be that the makers of ICQ have been watching too many Arnold Schwarzenagger movies?

Unregistering from a single machine (and keeping your membership)

Did the boss catch you chatting at work and now you have to stop using ICQ at the office? Follow these steps to unregister ICQ from a particular machine but keep your membership in ICQ:

1. **Click the ICQ button at the bottom of the ICQ window.**

2. **Choose Add/Change Current User⇨Remove ICQ # From Computer.**

   If you registered under more than one name, the names appear on a sub-menu.

3. **If necessary, choose the name of the person whose registration you want to remove from the computer.**

   The Remove User dialog box, shown on the left side of Figure 2-8, appears.

Figure 2-8:
Enter your
password
(left) and
then click
the Yes,
Please
Remove Me
option to
unregister
from a
single
computer.

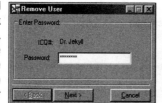 

4. **Enter your password in the Remove Password dialog box and click the Next button.**

   If you've forgotten your password, go to the `www.icq.com/password` Website and submit a request to obtain your password.

   The second Remove User dialog box asks if you really want to go through with it, as shown on the right side of Figure 2-8.

5. **Click the Yes, Please Remove Me radio button and then click Next.**

   A Warning box tells you that the registration will be removed from your computer.

6. **Click the Yes button.**

Uninstalling the ICQ software

So ICQ wasn't for you, after all? Too many chatterboxes trying to get your attention? Oh well, ICQ isn't for everybody.

Before you uninstall the software and rid yourself of ICQ forever, take the time to go online and unregister yourself. (Earlier in this chapter, "Unregistering Your Membership in ICQ" explains how.) By unregistering, you

remove your name from the ICQ computers. People who seek you online will
know that you withdrew your name from the ICQ masquerade. If you uninstall
ICQ without unregistering, your name will remain on ICQ's computers, wither,
and die a slow death.

Follow these steps to uninstall the ICQ software:

1. **Click the Start button and choose <u>P</u>rograms⇨Icq⇨Uninstall ICQ.**

   You see the Select Uninstall Method dialog box shown in Figure 2-9. The
   dialog box offers two means of uninstalling ICQ. You can select the
   <u>A</u>utomatic radio button and uninstall in a hurry, or you can click the
   <u>C</u>ustom radio button and pick and choose which ICQ files to uninstall.

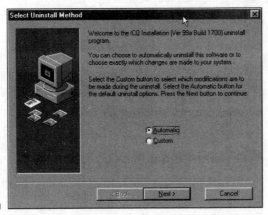

Figure 2-9:
Click the
<u>A</u>utomatic
radio button,
click <u>N</u>ext,
and then
click <u>F</u>inish
to uninstall
ICQ.

ICQ is one of those all-or-nothing programs. Unless you have an ulterior
motive and you want to keep a handful of ICQ files, you may as well
delete all of them.

2. **Click the <u>A</u>utomatic radio button and then click <u>N</u>ext.**

3. **Click the <u>F</u>inish button.**

   Twiddle your thumbs while the ICQ program files are removed from your
   computer.

Occasionally when you remove software, you see the Remove Shared
Component dialog box. This dialog box appears when files that more
than one program relies on are about to be removed. We suggest clicking
No to <u>A</u>ll in the Remove Shared Component dialog box to prevent shared
files from being removed. Keeping shared files on the computer does no
harm, but removing a shared file can do harm to a software program
that relies on the file.

Chapter 3

Up and Running with ICQ

In This Chapter

▶ Making the switch to Advanced mode

▶ Exploring the ways to start ICQ

▶ Closing ICQ — or putting the program into Sleep mode

▶ Moving and changing the size of the ICQ window

▶ Running ICQ from a floating Status button

▶ Declaring your online status to other ICQ members

▶ Configuring your browser to work with ICQ

*T*his chapter explains the things you need to know to get a good start with ICQ. In this chapter, you put your best foot forward, put the pedal to the metal, and charge ahead.

Chapter 3 explains how to switch to Advanced mode to take advantage of the features Advanced mode has to offer. You also discover techniques for starting and shutting down ICQ. When you run ICQ, you're connected to the Internet and the ICQ network, so starting and shutting down isn't as easy as clicking a couple of buttons.

This chapter offers advice for managing the ICQ window so it doesn't get in the way of your other work. And you also find out how to tell others when you are online and hide from bothersome ICQ chatters. Finally, this chapter describes how to configure your browser so that you don't get shut down automatically in the middle of an exciting ICQ chat.

Switching to Advanced Mode

When you first start working in ICQ, you land in Simple mode, but don't plan on staying here long. You can benefit by switching to Advanced mode. ICQ says that Simple mode is designed for beginners and is easier to use, but we think you should jump in and start with Advanced mode right away. The important features — the ones that make ICQ fun — are only available in Advanced mode. Besides, Advanced mode isn't as complicated as ICQ makes it out to be.

Follow these steps to switch to Advanced mode:

1. **Click the To Advanced Mode button in the ICQ window.**

   You can also click the ICQ button and choose Advanced Features from the pop-up menu. Double-click the ICQ flower in the lower-right corner of the screen if the ICQ window isn't displayed.

2. **In the Simple/Advanced Mode Selection dialog box, click the Switch to Advanced Mode button.**

   That's all there is to it! Figure 3-1 shows what the ICQ window looks like in Advanced mode and Simple mode.

Figure 3-1:
The ICQ
window in
Simple
mode (left)
and
Advanced
mode (right).

Besides more buttons — Icq Now! and Services — Advanced mode offers the ICQ iT! Search mechanism and two tabs at the top of the window for changing views of the Contact List.

Throughout this book, we assume that you are working in Advanced mode. If we instruct you to click a button or choose an option and the button or option isn't there, you're working in Simple mode. Switch to Advanced mode to take advantage of all the ICQ features.

Starting ICQ — and Choosing How You Want to Start the Program

When you install ICQ, you also install something called the ICQ NetDetect Agent. No, the NetDetect Agent doesn't work for a foreign spy syndicate. The NetDetect Agent hovers in the background, waiting to see when you connect to the Internet. When you connect, the NetDetect Agent starts the ICQ program automatically, opens your Web browser if you haven't already opened it, and sends you to the ICQ homepage (at www.mirabilis.com). If you look closely, you can see the ICQ NetDetect Agent icon on the right side of the Taskbar next to the clock when you are offline. (If you don't see it, click the Start button and choose Programs⇨Icq⇨ICQ NetDetect Agent.)

Not everybody wants ICQ to start automatically when they go on the Internet. Waiting for the ICQ program to start and waiting for the ICQ homepage to appear onscreen is a drag if all you want to do is go online for a minute and collect your e-mail or check out a baseball score.

To decide for yourself how you want to start the ICQ program, click the ICQ button in the ICQ window and choose Preferences from the pop-up menu. Then, in the Owner Prefs For dialog box, click the Connection tab, as shown in Figure 3-2. By checking or unchecking the two check boxes at the bottom of the dialog box, Launch Default Web Browser When Connection Is Detected and Launch ICQ on Startup, you can choose how and when to start ICQ. Here are the three strategies for starting ICQ:

Check or uncheck these boxes to choose how to start ICQ.

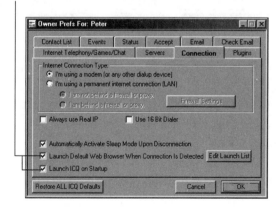

Figure 3-2:
Choosing
how and
when to
start ICQ.

Making certain you don't visit the ICQ homepage at startup

We suspect that ICQ wants you to visit its homepage whenever you go online. How do we know? Because, after you uncheck the Launch Default Web Browser When Connection Is Detected box in the Owner Prefs dialog box (refer to Figure 3-2), the ICQ NetDetect Agent dialog box shown here appears the next time you go online. If you click Yes in this dialog box, you check the Launch Default Web Browser When Connection Is Detected check box without knowing it. In other words, you tell ICQ that you *want* to open your browser and visit the ICQ homepage whenever you go online.

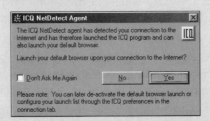

To make your decision not to visit the ICQ homepage stand, click the Don't Ask Me Again check box and then click the No button.

You can still change your mind about visiting the ICQ homepage when you go online: Click the ICQ button, choose Preferences, click the Connection tab in the Owner Prefs For dialog box (refer to Figure 3-2), and check the Launch Default Web Browser When Connection Is Detected check box.

Rather than visit the ICQ homepage whenever you go online, you can bookmark the page in your Web browser and thereby visit the page when you choose to do so. The address of the ICQ homepage is www.mirabilis.com.

✔ You go online, ICQ starts automatically, your Web browser starts automatically, and you go automatically to the ICQ homepage.

Make sure both boxes — Launch Default Web Browser When Connection Is Detected *and* Launch ICQ on Startup — are checked.

✔ You go online, ICQ starts automatically, but your browser doesn't start automatically, nor do you visit the ICQ homepage.

Uncheck the Launch Default Web Browser When Connection Is Detected check box, but leave the check in the Launch ICQ on Startup box.

✔ You go online, period. ICQ does not start automatically and you don't go to ICQ's homepage. To start ICQ, you have to click the Start button and choose Programs⇨Icq⇨ICQ. The NetDetect Agent is turned off — you don't see its icon in the lower-right corner of the screen.

> Uncheck the Launch ICQ on Startup check box (whether the other box is checked doesn't matter, since the NetDetect Agent is turned off).

No matter what you're doing or whether you're on the Internet, you can always start ICQ by clicking the Start button and choosing Programs⇨ Icq⇨ICQ. Whether your browser starts or you visit the ICQ homepage depends on which options you chose in the Owner Prefs For dialog box.

Disconnecting from the ICQ Network

When you are ready to shut down ICQ — suppose you've had your fill of online gab — you can disconnect from the ICQ network by shutting down the program or putting it to sleep. Or, if you want to maintain your connection to ICQ but lurk in the background, you can change your online status to Offline/Disconnect, Invisible, Away, or one of the other status descriptions that tells others you have been detained by interests above and beyond yakking on the Internet.

Do one of the following to disconnect from the ICQ network:

✔ **Shut down ICQ altogether:** Click the ICQ button and choose Shut Down from the pop-up menu. ICQ is closed for good, and the NetDetect Agent is put out of action (the previous section in this chapter describes the NetDetect Agent). Until the next time you shut down and restart your computer, the only way for you to reconnect to ICQ is to click the Start button and choose Programs⇨Icq⇨ICQ. You can also shut down ICQ by clicking the Close button (the *X*) in the upper-right corner of the ICQ window.

✔ **Put ICQ to sleep:** Click the ICQ button and choose Sleep Mode from the pop-up menu. Slip into Sleep mode if you close your connection to the Internet and want to start ICQ next time you go online. In Sleep mode, the ICQ window closes and the NetDetect Agent goes to work. Instead of the ICQ flower button in the lower-right corner of the screen, you see the NetDetect Agent icon. Next time you go online, ICQ will start automatically. By the way, ICQ puts you in Sleep mode without asking when you disconnect from the Internet.

✔ **Leave the ICQ window open but disconnect from the ICQ network:** Click the Status button — it's located in the lower-right corner of the ICQ window — and choose Offline/Disconnect. The ICQ window stays open when you choose Offline/Disconnect, but you're disconnected from ICQ.

Minimize the ICQ window to set it aside. When you want to connect to ICQ again, double-click the ICQ flower button in the lower-right corner of the screen to see the ICQ window, click the Status button, and choose Available/Connect from the pop-up menu.

The Status pop-up menu offers many choices besides Offline/Disconnect. Later in this chapter, "Telling Others What Your Online Status Is" describes the different ways to broadcast your status to other ICQ members. Be sure to read "Taking Charge of the ICQ Window," the next section in this chapter, to find out how to keep the ICQ window from interfering when you're trying to do other tasks at your computer besides chatting on ICQ.

If the NetDetect Agent ceases to work, you can make it work again by clicking the Start button and choosing Programs⇨Icq⇨ICQ NetDetect Agent. Sometimes the NetDetect Agent fails when you shut down your browser improperly or the computer hangs.

Taking Charge of the ICQ Window

Double-clicking the flower button in the lower-right corner of the screen opens the ICQ window. Everybody knows that. What most people don't know is that ICQ offers a bunch of different ways to handle the window. You can tuck the ICQ window into a side of the screen, slide it around, or change its size. You can even make it disappear after a certain amount of idle time has elapsed and pop up automatically when someone sends a message, chat invitation, or other item. Read on to find out strategies for handling the ICQ window.

Choosing how the window appears onscreen

One of the drawbacks of ICQ is that the ICQ window insists on being on top when you're running several programs at once. Normally, you get to choose which program window is on top by clicking a taskbar button or program window. The ICQ window, however, stubbornly stays on top no matter what.

You can do something about that. In fact, you can do a lot to make the ICQ window work your way. On the Contact List tab of the Owner Prefs For dialog box, shown in Figure 3-3, are a bunch of useful options for changing the way that the ICQ window works. To get to the Contact List tab, click the ICQ button, choose Preferences, and click the Contact List tab In the Owner Prefs For dialog box.

Choose options for handling the ICQ window

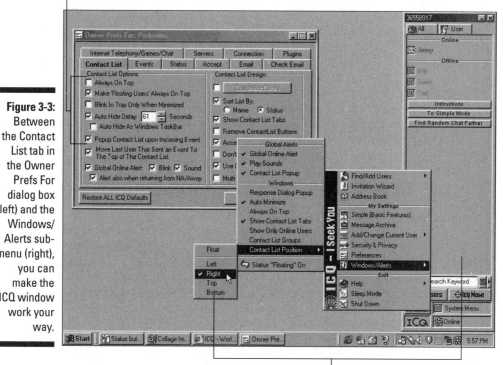

Figure 3-3:
Between
the Contact
List tab in
the Owner
Prefs For
dialog box
(left) and the
Windows/
Alerts sub-
menu (right),
you can
make the
ICQ window
work your
way.

Choose an option to fasten the window to the side of the screen.

While the Owner Prefs For dialog box is open to the Contact List tab, check out these strategies for taking charge of the ICQ window:

✔ **Make the window appear behind other windows:** Uncheck the Always On Top check box. The ICQ window will appear behind other program windows when you're working in other program windows.

A fast way to decide whether the ICQ window always appears in front is to click the ICQ button and choose Windows/Alerts⇨Always On Top.

✔ **Minimize the window automatically when you are not using ICQ:** Click the Auto Hide Delay check box and enter the amount of idle time you will tolerate. When you leave ICQ and work in another program for the amount of time you enter, the ICQ window is minimized. To see the window again, double-click the flower button in the lower-right corner of the screen.

A fast way to turn the Auto Hide mechanism on or off is to click the ICQ button and choose Windows/Alerts⇨Auto Minimize.

> ✔ **Make the window appear automatically when you are sent a message, chat invitation, or other item:** Check the Popup Contact List upon Incoming Event check box. With this strategy, the ICQ window appears onscreen automatically when someone sends you an invitation to chat, a message, a file, or other item.
>
> To turn this option on or off quickly, click the ICQ button and choose Windows/Alerts⇔Contact List Popup.

Chapter 7, which explains how to manage the Contact List in the ICQ window, describes other valuable options on the Contact List tab of the Owner Prefs For dialog box.

Choosing where the window appears onscreen

Except for refusing to yield to other windows and always wanting to stay on top, the ICQ window is no different from other program windows. Move it onscreen by dragging its title bar, the stripe along the top that lists your ICQ membership number. To change the window's height or width, carefully move the pointer over a border, click when you see the double arrows, start dragging, and release the mouse button when the ICQ window is the size you want it to be.

Besides dragging the ICQ window here and there, you can position it squarely against the left side, right side, top, or bottom of the screen, as shown in Figure 3-3, where it appears against the right side. Follow these steps to fasten the ICQ window to the side of the computer screen:

1. **Click the ICQ button.**

2. **Choose Windows/Alerts⇔Contact List Position.**

   You see a submenu with five position choices: Float, Left, Right, Top, and Bottom.

3. **Choose a position for the ICQ window from the submenu.**

Go back to the Contact List Position submenu and choose Float (see Figure 3-3) if you want to be able to move the ICQ window at will across the screen.

Running ICQ on a shoestring

Here's a trick that you may care to try if you're thoroughly familiar with the ICQ commands and you're tired of seeing the ICQ window appropriate valuable space onscreen: Reduce the ICQ window to a single button, the Status button. After you've performed this magic trick, you can click the Status button and get to most of the same commands that are found in the ICQ window.

Follow these steps to see if running ICQ on a shoestring is for you:

1. **Click the ICQ button.**

2. **Choose Windows/Alerts⇨Status "Floating" On.**

Look closely and you will see, somewhere on your screen, the Status button. Try dragging it into a corner to put it out of harm's way.

3. **Minimize the ICQ window.**

To do that, you can either click the Status button and choose Minimize ICQ from the pop-up menu or simply click the Minimize button in the upper-right corner of the ICQ window.

You're all set. When you want to give a command, click the Status button, choose a command on the pop-up menu, and choose a command from a submenu.

Miss the ICQ window? To get it back, click the Status button and choose Open ICQ from the pop-up menu. To remove the Status button, click it and choose "Floating" Off.

Telling Others What Your Online Status Is

When you go online, ICQ members who have added your name to their Contact Lists know it. They know it because, under the word _Online,_ your name appears in their ICQ windows. As the next chapter explains, someone who wants to invite you to chitchat can click your name on the Contact List and choose ICQ Chat from the pop-up menu.

But suppose you want to go online without anyone bothering you? For that matter, suppose you want to go online without other ICQ members knowing it? ICQ has many different ways of describing your online status while you're connected to the ICQ network. What's more, you can leave messages that describe why you're away or why you aren't receiving visitors. Keep reading.

Telling others whether you are available for chats

To tell others whether you're available for chatting or trading messages, click the Status button and choose an option from the pop-up menu. Table 3-1 describes the options on the Status menu (switch to Advanced mode to take advantage of all the options). After you choose an option, the icon that represents the option you chose appears next to your name on others' Contact Lists, as shown in Figure 3-4. Someone who has put your name on his Contact List can glance at the icon beside your name and know right away what your online status is.

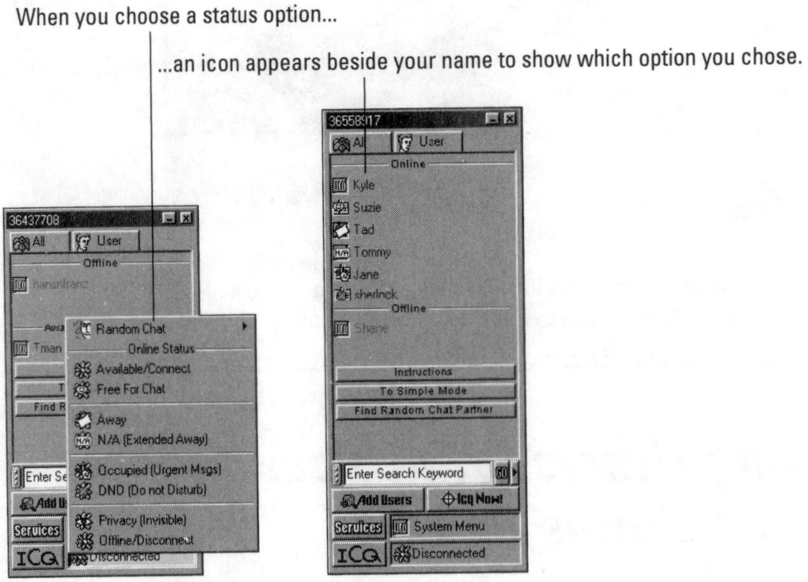

When you choose a status option...

...an icon appears beside your name to show which option you chose.

Figure 3-4:
Choose a
Status
option to tell
others
whether
you're avail-
able for
chats.

Table 3-1	**Status Menu Options**	
Symbol	*Status Option*	*What It Tells Others*
🌸 Available/Connect	Available/Connect	You're available for chatting and sending and receiving messages.
🌸 Free For Chat	Free For Chat*	You want to chat very much and will accept invitations to chat automatically.
🐾 Away	Away*	You're gone from your computer for the moment. ICQ switches to Away status automatically when your screensaver kicks in. What's more, you can tell ICQ to switch to Away status automatically after a certain number of idle minutes have elapsed. See the next section in this chapter.
N/A N/A (Extended Away)	N/A (Extended Away)*	You're gone from ICQ for an extended period of time. You can instruct ICQ to switch into N/A (Extended Away) status automatically after you have been in Away Status for a set amount of time. See the next section in this chapter.
🌸 Occupied (Urgent Msgs)	Occupied (Urgent Msgs)*	You're busy doing something else. Someone who attempts to send you an item is given the opportunity to mark it as urgent. When an urgent message arrives, you hear a sound and the message icon blinks on and off in the lower-right corner of the screen. When a normal item is sent, its icon does not blink on and off and no sound is heard.

(continued)

Table 3-1 *(continued)*

Symbol	Status Option	What It Tells Others
![DND (Do not Disturb)]	DND (Do not Disturb)*	You don't want to be disturbed, but you want others to know that you're online. Icons in the ICQ window and lower-right corner of the screen do not blink to get your attention when you switch to DND status.
![Privacy (Invisible)]	Privacy (Invisible)	Other ICQ members do not know that you're online. Choose this option when you don't want to be bothered by anyone. People who have added your name to their Contact Lists think that you're offline.
![Offline/Disconnect]	Offline/Disconnect	You want to disconnect from the ICQ network but retain your connection to the Internet. Your name appears under "Offline" in others' Contact Lists.

* The Change/Confirm Message dialog box appears when you select this option so you can enter a message explaining why you are away, are occupied, or don't care to be disturbed. Others can click your name on their Contact Lists, choose Read Message on the pop-up menu, and read the message you enter. See "Writing messages to describe why you are away or busy" later in this chapter.

You can still receive invitations to chat, messages, and other items while you are in Away, Occupied, N/A, or DND status. However, the chat request and other icons do not flash onscreen. Instead, they appear in the lower-right corner of the screen or next to the names of people on your Contact List, provided the sender is on your Contact List. In Occupied status, others can send you chat requests and items that flash on and off, but to do so they must mark the items as urgent when they are sent.

Switching to Away and N/A status automatically

To make sure that the icon next to your name on others' Contact Lists correctly describes your online status, you can tell ICQ to switch you to Away status or N/A (Extended Away) status after a certain amount of idle time has elapsed. In other words, if you step away from your computer for a while, ICQ can switch you automatically to Away status so that others know you're not available. And if you stay in Away status for too long, ICQ can then switch you automatically to N/A (Extended Away) status.

Follow these steps to tell ICQ to update your status automatically when you leave your computer to milk the cow or slop the hogs:

1. **Click the ICQ button.**

2. **Choose Preferences on the pop-up menu.**

    You see the Owner Prefs For dialog box.

3. **Click the Status tab.**

4. **Check the Automatically Set "Away" After check box and enter the number of minutes of idle time that are to elapse before ICQ switches you to Away status.**

    How much idle time can you tolerate? Enter **15**, for example, if you want ICQ to switch you to Away status after fifteen minutes.

5. **In the Automatically Set "N/A" After text box, enter the number of minutes you want to stay in Away status before switching automatically to N/A (Extended Away) status.**

6. **Click the OK button.**

Writing messages to describe why you are away or busy

When you switch to Free for Chat, Away, N/A, Occupied, or DND status, the Change/Confirm Message dialog box shown on the right side of Figure 3-5 appears so you can describe why you are away or busy. Someone who sees the Away, N/A, Occupied, or DND icon next to your name on his Contact List can click the icon, choose the Read Message option from the pop-up menu, and read a message to find out why you are incommunicado.

Figure 3-5:
In the
Owner Prefs
For dialog
box (left),
you can
enter status
messages
and spare
yourself
from having
to write
them in the
Change/
Confirm
Message
dialog box
(right).

Enter messages on the status tab...

...and be able to choose the messages in the Change/Confirm Message dialog box

Owner Prefs For: Pedrisimo

Internet Telephony/Games/Chat		Servers
Contact List	Events	**Status**	Accept

Enter Default Availability Mode Message For: N\A

Presets:

Gone Fishing ▼ | Gone fishing -- be back later.

Go Away
Outta Here
Gone Fishing
Coop Flown
Escaped
Bought the Farm
Exit Stage Right
Hasta La Vista

"Away" When Screen Saver is A

"Away" After 10 Minute

"N\A" After 20 Minute

☑ Show Messages in Tray in All Status Modes
☑ Disable "Online Alert" Messages in "Away","DND

Restore ALL ICQ Defaults

Change/Confirm N/A Message

This message will be displayed when you are marked as "N/A".
The message can be modified in your preferences.

Gone fishing -- be back later.

Select Message | OK

Go Away
Outta Here
Gone Fishing
Coop Flown
Escaped
Bought the Farm
Exit Stage Right
Hasta La Vista

Edit Messages

But instead of entering a message in the Change/Confirm Message dialog box, you can choose a message from the Select Message drop-down list, as Figure 3-5 shows. You can choose a message, that is, as long as you entered messages on the Status tab of the Owner Prefs For dialog box, which is also shown in Figure 3-5.

Being able to choose a message saves time. And by entering messages yourself, you don't have to rely on the bland, generic messages that ICQ offers in the Change/Confirm Message dialog boxes.

Follow these steps to write messages that describe why you are away or busy and be able to choose messages instead of write them in the Change/Confirm Message dialog box when you change your online status:

1. **Click the ICQ button and choose Preferences from the pop-up menu.**

   You see the Preferences dialog box (refer to Figure 3-5).

2. **Click the Status tab.**

3. **On the Enter Default Availability Mode Message For drop-down list, choose which type of status you want to write messages for.**

   For example, to write messages that describe why you chose Away status, choose the Away option.

4. **Enter the message in the text box.**

Declaring your online status to a particular person on the Contact List

By clicking the Status button and choosing an option on the Status menu, you tell everyone who has put your name on the Contact List what your online status is. Others know whether you're available for chats, occupied, or away, for example. And you can even make yourself invisible to people who have placed your name on their Contact Lists by choosing Privacy (Invisible) on the Status menu.

Suppose, however, that you want to be invisible to all ICQ members except a certain special someone. For that matter, suppose you want to be invisible to a particular bothersome person on your Contact List but not to everyone else.

For those occasions, ICQ offers a means of declaring your online status to a particular person on your Contact List, not to all the people on the list. You can also accept messages from a particular person but not accept messages from others.

Follow these steps to declare your online status to one person on your Contact List:

1. **Click the person's name on the Contact List and choose More (Rename, Delete)Í Alert/Accept Modes on the pop-up menu.**

2. **In the Alert/Accept Settings dialog box, click the Status tab.**

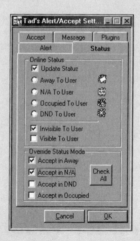

3. **Click the Update Status check box, and, by clicking a radio button, declare your online status. You can also click the Invisible To User or Visible To User check box to make your presence known or unknown.**

4. **Click any Override Status Mode check boxes if you want to be alerted to items others have sent to you while you are in Away, N/A, DND, or Occupied status.**

5. **Click the OK button.**

5. **Click the Rename button, and, in the Rename Location dialog box, enter a descriptive name for the message you entered; then click OK.**

   The name you enter will appear on the Presets drop-down list and make identifying the message easier when the time comes to choose it in the Change/Confirm Message dialog box (refer to Figure 3-5).

6. **Open the Presets drop-down list, choose a generic name, and repeat Steps 4 and 5 if you want to enter other messages.**

   You can enter as many as eight different messages.

7. **Choose another status message type on the Enter Default Availability Mode Message For drop-down list, and repeat Steps 4 through 6 to enter more messages.**

   While you're visiting the Status tab of the Owner Prefs For dialog box, you may as well enter a bunch of different messages.

8. **Click OK when you're done entering Change/Confirm messages.**

   Next time you change your online status, you can choose a message in the Change/Confirm Message dialog box or enter a message, as you wish.

What happens if you need to edit a message? Go back to the Status tab of the Owner Prefs For dialog box (refer to Figure 3-5), choose the message that needs editing from the Presets list and edit or rewrite the message. To rename a message, click the Rename button and enter a new name in the Rename Location dialog box.

Be careful about clicking the Restore ALL ICQ Defaults button in the Owner Prefs For dialog box. Click that button and all the work you did to write status messages is lost. Instead of the messages you worked so hard to write yourself, you get the bland, generic messages that you started with.

Telling Your Browser When to Disconnect Automatically

When you chat on ICQ, your browser thinks you have left the room. From the browser's point of view, you've left your chair, because no browser buttons are being clicked. Consequently, your browser may cut off your connection to the Internet — and the ICQ network — after a certain amount of idle time has elapsed. You might get cut off in the middle of a chat because your browser thinks you're not doing anything at your computer.

Whether your browser cuts you off automatically depends on whether you have configured your browser to shut down automatically after a certain amount of time. Follow these steps in Windows to see what your browser is configured to do and decide how many minutes of idle time you will tolerate before the browser ends your connection to the Internet and the ICQ network:

1. **Click the Start button and choose Settings⇨Control Panel.**

   The Control Panel window opens.

2. **Double-click the Internet icon.**

   You see the Internet Properties dialog box.

3. **Click the Connections tab.**

4. **Click the Settings button.**

   As shown in Figure 3-6, the Dial-Up Settings dialog box appears.

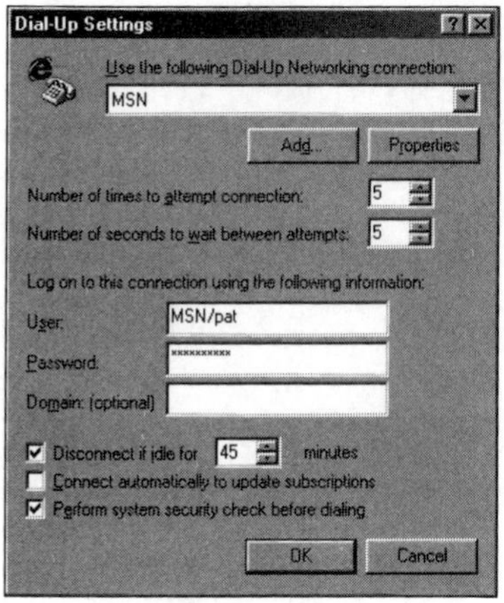

Figure 3-6: In this dialog box, you tell Windows how long to wait before disconnecting your computer from the Internet — and from the ICQ network.

5. **Either uncheck the Disconnect If Idle For check box, or check the box and enter the number of minutes of idleness to tolerate before you're disconnected from the Internet.**

   Serious ICQ chatters usually uncheck the box so they can chat away without running the risk of being disconnected unexpectedly. But you might consider entering a number in the Minutes box. Some people think that if you gab for more than an hour, you ought to be disconnected automatically for talking too much.

6. **Click OK to close the Dial-Up Settings dialog box and OK again to close the Internet Properties dialog box.**

Part II
Making Friends in the ICQ Community

In this part . . .

Part II is for everybody who has the gift of gab. In Part II, you kiss the Blarney Stone. Well, you kiss the digital Blarney Stone, anyway.

This part explains how to chat and chatter on ICQ. You also find out how to find new friends on the ICQ network, manage a Contact List with the names of your many friends, send and get stuff from ICQ members, and paint a picture of yourself in the White Pages.

Chapter 4

Chatting the Day Away

• •

In This Chapter

▶ Inviting someone from your Contact List for a chat

▶ Receiving chat invitations — and accepting or declining them

▶ Choosing a background color, text color, and font for the Chat window

▶ Exploring ways to make chatting more enjoyable

▶ Including a third (or fourth or fifth or sixth) person in a chat

▶ Booting someone out of a chat

▶ Replaying a chat from the Message Archive

• •

*T*his chapter is for the birds — it explains how to chatter. Actually, this chapter is about chatting, not chattering. It gets to the heart of the matter and explains how to chat in ICQ. Although ICQ offers a bunch of different services, the program is famous for its ability to help others hook up and start talking to one another.

In this chapter, you discover how to invite someone for a chat and how to handle a chat invitation that someone sends you. You will find many tips and tricks in this chapter for making chats more fun and pleasurable. Read on to find out how to change the look of the Chat window — the background color, font color, and font. If you want to include more than two people in a chat, this chapter explains how. And you also discover how to kick boorish people out of chats, replay chats, and put more pizzazz (not pizza!) in a chat.

The Four Ways to Start Chatting

ICQ offers four different ways to engage someone else in a rollicking good chat:

✔ Chat with someone whose name appears on your Contact List — or be invited to chat by someone who put your name on his or her list.

✔ Search at random for someone to chat with — or make yourself available to others who are looking at random (see Chapter 2).

     ✔ Join a chat room and chat with others who have joined (see Chapter 5).

     ✔ Go to the Chat Request Page in the PeopleSpace Directory and put out a request to chat with others (see Chapter 5).

To engage in a chat, both parties have to be online and connected to the ICQ network. You can invite someone from your Contact List to chat when he or she is offline, but doing so is pointless because the invitation won't be delivered until the other person is online. Send the other person a message instead (Chapter 8 explains sending messages).

Engaging in Idle Chatter

Chatting in ICQ is a bit like a dance party. You can boldly ask others to dance or you can stand on the sidelines looking coy until someone asks you. Either way, the name of the person being asked must appear on the asker's Contact List before the chat can begin. Read on to find out how to invite someone else to chat and what to do if you're invited.

Inviting someone else to chat

Follow these steps to invite someone on your Contact List for a chat:

1. **Click the Person's name on the Contact List and choose ICQ Chat on the pop-up menu.**

   You see the Send Online Chat Request dialog box, shown on the left side of Figure 4-1.

2. **Write an enticing invitation to chat in the Enter Chat Subject box.**

   As you can see on the right side of Figure 4-1, the words you write will appear in the Incoming Chat Request dialog box when the invitation arrives on the other side.

3. **Click the Chat button.**

   If the other party takes the bait, you soon see the Chat window (skip ahead to "Chatting Away in the Chat Window" if you need help managing the window). But if you got turned down, either a message box tells you why or nothing happens because the other party chose to ignore your request. Don't take it badly. Don't fret about it. There are lots of fish in the ocean.

Figure 4-1:
When you
invite
someone for
a chat (left),
the invitation
appears on
the other
side in the
Incoming
Chat
Request
dialog box
(right).

Click to see the invitation   Click to start chatting

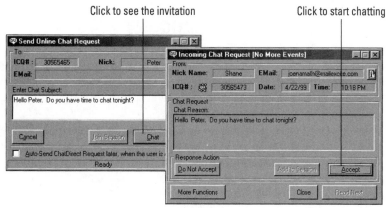

Receiving and accepting (or declining) an invitation to chat

You can tell when someone wants to chat with you because the Chat icon starts flashing in the lower-right corner of the screen where the flower button normally is. And if the name of the person who wants to chat happens to appear on your Contact List, the icon flashes next to his or her name there as well.

To see who has come a-calling and what the caller wants to chat about, either double-click the Chat icon or click the icon on your Contact List and choose Receive from the pop-up menu. The Incoming Chat Request dialog box appears (refer to Figure 4-1). Either accept or decline the invitation by clicking a button in the dialog box:

   ✔ **Accept the invitation:** Click the Accept button. Shortly, the Chat window appears and you can start gabbing (the next section in this chapter explains how to handle the Chat window).

   ✔ **Decline the invitation:** Click the Do Not Accept button. You see a pop-up menu with suggestions for how to turn down the offer to chat. Choose a canned reply, select Enter a Decline Reason and enter a reason of your own in the Decline User Request dialog box, or choose Away to change your online status to Away (Chapter 3 explains what Away and the other online status choices are).

Accepting (or declining) chat invitations automatically

In case you love to gab, ICQ gives you the opportunity to accept all chat invitations without reviewing them first in the Incoming Chat Request dialog box. And if you like to gab with a particular person on your Contact List, you can accept chat requests from him or her automatically as they arrive.

✔ **Accepting (or declining) all chat invitations automatically:** By clicking the Status button and choosing Free For Chat from the pop-up menu, you accept all invitations to chat. But suppose you want to accept invitations to chat automatically no matter what status you are in. To do so, click the ICQ button, choose Preferences, and click the Events tab in the Owner Prefs For dialog box. Make sure ICQ Chat is chosen in the Select Event to Configure drop-down list, and then click the Auto Accept ICQ Chat option button.

With this strategy, the Chat window appears right away when someone wants to chat with you. Click the Auto Decline option button if you're in a permanent bad mood and you want to decline all invitations to chat.

✔ **Accepting requests from certain people automatically:** Click the name of the person in your Contact List and choose More➪ Alert/Accept Modes. In the Alert/Accept dialog box, click the Accept tab, and then check the Auto Accept Chat check box.

Invitations to chat are accepted automatically when you click the Status button and choose Free For Chat from the pop-up menu (Chapter 3 explains how to tell others what your online status is). After you choose Free For Chat and someone asks to engage you in a chat, the Chat window appears automatically.

Chatting Away in the Chat Window

All chats take place in the Chat window, and this part of the chapter is devoted to that venerable place. Here, you find out how the Chat window works and how you can change the look of the Chat window. We've included many tips and tricks on these pages to turn you into a first-class chatterbox. You will find instructions here for closing a chat and including actions and emotes to make your chatter livelier.

How the Chat window works

The Chat window, shown in Figure 4-2, appears when you accept an invitation to chat or your invitation to chat is accepted. Now you can start chatting — typing, actually — to your heart's content. The contributions you make to the conversation appear in the topmost window; other people's contributions appear in the other windows (later in this chapter, "Including a Third Party in a Chat" explains how to chat with more than one person). If you forget with whom you're chatting, read the name above your partner's window.

Notice the menu and toolbars in the Chat window, one across the top of the window and the other — it has only three buttons — along the top of your partner's window. The next few pages explain how useful the menu and toolbars are.

Names of people in the chat

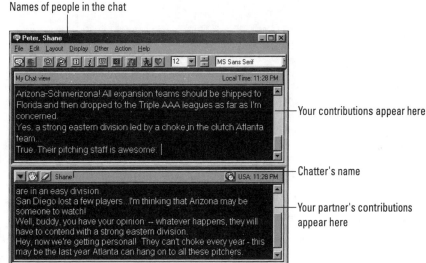

Your contributions appear here

Chatter's name

Your partner's contributions appear here

Figure 4-2: Conversations take place in the Chat window.

The Chat window is like any other program window. You can drag it from place to place, change its size by dragging a border, and minimize or maximize it. Place the Chat window in a corner of the screen and you can chat while you do other work. Drag the division mark between the halves of the window to make one side larger or smaller. If you stretch the window out of shape, you can always get a normal-size window by choosing Layout⇨Reset.

The split screen versus the IRC screen

The first time that the Chat window appears, a dialog box asks if you want a split screen or IRC (Internet Relay Chat) screen. Most people prefer the split screen. In the split screen, your comments appear in the top half of the Chat window and your partner's appear in the bottom half (refer to Figure 4-2). In an IRC screen, as all America Online members know, text appears in the order in which it was entered and talkers' names appear beside their contributions to the discussion.

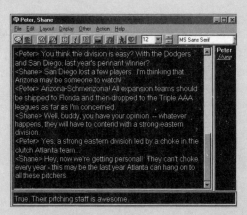

Some people are accustomed to IRC screens and prefer them to split screens. If you are one of those people, choose Layout⇨IRC Style in the Chat window (choose Layout⇨Split if you change your mind and want to go back to a split screen). You can also click the Style button to choose a different screen style.

To contribute to a chat on an IRC screen, you have to press the Enter key after you type your contribution in the space along the bottom of the window. In a split screen, nobody has to press the Enter key unless they want to in order to jump down a line. ICQ switches to an IRC screen automatically when six or more people are chatting with one another (choose Display⇨Auto Color when that many people are chatting to assign a different color to each chatter's contributions).

Besides splitting the screen horizontally, you can split it vertically, as this illustration shows. Choose Layout⇨Vertical to split the screen vertically (and Layout⇨Horizontal if you don't like a vertical screen and want to see the horizontal screen again).

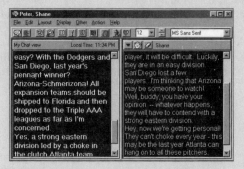

Changing the appearance of the Chat window

To begin with, the appearance settings you chose for your side of the window — the background color, text color, and font — appear on your side, and the settings your partner chose appear on his or her side. By clicking toolbar buttons and choosing menu commands, you can do a lot to change the Chat window's appearance:

  ✔ **Imposing your choices on your partner:** Click the Override Font & Color button (or choose Display⇨Override Format) to make your partner's side of the Chat window look like yours. As long as the Override Format button is "pressed down," the background color, text color, and font you chose for your side of the window appear on your partner's side as well. Click the button a second time to see your partner's choice of background color, text color, and font. By the way, the colors you choose for your window have no bearing on what your partner sees. Sorry, you can't control the color or font in his or her window.

  ✔ **Choosing a background color:** Click the Background Color button and select a color from the drop-down menu. You can also choose Display⇨Back Color.

  ✔ **Choosing a color for text:** Click the Color button and select a color from the drop-down menu, or choose Display⇨Color and select a color. If the text disappears when you choose a new color for text, it did so because you chose a color that is identical or nearly identical to the background color. Choose a new font color to solve the problem.

  ✔ **Changing the font and font size of the letters:** Click the down arrow to open the Font drop-down menu and choose a font. To change the size of the letters, make a choice from the Font Size drop-down menu. You can also choose Display⇨Font to change the appearance of text by way of the Font dialog box. A *font* is a typeface design.

Tricks for handling long chats

As chats start to drag on, especially when you are trying to do one or two other things as well as chat, the Chat window can be hard to handle. Here are a few tricks for handling the Chat window:

  ✔ **Minimize the window until your partner starts typing again:** For those occasions when your chat partner leaves to take out the trash or the cat, click the Sleep button or choose Other⇨Sleep (or press Ctrl+S). The Chat window is minimized until your partner starts typing or you click the Chat window button on the taskbar. When you partner decides to rejoin the conversation, the Chat window leaps onscreen.

✔ **Beep your chat partner to get his or her attention:** Choose Other⇨Beep Users (or press Ctrl+G). The person with whom you're chatting will hear two beeps and, to underscore the point, see the words "Beep Beep" on his or her screen. Beep your partners when you think they have gone to sleep on you. (Your partner must have chosen Other⇨Enable Sounds to hear the beeps.)

✔ **Let others know when you have minimized the Chat window:** Choose File⇨Send Focus to tell others when you have minimized the Chat window and you're not paying attention. The person with whom you're chatting will see your name in italics on his or her Contact List, know that you minimized the window, and understand that you can't read new contributions to the chat. Well, your partner will know that you minimized the window as long as he or she knows what an italicized name on the Contact List means...

✔ **Keep the Chat window on top:** Choose Layout⇨Always on Top to keep the Chat window in front of other program windows and always be able to see the window.

 ✔ **Freeze the text so you can read it more easily:** On the off chance that you encounter someone who can type faster than you can read, click the Freeze button atop his or her side of the Chat window. Clicking the button stops the text from scrolling in the window. Click the Freeze button a second time to make the text start moving again.

 ✔ **Clear the text from a Chat window and start with a clean slate:** Click the Clear button to empty the text from your partner's side of the window. To empty the text from both sides, choose File⇨Clear Buffer.

Putting some oomph (sort of) in your chatter

In the For What It's Worth Department, words aren't the only things you can hurl during a chat. You can also express yourself with actions and emotions, or *emotes,* as they're known in ICQ. Well, ICQ calls them actions and emotes. We wouldn't go that far. To be precise, you can decorate your chatter with cartoon-like descriptions of actions and various emotional states.

Figure 4-3 shows an example of an action and an emote. Actions are accompanied by the word *Action* and a dramatic description of some kind. Emotes come in several different descriptions — jokingly, shocked, and annoyed, among others. When you enter an emote, you get the chance to describe your emotional state to your chat partner.

Follow these instructions to send an action or a so-called emote:

✔ **Sending an action:** To quickly describe an action of some kind, click the Send Action button and choose an action from the drop-down list.

To describe the action yourself, choose Action⇨Send Action (or press Ctrl+A). In the Action Event dialog box (refer to Figure 4-3), describe the action you want to convey to your chat partner and click the Send button. *Do not* include your name in the description, because ICQ enters it for you. For example, if your name is Joe and you enter "Joe does this and that," ICQ enters the following description: "Joe Joe does this and that."

Click a button or check an option from the Action menu

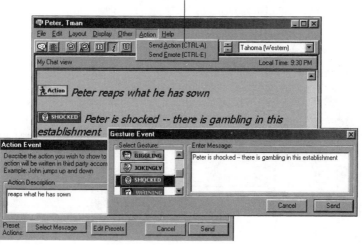

Figure 4-3:
Put actions and emotes in a chat to give it a bit of pizzazz.

 ✔ **Sending an emote:** Either click the Send Emote button or choose Action⇨Send Emote (or press Ctrl+E). In the Gesture Event dialog box (refer to Figure 4-3), click a gesture and then enter a message to describe your emotional state. Click the Send button when you're done.

As you know if you selected an action by clicking the Send Action button, the actions that ICQ enters from the Send Action drop-down menu are hard to figure. The brief descriptions on the menu don't do a very good job of describing what is entered in the Chat window when you choose an option. To remedy this problem, you can enter your own actions for the Send Action menu or edit ICQ's. To do so, choose Action⇨Send Action (or press Ctrl+A) to open the Action Event dialog box, and then click the Edit Presets button. You see the Edit Action Presets dialog box, where you can rename the options on the Send Action drop-down menu or enter action descriptions of your own.

 A better but somewhat old-fashioned way to lay emphasis on the words you type in the Chat window is to click the Bold, Italic, or Underline button on the toolbar and boldface, italicize, or underline text. These buttons work the same as they do in a word processor.

Closing down a chat

How a chat gets closed down depends on whether you close it down or the other party does. Either way, as shown in Figure 4-4, the Chat Session Ended dialog box appears if you decide to keep the chat for posterity, and you get the opportunity to save the text of the chat in the Message Archive. Chats and messages that have been stored in the archive can be recovered and re-examined on rainy days when you have nothing better to do (later in this chapter, "Revisiting a Chat" explains how to review a chat for old time's sake).

Uncheck if you don't want to save the chat   Choose quit

Figure 4-4:
When
you're
finished
chatting,
you can
deposit a
copy of the
chat in the
Message
Archive
and read
the chat
later on.

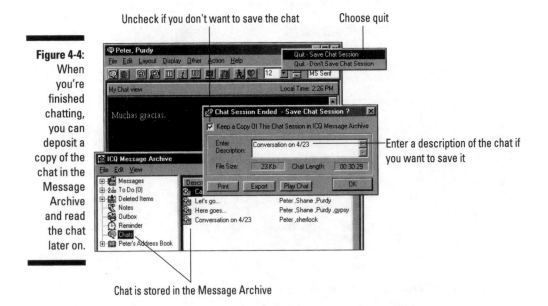

Enter a description of the chat if
you want to save it

Chat is stored in the Message Archive

Follow these steps when the time has come to finish chatting:

1. **As shown in Figure 4-4, click the Close button (the *X*) in the Chat window and choose Quit – Save Chat Session or Quit – Don't Save Chat Session if you're the one who decides to end the chat.**

   If the other person ends the chat before you, skip to Step 2. Besides clicking the Close button, you can end a chat by choosing File➪Quit➪Save Chat, or File➪Quit➪Don't Save Chat.

   If you decided to save the chat, the Chat Session Ended – Save Chat Session dialog box, shown in Figure 4-4, appears. You're done if you opted not to save the chat in Step 1.

2. **Enter a description of the chat in the Chat Session Ended dialog box if you want to save the chat; if you don't want to save it, uncheck the Keep a Copy of This Chat Session in ICQ Message Archive check box.**

To start with, the dialog box lists the invitation you or the other party entered to begin the chat. Enter a descriptive name or description — something to help you recognize the chat in the Message Archive if you want to open and read it someday.

3. Click OK.

That's all there is to it. Later in this chapter, "Revisiting a Chat" explains how you can go to the Message Archive and read the text of a chat you saved.

Including a Third Party in a Chat

Suppose you're invited for a chat, you're already chatting with someone else, and you would like to include the person who invited you to chat in the chat you're already having. Or, looking at it from the other side, suppose you're chatting away about tuber roses or Grecian urns and it dawns on you that someone on your Contact List ought to be in the discussion.

More than two people can participate in a chat. "The more the merrier" is ICQ's philosophy. To include another person in a chat, follow the usual routine of inviting the other person (click his or her name on the Contact List and choose ICQ Chat on the pop-up menu), or double-click the chat icon to accept an incoming request to chat. Then follow these instructions:

- **Include someone from your Contact List in a chat:** In the Send Online Chat Request dialog box, click the Join Session button. A drop-down menu appears with the names of people who are already chatting, as shown in Figure 4-5. Click the chat to which you want to invite another person.

- **Invite the person who invited you to chat to participate in a chat you are having:** In the Incoming Chat Request dialog box, click the Add to Session button. On the drop-down menu, click the chat in which you want to include the other person.

As Figure 4-5 shows, another area is added to the Chat window to make room for the newcomer. When six or more people are chatting, ICQ switches to an IRC (Internet Relay Chat) screen instead of a split screen.

As Chapter 3 explains, you can click the Status button in the ICQ window and choose Free For Chat to accept all chat invitations without reviewing them first. Accepting invitations to chat without first seeing who has invited you is fine and dandy, except if you want to include third parties in a chat. In order to include someone who has invited you to chat in a chat you are having already, you have to click the Add to Session button in the Incoming Chat Request dialog box, and that dialog box doesn't appear if you are connected to ICQ under Free For Chat status. It doesn't appear because chat requests are accepted automatically. The moral: If you want to include outside parties in chats you are having already, click the Status button and choose Available/Connect instead of Free For Chat status.

Figure 4-5:
Click the
<u>J</u>oin
Session
(or Add to
<u>S</u>ession)
button in
the Send
Online Chat
Request
(or Incoming
Chat
Request)
dialog box
to include
another
person in
a chat.

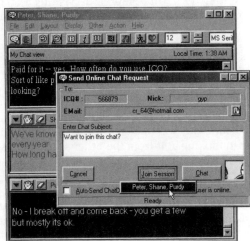

Kicking a Bore out of a Chat

The Internet brings out the worst in some people. Under the cloak of anonymity, otherwise mild-mannered individuals can turn into beasts. Or bores. Or cantankerous grumblers. Or bad-tempered crackpots. Or, worst of all, conspiracy theorists!

To help maintain civility in a chat, ICQ offers you the opportunity to kick someone out. That's right — you can kick someone out of a chat by majority vote. Chatters see a box in which they can vote yeah or nay to kick someone out. And if the majority votes to give someone the boot, the offensive lout is sent packing!

If someone else starts the procedure for kicking someone out, you see a dialog box in which you can vote yeah or nay, and that's all there is to it. Follow these steps if you decide to do the booting:

1. Choose <u>F</u>ile⇨<u>K</u>ick User.

The ChatDirect Session – Kick User dialog box appears with a list of everyone in the chat except yourself, as shown in Figure 4-6. (In the figure, the vote has already been taken.)

2. **Either double-click the name of the person you want to kick out or click the person's name and then click the Kick User button.**

3. **Click OK in the dialog box that asks if you really want to be so bold as to kick somebody out of a chat.**

   After you click OK, other chatters vote whether or not to give the person the heave-ho. Your vote has already been counted. The results of the vote appear in the ChatDirect Session – Kick User dialog box.

Figure 4-6:
Choose
File⇨Kick
User to
remove an
unruly
grump from
a chat.

If your bid to kick the offensive person succeeds, you see the User Kicked dialog box shown in Figure 4-6. If your bid fails, a different dialog box tells you as much.

Rather than attempt to boot someone from a chat, we suggest leaving if you are offended by the conversation. Your absence usually does more to reprimand someone than storming away from the discussion. Some people get their kicks from offending others. We suggest not giving them the opportunity to do that.

Revisiting a Chat

Earlier in this chapter, "Closing down a chat" explained how you can save the text of a chat for posterity in the Message Archive. As long as you saved the chat session, you can recover it again. You can open the Message Archive and read your words of wisdom and witty repartees.

Follow these steps to revisit a chat you saved in the Message Archive:

1. **Click the ICQ button in the ICQ window.**

2. **Choose Message Archive.**

   The ICQ Message Archive window appears. (If you're curious about all that stuff in the Message Archive, have a look at Chapter 15, which explains the Archive in detail.)

3. **On the left side of the window, double-click the Chats icon.**

   Chats that you saved in the Message Archive appear on the right side of the window. You named these chats when you saved them in the Chat Session Ended dialog box (refer to Figure 4-4).

4. **Right-click the chat that you want to revisit and choose Playback Chat on the shortcut menu.**

   As shown in Figure 4-7, the Chat window opens, as does the ICQ Chat File Player. The File Player looks kind of like boombox, doesn't it? By using the controls in the Chat File Player, you can literally play back the chat in the Chat window. In fact, if you leave the Speed Slider mechanism on the left side, the chat is played back at the same speed in which it took place originally.

Figure 4-7: In the ICQ Chat File Player, you can revisit a conversation you had before.

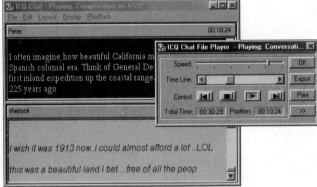

5. **Drag the Speed Slider to the right to adjust the speed at which the chat is played and then click the Play button and read the text as it appears in the Chat window.**

   When the chat finishes playing, the Restart button appears in case you want to click Restart and watch the chat text scroll down the screen a second time.

Clicking the Play button and reading the chat text in the window is the slow way of reliving a chat. Maybe you want to find a passage or two, perhaps to copy them to the Clipboard. The fastest way to skim or speed-read a chat is to drag the scroll box or click the left arrow button in the Time Line scroll bar. By doing so, you can move forward through the chat by leaps and bounds. Unfortunately, you can't drag the scroll box to the left or click the left arrow button to scroll upward in the Chat window. If you overshoot the mark, click the To Beginning button to go to the start of the chat and start scrolling all over again.

In sum, the Chat File Player offers these buttons for going here and there in a chat:

 ✔ **Rewind:** Goes directly to the start of the chat.

✔ **Pause:** Stops the screen from scrolling so you can read a passage and perhaps copy it to the Clipboard. (To copy a passage, drag over the text to select it, right-click, and choose Copy from the shortcut menu.)

✔ **Play:** Plays the chat at the speed marked on the Speed slider.

✔ **Fast Forward:** Goes directly to the end of the chat.

Click OK in the Chat File Player or click the Close button in the Chat window when you want to close both the window and the Chat Player.

Saving a Chat in a Text File

As "Closing down a chat" explained earlier in this chapter, chats are saved for posterity in the Message Archive. As long as you saved the text of the chat when the chat ended, you can go back to the conversation and save it as a text (.txt) file. Follow these steps to do so:

1. **Click the ICQ button and choose Message Archive.**

   The Message Archive window opens. Chapter 15 is devoted to the Message Archive, in case you are curious about this place in which so many of your adventures in ICQ are stored for posterity.

 2. **Double-click the Chats icon.**

   A list of the chats you saved appears on the right side of the window.

3. **Click the chat that you want to save as a text file.**

4. **Chose File⇨Save As.**

   The Save As dialog box appears.

5. **Using the usual methods, find the folder in which to store the file, make sure the folder's name appears in the Save In box, enter a name in the File Name text box, and click the Save button.**

   You can open the file with any word-processing program.

Chapter 5
More Chat Topics

. . . .

In This Chapter

▶ Finding someone to chat with on the Chat Request page

▶ Inviting others to chat on the Chat Request page

▶ Finding a chat room of interest in the Chat Room Directory

▶ Creating your own chat room — and registering it in the Chat Room Directory

▶ Opening and closing chat rooms

▶ Making sure your chat room runs smoothly

. . . .

*T*his chapter picks up where Chapter 4 left off and describes more techniques for chatting with others. In this chapter, you learn how to find your way around the Chat Request page, the place where ICQ members can go to find like-minded people to chat with. This chapter also takes on chat rooms. You are hereby encouraged to visit chat rooms and even to create a chat room of your own. The end of this chapter gives you directions for finding chat rooms outside of ICQ, in case ICQ chatter isn't intelligent enough or exciting enough for you.

This chapter closes out the subject of chatting in ICQ. By the time you finish reading Chapter 5, you will be a full-fledged Internet blabbermouth.

Visiting the Chat Request Page

One of the best ways to find and start chatting with people whose interests are similar to yours is to visit the Chat Request page, shown in Figure 5-1. As "Putting out a request to chat with others" explains later in this chapter, ICQ members can go to the Chat Request page and post an invitation to chat about their favorite topics — the ineluctable modality of the visible, manchego cheese, the Spice Girls, or whatever. People who hanker to chat about similar topics can find one another on the Chat Request page.

Figure 5-1:
Go to the
Chat
Request
page to find
or attract
people who
want to talk
about the
same
subjects
as you.

Click View to see who wants to chat.

Click Request to put in your request for a chat.

Read on to find out how to visit the Chat Request page, see who wants to talk about what, and perhaps engage somebody in a chat. You will also find instructions for finding out how to issue your own invitation to chat on the Chat Request page.

Finding someone to chat with on the Chat Request page

Follow these steps to get to the Chat Request page, play the field, and maybe engage somebody in a passionate discussion:

1. **Click the Add Users button to open the Find/Add Users to Your List dialog box.**

2. **Click the Chat tab in the dialog box.**

   The Chat tab presents a bunch of confusing hyperlinks that either help you find others to chat with or take you to instructional pages. All links on the Chat tab lead to a page on the Internet.

 3. **Click the Chat Request hyperlink.**

   After a moment, your browser opens to the Chat Request page (refer to Figure 5-1). Scroll down the page and you see a table that lists topics and the number of people who have signed on to chat about each topic.

4. **Find a topic that interests you, and, in the Action column, click the View button beside the topic's name.**

As shown in Figure 5-2, you go to the View Chat Request page, where you see a list of people who have submitted requests to chat about the topic you chose.

Figure 5-2:
Click the
Chat Me
button to
start
chatting
with
someone
on the
View Chat
Request
page.

You can request a Chat Now, <u>GO!</u>

Post a Chat Request for a given period (up to 90 minutes). Your posting will be automatically deleted after that period. <u>Try It Out.</u>

<u>View the Most Requested Topics</u>

NICK NAME	ICQ#	CHAT SUBJECT	CHAT INFO	AVAILABLE UNTIL	INTERNET-TELEPHONY
marianne	06787000	Wish Me Happy Birthday	iedereen is welkom voor een borrelop 17 december!	3:14 EST	
		Page Me	Zoom Me	Add Me	ICQ Me	Chat Me	Disabled
Karianne	04436000	Wish Me Happy Birthday		3:47 EST	
		Page Me	Zoom Me	Add Me	ICQ Me	Chat Me	Online

Total Requests: 2

If none of the invitations interests you, click the Back button in your browser to return to the Chat Request page and start the search anew. Otherwise, keep reading to find out how to engage someone in a chat.

By the way, if Internet-Telephony, the right-hand column on the View Chat Request page, shows the Online icon, the person who requested the chat is capable of chatting with a telephony application as well as by conventional means. Chapter 16 describes telephony applications that work with ICQ.

Be sure to click the Refresh/Reload button on the Chat Request page from time to time. Clicking that button updates the page so you can see how many want to chat and what they want to chat about.

Chatting with someone from the View Chat Request page

After you have found someone to chat with on the View Chat Request page (refer to Figure 5-2), the next step is to click the Chat Me button. In the File Download dialog box that appears onscreen, make sure the first option button, Open This File from Its Current Location, is selected, and then click OK. After the contact information has been downloaded to your computer (it takes only a couple of seconds), you see the Send Online Chat Request dialog box. Enter a word or two and click the <u>C</u>hat button. Soon, if the other party is online and accepts your bid to chat, the Chat window appears and you can start gabbing. Chapter 4 explains the Chat window.

ICQ for people who don't speak English

You can usually find many topic categories for people who don't speak English or want to chat in a language apart from English on the Chat Request page (refer to Figure 5-1). And if the language you want to chat in can't be found on the page, you can introduce a new language topic, as "Putting out a request to chat with others" explains later in this chapter. ICQ members who want to chat in languages other than English tend to hang out on the Chat Request page, because that's where they are most likely to find one another.

ICQ offers another aid to people who don't speak English: the ICQ Languages Center. To find out about the Languages Center and discover chat rooms and user lists where English is not the lingua franca, do the following:

1. **Click the Add Users button in the ICQ window.**

2. **In the Find/Add Users to Your List dialog box, click the ICQ International tab.**

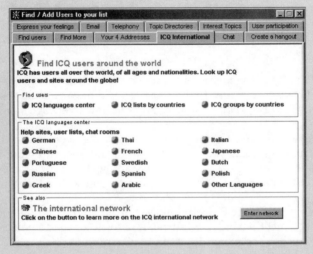

Before you start chatting, however, you might click the Zoom Me button. Clicking Zoom Me takes you to the ICQ White Pages, where you can learn more about the person who is so anxious to chat. The White Pages list the information that ICQ members divulge when they register — or when they update their profiles in the Global Directory (click the ICQ button and choose Add/Change Current User⇨View/Change My Details to find out what the White Pages have to say about you).

By the way, if a topic on the Chat Request page happens to be one you're enamored of, you can click the Related ChatRoom hyperlink and see if any chat rooms are open for discussing your favorite topic. Related ChatRoom hyperlinks can be found in the right side of the topic table.

Putting out a request to chat with others

If the invitations to chat on the Chat Request page don't do anything for you, you can always submit a request of your own. Others who read your request and are enticed by it can heed the call and ask you for a chat.

Starting from the Chat Request page (refer to Figure 5-1 and "Finding someone to chat with on the Chat Request page" earlier in this chapter), follow these steps to offer yourself to other people who are looking for a good chat:

[Request] 1. **Find the topic name that best describes what you want to chat about and click its Request button.**

Be sure to read both tables on the Chat Request page before you choose a topic and click the Request button. At the top of the page, under "Current Requested Chats," are topics that other members want to chat about, but you can find more topics by scrolling to the bottom of the page and looking under "Other Dynamic Chat Request Topics." Dynamic? Hope your chat request can live up to that billing.

After you click Request, you see the Request form shown at the top of Figure 5-3. The topic category you chose appears on the form under the word "Subject."

Figure 5-3:
Fill out the
Request
form (top) to
submit a
chat invita-
tion to the
View Chat
Request
page
(bottom).

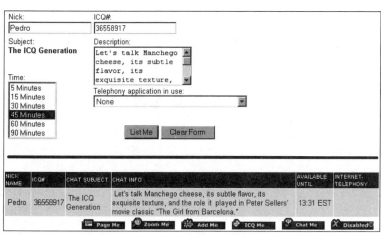

2. **Enter your name or nickname in the Nick box.**

3. **Enter your ICQ number in the ICQ# box.**

Be sure to enter the correct number. Others won't be able to find you, if you don't.

4. **In the Description box, write an enticing description of the subject you want to chat about.**

What you enter in the Description box will help others decide whether chatting with you is a worthwhile venture.

5. **In the Time box, choose how long you intend to stay online and field invitations to chat.**

   By making a choice, you commit to staying online for 5 to 90 minutes. Be sure to keep your commitment. Going to the trouble to find someone to chat with on the Chat Request page and then discovering that the person is offline is disappointing.

6. **In the Telephony Application to Use drop-down menu, choose an application name if you propose to chat by means of an application such as Microsoft NetMeeting or NetSpeak.**

   Chapter 16 describes telephony applications that work with ICQ.

7. **Click the List Me button.**

   ICQ informs you that your invitation has been listed on the Chat Request page and at what time your invitation will expire.

8. **Click the View List button.**

   You go to the View Chat Request page, as shown on the bottom of Figure 5-3, where you can see precisely what your invitation looks like.

If anybody takes the bait, you soon see the Incoming Chat Request dialog box. Or, if you chose Free For Chat status from the Status menu, the Chat window appears right away when someone wants to chat with you. Chapter 4 explains the Chat window and how to chat with others.

Finding and Joining a Chat Room

One way to find and chat with like-minded people is to join a chat room. Anybody who is registered with ICQ can start a chat room, as "Creating and Managing Your Own Chat Room" explains later in this chapter.

After you join a chat room, its name appears on your Contact List. Like the names of ICQ members who are online, the names of chat rooms that are online and ready to receive visitors appear in the Contact List under the word "Online." Chat room names are preceded by an ampersand (&) in the Contact List to distinguish them from the names of ICQ members. When the members of a chat room see on their Contact Lists that the room is up and running, they can congregate in the room and have a rollicking good time.

Unfortunately, ICQ doesn't provide a master list of the chat rooms that members have created. To search for chat rooms, you can look in the Chat Room Directory, but the directory only presents chat rooms that are online and connected to the ICQ network. Therefore, the only way to find and join a chat room is to find and join it while it is online. In other words, you have to get lucky. Even when you find a category in the Chat Room Directory that interests you, your chances of being able to join a chat room in the category are pretty slim, because the chat room has to be online while you're searching for you to find it.

Oh well. When you find a good chat room — when you find one that keeps regular hours and whose members are interesting and given to lively discussion — the search is worth the effort. Read on to find out how to search for a chat room that suits your taste, join a chat room, and start impressing the people in the room with your bon mots and witty repartee.

Follow these steps to search for a chat room to join:

1. **Click the Add Users button in the ICQ window.**

   The Find/Add Users to Your List dialog box appears. You have to be in Advanced mode to see the Add Users button.

2. **Click the Chat tab.**

3. **Click the Chat Room Directory hyperlink.**

   Your browser opens to the Chat Room Directory page on the Internet (`www.icq.com/icqchat`). This page lists chat rooms by group, category, and subcategory.

4. **Scroll through the list, find a group that seems promising, and then click a category hyperlink under the group's name.**

   You see a list of subcategories similar to the one at the top of Figure 5-4. For the figure, we clicked, under the Local group, the By Languages category.

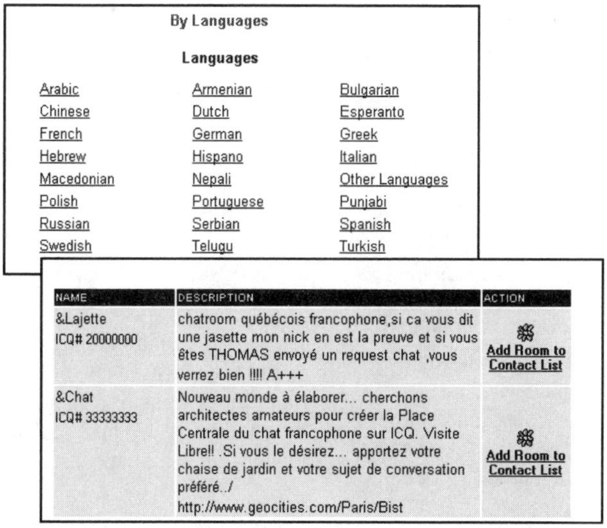

Figure 5-4: To find and perhaps join a chat room, start from the Chat Room Directory and keep clicking categories and subcategories.

By Languages

Languages

Arabic	Armenian	Bulgarian
Chinese	Dutch	Esperanto
French	German	Greek
Hebrew	Hispano	Italian
Macedonian	Nepali	Other Languages
Polish	Portuguese	Punjabi
Russian	Serbian	Spanish
Swedish	Telugu	Turkish

NAME	DESCRIPTION	ACTION
&Lajette ICQ# 20000000	chatroom québécois francophone,si ca vous dit une jasette mon nick en est la preuve et si vous êtes THOMAS envoyé un request chat ,vous verrez bien !!!! A+++	Add Room to Contact List
&Chat ICQ# 33333333	Nouveau monde à élaborer... cherchons architectes amateurs pour créer la Place Centrale du chat francophone sur ICQ. Visite Libre!! .Si vous le désirez... apportez votre chaise de jardin et votre sujet de conversation préféré../ http://www.geocities.com/Paris/Bist	Add Room to Contact List

5. **Click a subcategory to see if any chat rooms are open and can be joined.**

   More often than not, a message tells you, "No online ICQ chat rooms were found under your chosen category," but sometimes you get lucky and see a couple of chat rooms, as shown at the bottom of Figure 5-4.

   Don't get frustrated if your search proved fruitless. Instead, click the Back button in your browser to return to the group-and-category page and turn your search for chat rooms in another direction (or read the sidebar "A sure way to find chat rooms that are open and online," which describes a way to find chat rooms that are certain to be online).

6. **Click the Add Room to Contact List hyperlink next to a chat room description, if you care to join a chat room you have found.**

7. **In the File Download dialog box, make sure the first option button, Open this File from Its Current Location, is chosen; then click OK.**

   ICQ downloads a contact information file to your computer.

   What happens next depends on whether you need authorization from the person who manages the chat room to become a member. If you need authorization, a dialog box asks you to explain why you want to join the chat room. Enter a reason and click the Request button.

   If authorization isn't required, a message box informs you that you have joined and the name of the chat room appears on your Contact List.

To enter a chat room you have joined, click its name on the Contact List — an ampersand (&) appears in front of chat room names on the list — and choose ICQ Chat from the pop-up menu.

A sure way to find chat rooms that are open and online

Searching for chat rooms in the Chat Room Directory can be frustrating because often the subcategories are empty and you can't find an online chat room to join. However, ICQ offers a chat room equivalent to the random chats that you can get by clicking the Find Random Chat Partner button in the ICQ window. By clicking the View The Random Open Chat Rooms hyperlink, which is found throughout the Chat Room Directory pages, or by clicking the Find a Random Chatroom link on the Chat tab of the Find/Add Users to Your List dialog box, you can see a random list of online chat rooms that are open.

The list you see is generated at random. If nothing on the list interests you, click the View The Random Open Chat Rooms hyperlink again. Maybe the next list will turn up a chat room you care to join.

Suppose you regret putting a chat room on your Contact List. No problem. To take the chat room off your list, click its name and choose More (Rename, Delete)⇨Delete on the pop-up menu.

Creating and Managing Your Own Chat Room

Before you know anything about creating a chat room, you should know that running a chat room can be very rewarding, but it also represents a big commitment. Last time we looked, 30 million people had registered with ICQ. If you create a chat room, more than a few ICQ members will find your room and join up. Your loyal following will expect you to be online, not always necessarily, but during regularly scheduled times. ICQ users don't like to be disappointed! If you make the commitment to running a chat room, be prepared to stick to it.

We recommend checking out the many chat rooms in the Chat Room Directory if an occasional chat is all you're after (see the previous section in this chapter). There, you can probably find a chat room to your liking.

Read on to find out how chat rooms work, what running a chat room entails, how to create a chat room, and other chat room particulars.

How chat rooms work

Apart from having to be online at regularly scheduled times, running a chat room is not very different from being a run-of-the-mill member of ICQ. People who have joined your chat room can tell when it is up and running because its name appears under "Online" on the Contact List. To enter your chat room, others click its name on the Contact List and choose ICQ Chat on the pop-up menu. Sounds familiar, doesn't it? Each chat room, like each ICQ member, is given a number. Even registering a chat room is pretty much the same as registering under your own name.

As part of registering, you tell ICQ where to put your chat room in the Chat Room Directory. You get to choose the subcategory (the previous part of this chapter explains how to search for chat rooms by category in the Chat Room Directory). Besides the Chat Room Directory, your chat room sits for a spell in the Newly Created Chat Rooms page, a list of newly minted chat rooms.

To make your chat room available to others, all you have to do is go online under the name of the chat room, not under your own name. As the owner and sole proprietor of a chat room, you decide whether others need permission to join. You can also bar someone from entering the room and close the room to new members. As far as we can tell, the Chat window can accommodate as many as 20 visitors to a chat room (the most we've ever seen), although the Chat window switches to IRC (Internet Relay Chat) mode when more than 6 people are aboard. See Chapter 4 for instructions in handling the Chat window, including how to kick someone out of a chat.

Pretty simple, isn't it? If you're already registered under more than one name and are accustomed to switching from alter ego to alter ego, you will find managing a chat room especially easy.

Creating and registering a chat room

Before you register a chat room, go to the Chat Room Directory, study the subcategories, and decide which subcategory is the best fit for the chat room you will create. As part of registering, ICQ will ask you for the name of the subcategory you choose. You must enter the subcategory name exactly.

Others will search the Chat Room Directory for chat rooms to join, so choose a subcategory carefully. To get to the Chat Room Directory, click the Add Users button, click the Chat tab in the Find/Add Users to Your List dialog box, and click the Chat Room Directory hyperlink. Figure 5-5 demonstrates what a subcategory in the Directory is.

Group

Figure 5-5:
When you create a chat room, ICQ asks which subcategory to put it under in the Chat Room Directory.

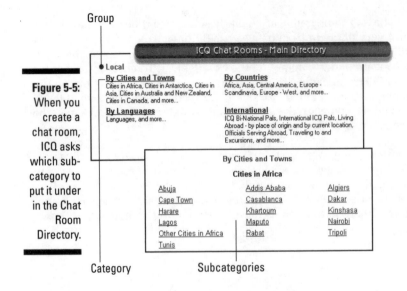

Category   Subcategories

Follow these steps after you have chosen a subcategory to create and register a chat room:

1. **Click the ICQ button in the ICQ window.**

2. **On the pop-up menu, choose Add/Change Current User⊅Register A New User (ICQ#).**

   A message box tells you that registering under more than one name isn't healthy. Don't worry about it — you're registering a chat room.

3. **Click OK in the message box.**

   You see the first Registration Wizard dialog box. We trust you've encountered this box before when you registered the first time. See Chapter 2 if you need help with registering details.

4. **Under Connection Type, choose the option that describes how you are connected to the Internet (probably <u>M</u>odem User), and then click Next.**

5. **In the second Registration Wizard dialog box, shown in Figure 5-6, choose ChatRoom from the User Type drop-down menu.**

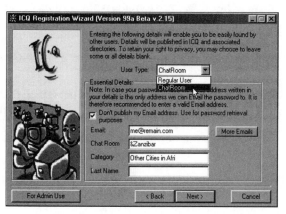

Figure 5-6:
To create and register a chat room, choose ChatRoom from the User Type drop-down menu.

Notice how an ampersand (&) appears in the Chat Room text box when you choose the ChatRoom option in the User Type drop-down menu. That is because all chat room names must begin with an ampersand.

6. **In the Chat Room text box, enter a descriptive name after the ampersand (&).**

   Your chat room will be known in the Chat Room Directory by the name you enter (refer to Figure 5-4 to see what chat room names look like). People who join your chat room will see the name you enter now on their Contact Lists.

7. **In the (misnamed) Category text box, enter the name of the subcategory where you want your chat room to appear in the Chat Room Directory.**

You must enter the name exactly as it is found in the Chat Room Directory (refer to Figure 5-5). If the name doesn't fit in the Category text box, enter the first 20 characters.

Chapter 2 explains how to handle the Email text box (enter your address and click the check box if you don't want your address to be made public).

8. **Click the Next button and describe your chat room in the following Registration dialog box.**

Because you're registering a chat room, most of the information doesn't pertain to you. *But be sure to click the Add Your Own Personalized Message button and describe your chat room in the dialog box that appears.* Doing so is essential because the words you enter will appear in the Chat Room Directory next to your chat room's name under Description (refer to Figure 5-4). Far too many people forget to describe their chat rooms — yet reading the description is the only way for others to know whether they care to join. While you're writing the description, you might enter your "office hours," the times during the week or day in which your chat room will be up and running.

9. **Click the Next button and fill out the rest of the Registration dialog boxes.**

Turn to Chapter 2 if you need help filling in the rest of the dialog boxes. When you come to the Privacy Level options, click the My Authorization Is Required radio button if you want to pick and choose who gets to join your chat room. Uncheck the option if your little club is open to everyone who wants to join.

Later in this chapter, "Caring for and feeding a chat room" explains how to change the particulars of your chat room — its description in the Chat Room Directory and whether authorization is needed to join — after you have registered it.

By the way, if no subcategory adequately describes your chat room, you can ask ICQ to post a new subcategory in the Chat Room Directory. To do so, send an e-mail message to icqlist@icq.com and politely ask for a new subcategory. Explain why the subcategory is so essential to your well being. "Caring for and feeding a chat room" explains how to choose a new subcategory for a chat room, in case the subcategory you requested turns out to be the wrong one.

To unregister a chat room and close it down for good, turn to Chapter 2 and follow the instructions for unregistering a membership in ICQ.

Opening and closing a chat room

Your chat room is open and can receive visitors whenever you go online with it. In other words, when you connect to ICQ under your chat room name instead of your own name, the chat room is open. Others see the name of your chat room on their Contact Lists under "Online." They can click the chat room name and choose ICQ Chat from the pop-up menu to enter your room.

Follow these steps to open or choose a chat room by going online under your own name or the name of your chat room:

1. **Click the ICQ button and choose Add/Change Current User.**

2. **Choose Change the Active User on the submenu.**

3. **On the following submenu, choose either your name or the name of your chat room.**

   A check mark appears beside the name of the creature — person or chat room — that is online at present.

4. **Click Yes in the Confirm Change User (ICQ#) message box.**

Caring for and feeding a chat room

A chat room is a bit like a furry animal — it requires care and needs to be fed from time to time. Here are instructions for making sure your chat room purrs:

✔ **Choosing whether others need authorization to join:** Click the ICQ button and choose Security & Privacy. In the Security For dialog box, click the Security tab. Click the All Users May Add Me to Their Contact List option button if you want anyone to be able to join your chat room, or click the My Authorization Is Required option button to pick and choose who gets to join. Then click the Save button.

✔ **Barring someone from entering your chat room:** Take note of the person's ICQ number and nickname. Then click the ICQ button, choose Security & Privacy, and click the Ignore List tab in the Security For dialog box. Next, click the Add To Ignore List button, enter the details about the person in the Search dialog box, and click the Search button. When the person's name appears at the bottom of the Search dialog box, right-click the name and choose Move To Ignore List. Finally, click the Save button. Ignoring someone this way removes his or her name from your Contact List.

✔ **Changing the chat room description in the Chat Room Directory:** Click the ICQ button and choose Add/Change Current User⇨View/Change My Details. Then click the Info/About tab in the Global Directory dialog box, enter a new description, and click the Save button.

✔ **Choosing a new subcategory for your chat room:** If you don't like the subcategory to which you assigned your chat room when you created it, you can change subcategories. To do so, click the ICQ button and choose Add/Change Current User⇨View/Change My Details. In the Global Directory dialog box, go to the Main tab, enter a new subcategory name in the (misnamed) Category text box, and click the Save button.

Be sure to check the Chat Room Directory from time to time — ICQ has a habit of changing the Directory listings without notice. See if your chat room got moved to a new subcategory and if a new subcategory is more suitable for your chat room, and change subcategories if necessary.

✔ **Closing a chat room to new members:** You can't really close the door of a chat room to new members, but you can remove your chat room's name from the Chat Room Directory and keep others from finding it there. To do so, click the ICQ button and choose Add/Change Current User⇨View/Change My Details. In the Global Directory dialog box, go to the Main tab, remove the subcategory name from the (misnamed) Category text box, and click the Save button.

Seeking a Chat Room Outside the ICQ Network

Hungry for a chat and can't find a good one in the ICQ network? You can always leave ICQ and try out a different chat service. Follow these steps to test the waters at Lycos Chat, Talk City, or another chat service on the Internet:

1. **Click the ICQ button in the ICQ window.**

2. **Choose Find/Add Users⇨Locate People.**

   Your Web browser opens to the Web Directories page (`www.icq.com/directories/`).

3. **Scroll to the bottom of the page to Chat Services, and click the Chat Services hyperlink.**

   You go to the Chat Services portion of the Web Directories page (`www.icq.com/directories/directory.html#chatServices`), as shown in Figure 5-7. From here, you can click a hyperlink, forsake ICQ, and try chatting elsewhere.

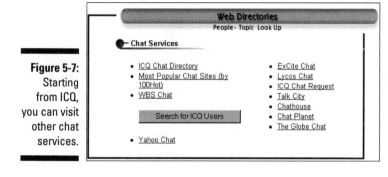

Figure 5-7:
Starting
from ICQ,
you can visit
other chat
services.

Chapter 6

Managing Your Contact List

• •

In This Chapter

▶ Authorizing or not authorizing your Contact List name

▶ Adding names to the Contact List

▶ Deleting names from the Contact List

▶ Viewing Contact List names in different ways

▶ Sending Contact List names to others

▶ Organizing Contact List names into groups

• •

The Contact List is to ICQ what place names are on a long banquet table — the Contact List is a gathering of all the people you have made friends with in ICQ.

This chapter explains everything you need to know to manage a healthy and happy Contact List. Read on to discover the ins and outs of giving permission to others to put your name on their Contact Lists. This chapter also explains how to add names to your Contact List and what happens when others add your name to their lists. Here, you learn ways of viewing the Contact List, how to remove names and change the names of people on the list, and how to send Contact List names to other people. This chapter explains how to file away Contact List names in groups to make the names easier to find. Finally, you will get the chance to play interior decorator in this chapter as you discover how to change the colors on the Contact List.

How the Contact List Works

Before you plunge in and find out all there is to know about the Contact List, you may as well know how the Contact List works. Figure 6-1 shows a typical Contact List.

Online status icons

Tab buttons

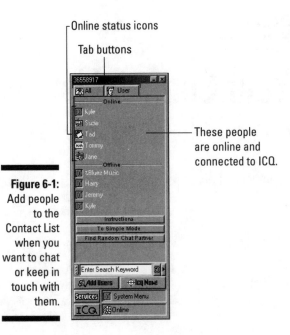

These people
are online and
connected to ICQ.

Figure 6-1:
Add people
to the
Contact List
when you
want to chat
or keep in
touch with
them.

The Contact List is where you keep the names of friends you have made on
the ICQ network. As you putter around in ICQ, you occasionally run into
somebody you want to know better or keep in touch with. When that happens, add the person to your Contact List.

You can tell when someone on your list is online and connected to ICQ
because his or her name turns blue and appears under the word *Online* on
the Contact List. What's more, an icon beside the person's name tells you
what the person's online status is and whether he or she is available for chatting (Chapter 3 explains how to tell others what your online status is).

Click a name on the Contact List and you see a pop-up menu with commands
for doing any number of things — sending chat invitations and messages, getting information about the person, and requesting a phone number, for
example. You can only invite someone to chat if his or her name is on your
Contact List.

To protect members' privacy, each ICQ member decides whether others need
permission to put their name on a Contact List. When you attempt to put
someone on your list, you may need permission first. If that's the case, a
dialog box appears so you can send a message to the other person and ask to
put his or her name on your list. Likewise, if you require others to get permission to put your name on their Contact List, you occasionally receive
messages asking for permission.

Even if you decide that others don't need permission to put your name on their Contact List, you're informed whenever someone puts your name on his or her list.

By clicking the two tab buttons above the Contact List, you can view the names on the list in different ways. When the Groups tab is displayed, names on the Contact List are arranged by group. ICQ offers four groups to begin with — General, Family, Friends, and Co-Workers — but you can create groups of your own as well to keep track of the names on your Contact List.

Choosing Whether to Authorize Your Name for Others' Contact Lists

When you registered with ICQ, you declared whether others need permission to put your name on their Contact List. ICQ offers two ways to handle Contact List names. You can either let others put your name on their list right away or you can make them get permission first.

Suppose you change your mind about putting your name on others' Contact Lists. Follow these steps to declare to ICQ how you want your name to be handled:

1. **While you're online and connected to ICQ, click the ICQ button and choose Security & Privacy on the pop-up menu.**

    You see the Security For dialog box.

2. **Click the Security tab.**

3. **Choose an option under Change Contact List Authorization:**

    • **All Users May Add Me to Their Contact List:** Your name goes straight onto others' Contact Lists whether you want it to or not.

    • **My Authorization Is Required:** You see the Incoming Request For Authorization dialog box when someone wants to put your name on his or her Contact List (see "When someone wants to put your name on his Contact List..." later in this chapter). In the dialog box, you can click a button to authorize or reject the request.

4. **Click the Save button and then the Done button.**

Adding a Name to the Contact List

Maintaining a healthy and happy Contact List is important if you want to stay in touch with the friends you make on the ICQ network. These pages explain how to put someone's name on your Contact List. You also discover the ins and outs of getting your name on others' Contact Lists.

Adding someone's name to your Contact List

Throughout ICQ, you'll find many opportunities to add people to your Contact List. In the Global Directory dialog box, right-click a name and choose Add to Contact List from the pop-up menu to put someone's name on your Contact List. Many dialog boxes offer an Add to Contact List button. Keep your eyes pealed and you will find many opportunities to put people on your Contact List.

What happens after you choose the Add to Contact List command depends on whether you need permission to place the person's name on your Contact List. Better read on.

Permission is required

If you need permission to put someone's name on your Contact List, you see the Privacy — User's Authorization Is Required dialog box, shown at the top of Figure 6-2. Follow these steps to seek permission to put a name on your Contact List:

1. **In the Enter Request Reason text box, introduce yourself and say that you want to put the other person on your Contact List.**

2. **Click the Request button.**

3. **In the Request For Authorization Was Sent message box, click OK.**

   The name appears on your Contact List under "Awaiting Authorization."

Meanwhile, whomever you sent the request to sees the Incoming Request For Authorization dialog box, shown on the bottom of Figure 6-2. Your name appears prominently in the dialog box. By clicking the Info button (the "i" in the upper-right corner), the person who receives your request can open the User Info On dialog box and find out everything there is to know about you in the White Pages.

Figure 6-2:
When
permission
is needed to
place a
name on the
Contact List,
the reques-
ter fills out
the Privacy
dialog box
(top); the
request
arrives on
the other
side in the
Incoming
Request For
Authoriza-
tion dialog
box
(bottom).

Enter an introductory message.

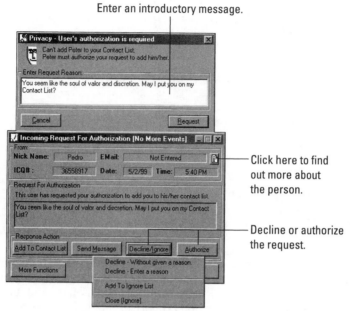

Click here to find
out more about
the person.

Decline or authorize
the request.

How do you know if your request is accepted or rejected? If the person
replies to your request, you see a System message icon (a red checkmark)
beside the person's name under Awaiting Authorization on your Contact List.
Either double-click the icon or click it and choose Receive to read the reply:

- ✔ **The person agrees to your request:** You see the Incoming
  "Authorization" Request Accepted dialog box, shown at the top of Figure
  6-3. Click the Close button. You have permission, and the name is
  entered on your Contact List.

- ✔ **The person denies your request:** You see an Incoming "Authorization"
  Request Denied dialog box, similar to the one at the bottom of Figure
  6-3. Sometimes the person explains why permission wasn't granted;
  sometimes not. Click the Close button. Then click the person's name
  under "Awaiting Authorization" on the Contact List and choose Delete
  on the pop-up menu. Better luck next time.

Sometimes nothing happens when you ask to put another's name on the
Contact List. You wait and wait and wait. It could be that the person ignored
your request. Or it could be that the other person neglected to respond to it.

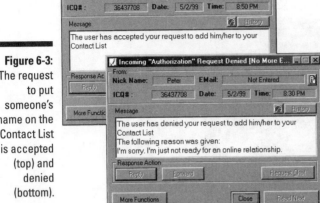

Figure 6-3:
The request
to put
someone's
name on the
Contact List
is accepted
(top) and
denied
(bottom).

To encourage the other person to get on the stick and authorize or reject your request, click the person's name under "Awaiting Authorization" on the Contact List and choose Re-Request Authorization on the pop-up menu. The Resent Request For Authorization From User dialog box appears. Send the request again.

But if the person's name sits under "Awaiting Authorization" for days and days and days, chances are you're being ignored. Click the person's name on the Contact List, choose Delete on the pop-up menu, and move on.

Permission isn't required

If you don't need permission to put someone's name on your Contact List, you see the User Has Been Added message box as soon as you choose the Add to Contact List command, as shown on the top of Figure 6-4, and the name is entered on your Contact List.

Meanwhile, the person whose name you entered on your list gets a System menu message in the form of the Incoming "You Were Added" dialog box, shown at the bottom of Figure 6-4. If the person whose name you entered wants to know about you, he or she can click the Info button (the "i") or the Get User Info button. By clicking the Add To Contact List, the other person can enter your name on his or her Contact List.

Figure 6-4:
When
permission
isn't
required to
enter a
name on the
Contact List,
the name is
entered
right away
(top), and
the person
whose
name was
entered
sees the
"You Were
Added"
dialog box
(bottom).

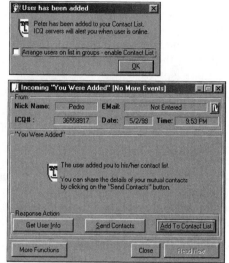

When someone wants to put your name on his Contact List . . .

What happens when someone puts your name on his Contact List depends on whether others need permission to put your name on their lists (see "Choosing Whether to Authorize Your Name for Others' Contact Lists" earlier in this chapter). Keep reading.

Permission is required

If someone wants to enter your name on his Contact List and he needs permission to do so, you get a System Menu message. Open the message and you see the Incoming Request For Authorization dialog box (refer to the bottom of Figure 6-2). In the dialog box, a message tells you why the other person wants your name for his or her Contact List.

 To find out whether you want your name to grace this person's Contact List, click the Info button (the "i" in the upper-right corner). Doing so brings up the User Info On dialog box, where you can read what is known about the person in the Global Directory.

Click the <u>A</u>uthorize button if you give permission to put your name on the other's Contact List.

But if you decide to decline the request, click the Decline/Ignore button. Doing so opens a drop-down menu (refer to Figure 6-2) with options for delivering the bad news:

- ✔ **Decline — Without given (*sic*) a reason:** Choose this option and the other person sees the Incoming "Authorization" Request Denied dialog box. The dialog box tells the other party that his or her request was turned down and gives no reason why.

- ✔ **Decline — Enter a reason:** Choose this option and you get a dialog box for explaining why the request was turned down. Later, when the other person sees the Incoming "Authorization" Request Denied dialog box (refer to Figure 6-3), your explanation appears at the bottom of the dialog box.

- ✔ **Add To Ignore List:** Places the person's name on the list of people you are ignoring. Never again will you receive messages, chat requests, or other communications from this person. Chapter 14 explains in detail how to ignore others.

- ✔ **Close (Ignore):** Closes the Incoming Request For Authorization dialog box. Your name remains under "Awaiting Authorization" on the other person's Contact List. The other person doesn't hear from you and concludes either that you're ignoring him or her or that you never received the request for authorization message.

Click the Send Message button if you want to send a message and ask the other person why he or she is so eager to have your name on the Contact List. Click the Add to Contact List button to add the requester's name to your Contact List.

Permission isn't required

If others don't need permission to put your name on their Contact Lists, your name is entered right away. Next time you go online and connect to the ICQ network, you get a System Menu message, the Incoming "You Were Added" dialog box appears, and you learn that your name was entered on someone's Contact List (refer to the bottom of Figure 6-4).

In the dialog box, click the Get User Info or Info button if you care to learn more about the person who has put your name on his list. Click the Add to Contacts button to add the requester's name to your Contact List.

Locating someone on your Contact List

In a long Contact List, especially one that has been divided into many groups, sometimes a name gets lost. Sometimes you lose track of a name and can't find it by reading the Contact List. For those times, ICQ offers the Find User and Sort commands.

If you happen to know the lost soul's name, nickname, e-mail address, or ICQ number, you can find him or her by following these steps:

3. Right-click the person's name and choose an option from the shortcut menu — ICQ Chat or Message, for example — if you want to get in touch with the person. The menu offers all the commands that you get when you click a person's name on the Contact List.

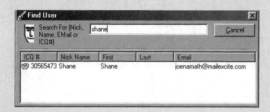

1. Right-click a Contact List tab — All, Online, User, or Groups — and choose Find User from the shortcut menu.

   The Find User dialog box appears.

2. In the text box, enter the person's nickname, name, e-mail address, or ICQ number.

   If ICQ can find the person you're looking for, the bottom of the dialog box opens and you find information about the person.

The Sort command is for arranging names on the Contact List by alphabetical order. When someone sends you a message or a request to chat, his or her name is moved to the top of the Contact List. But if you want to see the names in alphabetical order, right-click a tab — All, Online, User, or Groups — and choose Sort⇨By Name.

Removing Names from the Contact List

Contact Lists have a habit of getting crowded. May as well remove the names of long-lost people you don't hear from anymore. Follow these steps to remove someone's name from the Contact List:

1. **Click the person's name on the list.**

   If you have any doubts about who you're removing from the list, click the Info command on the pop-up menu to find out the person's interests and other information from the White Pages.

2. **Choose More (Rename, Delete)⇨Delete on the pop-up menu.**

   You see the Confirm Delete User dialog box.

3. **Click Yes to remove the person from your Contact List; check the Delete User from the Address Book check box as well if you also want to remove the person from your Address Book.**

As long as a person's name is on file in the Address Book, you can put him or her on the Contact List. So leave the person's name in the Address Book if you anticipate having to put him or her back on the Contact List someday. To place the name of someone in the Address Book on the Contact List, right-click the person's name in the Address Book and choose Add to Contact List. Chapter 15 explains the Address Book.

Changing Someone's Name on the Contact List

Go ahead — change the names of people on the Contact List. Give them descriptive names that help you tell one person from another. The people whose names you change will never be the wiser.

To change someone's name, click it in the Contact List and choose More (Rename, Delete)➪Rename. The person's name is highlighted on the Contact List. Type a new name and press the Enter key.

Another way to change someone's name on the Contact List — and find out what someone's real name is, for that matter — is to click his or her name on the Contact List and choose Info. As shown in Figure 6-5, the Main tab in the User Info On dialog box appears. On this tab, you can read the person's real name. And you can also open the Display drop-down menu and choose the person's first name, last name, or combination of first and last name. The name you choose will appear on the Contact List.

Figure 6-5:
Choose a
Display
option in the
User Info On
dialog box
to list
someone on
the Contact
List in a
different
way.

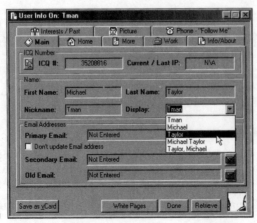

Ways of Viewing the Contact List

When you're online and connected to the ICQ network, names on the Contact List appear in blue or red. A blue name means that the person is online and connected to ICQ; a red name means the person is not connected to ICQ or is in Invisible status. Look for blue names when you want to chat with someone, since people whose names are blue are online and can receive invitations to chat.

To help you tell who is and isn't online, and to arrange Contact List names by group, you can click the tab buttons at the top of the ICQ window and view your Contact List in different ways:

- ✔ **All tab:** Displays all names whether they are connected at present to ICQ.

- ✔ **Online tab:** Shows only the names of people who are connected to ICQ.

- ✔ **User tab:** Lists names, not groups and names.

- ✔ **Groups tab:** Shows names arranged by group (later in this chapter, "Groups for Keeping Track of Contact List Names" explains what groups are).

By clicking different combinations of tab buttons, you can see the names on your Contact List in different ways, as shown in Figure 6-6. Here are the five different ways to view the names in the Contact List:

Figure 6-6:
Ways of viewing the Contact List: All | User; Online | User; Online | Groups; All | Groups (Group mode 1); and All | Groups (Group mode 2).

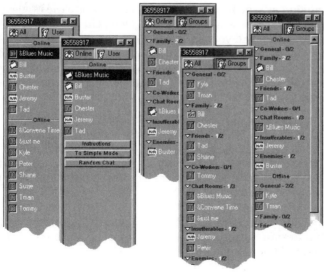

✔ **Online | User:** Displays the Online and User tab so you see only the names of people who are currently online and connected to ICQ.

✔ **All | User:** Shows everyone on your Contact List by name. The names of people who are connected to ICQ are listed under the word *Online;* the names of others appear on the bottom of the list under the word *Offline.*

✔ **Online | Groups:** Shows, arranged by group, only the people who are online at present.

✔ **All | Groups (Group mode 1):** Shows, by group, every name on the Contact List. Within each group, the names of people who are connected to ICQ appear first; the names of people who are not connected come next.

✔ **All | Groups (Group mode 2):** Shows every name arranged by online group and offline group. In mode 2, each group name is listed twice, first at the top of the list under *Online,* and next on the bottom of the list under *Offline.* The names of people who are connected to ICQ appear by group at the top of the list; the names of the others appear by group on the bottom.

To switch back and forth between group modes, either right-click the Groups tab or click a group name, choose Group Mode on the pop-up menu, and then choose Mode 1 or Mode 2.

ICQ offers a couple more commands for tinkering with the appearance of the Contact List. These commands are hardly worth mentioning, but for all we know you are a stickler for details and you want to cook your Contact List to perfection:

✔ **Removing or viewing separators:** *Separators* are the tiny white lines that appear beside the words *Online* and *Offline* in the Contact List. Turn off the separators and you get a little extra room for Contact List names in the ICQ window, although the division between online and offline names isn't as pronounced. To turn the separators on or off, either right-click the Groups tab or click a group name, choose Separators, and then choose On or Off on the submenu.

✔ **Removing or viewing "extra icons":** So-called extra icons are the tiny icons that appear to the right of names on the Contact List to show that a person has an ICQ homepage, for example. We can think of no reason whatsoever to turn these off, but if you they offend you, right-click a tab button and then click Show Extra Icons on the pop-up menu to remove the checkmark.

See "Changing the Appearance of the Contact List" at the end of this chapter if you want to know how to change the color of names on the list or the background color of the ICQ window.

Making a Contact List name "float" onscreen

Odd as it may seem at first, you can drag a name from the Contact List, plop it in a corner or side of the screen, and let it float there. Why would anyone do such a thing? Because letting a name float is one of the best ways to chat in ICQ while you are doing other tasks.

In effect, the name acts as a mini-window. When you see the chat icon or message icon next to the name, you know you have received a chat invitation or message from the person whose name you dragged off the Contact List. You can click the person's name and see a pop-up menu — the same menu you get when you click the person's name on the Contact List. Instead of the Contact List inhabiting a big chunk of the screen, only the names of people with whom you are trading messages or chatting appear.

To make a name float, either drag it from the Contact List or click it and choose More (Rename, Delete)⇨"Floating" On.

To move a name back onto the Contact List when you no longer want it to be footloose and fancy free on the desktop, either drag it back to the ICQ window or click it and choose "Floating" Off on the pop-up menu. You can also choose All "Floating" Off to move all names back into the ICQ window.

Sending and Receiving Contact List Names

Turns out Contact List names can be handed around like baseball cards. As long as your name is on someone else's Contact List, he or she can send you the other names on the list so that you can put them on your Contact List. And you can send the names on your Contact List, too. You can send them to anyone whose name appears on your Contact List. ICQ offers a special command for sending the names on a Contact List to other people: the Contacts command.

Seems strange, doesn't it, to be able to pass around Contact List names? However, you still need authorization to put someone's name on your list if authorization is required ("Choosing Whether to Authorize Your Name for Others' Contact Lists" earlier in this chapter explains how Contact List authorization works). If authorization is what the person wants, you have to get permission to add his or her name to your Contact List, no matter how you got the name. Passing around names with the Contacts command doesn't excuse you from getting others' permission to put names on your list.

Read on to find out how to send names on your Contact List to someone else and how to add names that were sent to you to your list.

Sending names on your Contact List to someone else

Follow these steps to send names on your Contact List to someone else:

1. **Click the person's name on your Contact List and choose Contacts from the pop-up menu.**

   The Export Users on Your Contact List to a Member dialog box, shown in Figure 6-7, appears. The dialog box lists all the people on your Contact List.

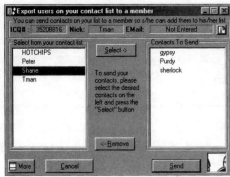

Figure 6-7: With the Contacts command, you can send names on your Contact List to someone else.

2. **Click a name on the left side of the dialog box and then click the Select button to choose a name to send.**

   The name appears on the Contacts To Send side of the dialog box.

3. **Keep clicking names and clicking the Select button until you have chosen all the names you want to send.**

   If you change your mind about sending a name, click it on the Contacts To Send side of the dialog box and then click the Remove button.

4. Click the Send button.

The person to whom you send the list can decide whether to put the names on his or her Contact List. Keep reading to find out what to do when you receive Contact List names from someone else.

By the way, the Incoming "You Were Added" dialog box — the one you see when someone puts you on his Contact List (refer to Figure 6-4) — offers a button called Send Contacts for sending the names on your list to the person who recently put your name on his or her Contact List. Click the Send Contacts button and you see the Export dialog box shown in Figure 6-7, where you can send names on your Contact List to your newfound friend.

Getting Contact List names from someone else

You can tell when someone has sent you names from a Contact List because the Contacts icon appears beside the person's name on your Contact List and in the lower-right corner of the screen. Follow these steps to retrieve the names and perhaps put them on your Contact List:

1. Either double-click the Contacts icon or click the icon and choose Receive from the pop-up menu.

You see the Incoming Contacts List dialog box, shown in Figure 6-8. The dialog box lists names you can add to your list.

Do you really want to crowd your Contact List with these names? To find out whether a name is worth putting on your Contact List, click the name and then click the Get User Info button. You see the User Info On dialog box, which describes all that is known about the person in the White Pages.

2. Place a name on your Contact List by clicking a name in the dialog box and then clicking the Add To Contact List button.

That's all there is to it if you don't need permission from the person to put his or her name on your Contact List. But if authorization is needed, you see the Privacy – User's Authorization Is Required dialog box (refer to Figure 6-2). Write a note in the dialog box, click the Request button, and click OK in the message box that tells you the request was sent. Later, if you get permission to put the person's name on your list, the Incoming "Authorization" Request Accepted dialog box will tell you so (refer to Figure 6-3).

3. Repeat Steps 1 and 2 for each name you want to put on your Contact List.

4. Click the Close button.

Click to find out more about someone.

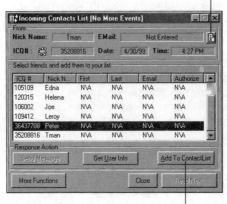

Figure 6-8:
The
Incoming
Contacts
List dialog
box lists the
names of
people you
can add to
your
Contact List.

Click to put the person's name on your Contact List.

Groups for Keeping Track of Contact List Names

You don't know it yet if you are new to ICQ, but a Contact List can get very long. And when the list gets too long and is crowded with names, the time has come to start putting the names in groups. Come to think of it, putting names in groups is a good idea no matter how long your Contact List is, because groups are the best way to distinguish one person from another. Co-workers can go in the Co-Worker group and friends can go in the Friends group. As for enemies and insufferables, you can create an Enemies group and Insufferables group for them. As Figure 6-9 shows, group names appear on the Contact List when you click the Groups tab in the ICQ window.

To start with, ICQ gives you four groups: General, Family, Friends, and Co-Workers. But you can create groups of your own. Names you add to your Contact List are put in the General group unless you tell ICQ to put them in a different group. You can also move names from group to group, view the names in some groups but not in others, change the names of groups, delete groups, and change the way that the names in groups are displayed. Better read on.

Triangle pointing right means the group is closed.

Triangle pointing down means the group is open.

Number of people online/people in group.

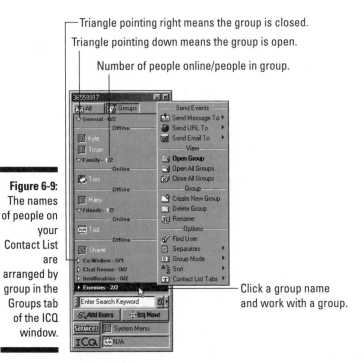

Figure 6-9:
The names
of people on
your
Contact List
are
arranged by
group in the
Groups tab
of the ICQ
window.

Click a group name
and work with a group.

Displaying groups and reading the Groups tab

As "Ways of Viewing the Contact List" explained earlier in this chapter, you have to display the Groups tab to arrange the names on the Contact List by group. To display the Groups tab, click the User tab button, if necessary — the Group tab appears right away and you can see the names of groups in the ICQ window (refer to Figure 6-9).

As always, the names of people who are online appear in blue on the Groups tab, and you can click the Online tab button to see only the names of people who are online, or the All tab button to see online and offline names (refer to Figure 6-6).

What's more, the Groups tab offers two so-called modes for displaying all the names on the Contact List. Right-click the Groups tab or click a group name and choose Group Mode⇨Mode 1 to display online and offline Contact List names by group. To clearly distinguish between online and offline names in groups, choose Group Mode⇨Mode 2, which shoves offline names to the bottom half of the ICQ window.

An arrow pointing to the right beside a group name means the group is closed; an arrow pointing down means the group is open and you can see the names of all its members or all its members who are online, depending on which tab button you clicked (All or Online). Notice the numbers beside group names. The first number tells how many people in the group are currently online. The second number tells how many people are in the group altogether.

Opening and closing groups so you can see or hide names

A Contact List in which all the groups are open can be as long as your arm. If you hang out on the Groups tab, you need to know how to open and close groups so you can see only the Contact List names you need to see. Follow these instructions for seeing or hiding the names in a group:

- ✔ **Opening a group:** Click the name and choose Open Group on the pop-up menu. Names in the group appear on the Contact List.

- ✔ **Closing a group:** Click the name and choose Close Group on the menu. The names disappear and the Contact List grows shorter.

- ✔ **Opening or closing all the groups on the Groups tab:** Either right-click the Groups tab button or click the name of a group, and then choose Open All Groups or Close All Groups on the pop-up menu.

The fastest way to open or close a group on the Groups tab is to double-click the name of the group whose names you want to see or hide.

Creating a new group

Create a new group on the Groups tab whenever you need to categorize the people on your Contact List in a new way. Create a Lost Souls, Close Personal Friends, or Sworn Enemies group, for example. Follow these steps to create a new group for categorizing the people on your Contact List:

1. **Click the name of a group and choose Create New Group from the pop-up menu.**

   You see the Create New Group dialog box.

2. **Enter a name for the group in the text box.**

   Choose a descriptive but short and sweet name that will fit easily in the ICQ window.

3. **Click the Create button.**

   The name of the group appears at the bottom of the list.

Putting names in one group or another

ICQ offers no less than three different ways to put a name on the Contact List in one group or another:

✔ On the Groups tab, click the name of the ICQ member you want to move to a different group, choose Move To Group on the pop-down menu, and then click the name of the group on the submenu.

✔ On the Groups tab, click a name, drag it over the name of the group you want to move it to, and release the mouse button.

✔ In the User Has Been Added dialog box shown in Figure 6-10, the dialog box you see when you add a name to your Contact List, click the Arrange Users on List in Groups check box, click the To an Existing Group option button, and choose the name of the group from the drop-down menu.

Figure 6-10:
As you add names to your Contact List, you can file them away by group.

Rearranging the names on the Groups tab

Suppose you want to change the order of group names on the Contact List. To move a group name up or down the list, start by clicking a name and choosing Close All Groups on the pop-up menu so you can see only group names on the Contact List. Then click the group name you want to move and drag it up or down the list to move it to a new location. As you drag, a plus sign appears below the pointer so you know you are moving a group name on the list.

Deleting and renaming groups

Deleting and renaming groups on the Groups tab of the ICQ window is pretty darn simple. Click the name of the group that needs deleting or renaming and follow these steps:

✔ **Deleting a group:** Choose Delete Group on the pop-up menu. You see the Confirm Delete Group dialog box. Choose a group from the drop-down menu if you want to move all the names in the group to another group before you delete the group in question. Then click the Yes button.

If you want to delete the names in the group as well as the group itself, click the Delete Group & All Users option button, and click the check box as well if you want to remove these people's names from your Address Book. Then click the Yes button.

✔ **Renaming a group:** Choose Rename on the pop-up menu. In the Rename Group dialog box, enter a new name and click OK.

Changing the Appearance of the Contact List

For the interior decorator that is waiting to be born inside everybody, ICQ offers the ability to change the appearance of the Contact List. Does the gray background make you feel gloomy? Instead of blue, do you think the names of people on the Contact List who are online should be green or purple? Do not despair, because you can decorate the Contact List to suit your taste.

Follow these steps to play interior decorator with the ICQ window:

1. **Click the ICQ button and choose Preferences.**

   You see the Owner Prefs For dialog box.

2. **Click the Contact List tab.**

3. **Under "Contact List Design" on the right side of the Contact List tab, click the check box beside the Customize Colors button, and then click the Customize Colors button.**

   You see the Colors dialog box, shown on the left side of Figure 6-11. The dialog box shows which color is assigned to the names of people on the Contact List who are online, offline, waiting to be authorized for the Contact List, and so on. The last color, the one beside the word *Background,* is the background color of the ICQ window.

   By clicking the color squares, you can open the Color dialog box and choose a new color for part of the Contact List or the background of the ICQ window.

Click a square.   Pick a color, any color.

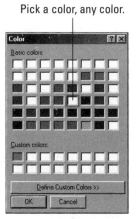

Figure 6-11:
Choosing
new color
assignments
for the parts
of the
Contact List
and the ICQ
window.

4. **Click the color square beside the part of the Contact List you want to change; click the Background check box and then click the gray square to change the background color of the ICQ window.**

   You see the Color dialog box shown on the right side of Figure 6-11.

5. **Click a color square in the Color dialog box and then click OK.**

   If none of the colors suits you, you can click the Define Custom Colors button. Doing so brings up a red-green-blue color array box. Keep clicking in the box and dragging the slider arrow to its right until the Color | Solid box displays a color you are happy with. You can click the Add to Custom Colors button to place the color you found in the Custom Colors list in the dialog box. That way, you can choose the color again simply by clicking its color box.

6. **Repeat Steps 4 and 5 as many times as you want to decorate other parts of the Contact List.**

7. **Click the Save button in the Colors dialog box.**

8. **Click the OK button in the Owner Prefs For dialog box.**

If you discover to your regret that you don't like the decorating changes you made to the Contact List, you can get the original colors back. To do so, open the Owner Prefs For dialog box (click the ICQ button and choose Preferences), go to the Contact List tab, and uncheck the check box beside the Customize Colors button.

You can also click the Restore ALL ICQ Defaults button to get the original colors back, but we don't recommend doing that because all the work you did in the Owner Prefs For dialog box, if you did any work, is undone when you click that button. For example, if you wrote customized status messages (on the Status tab), you have to rewrite them.

Chapter 7

Finding People Who Share Your Interests

• •

In This Chapter

▶ Appraising the different ways to find friends in ICQ

▶ Locating someone whose name or ICQ number you know

▶ Searching the White Pages for like-minded people

▶ Finding a good discussion on the Message Board

▶ Posting a message and starting a new discussion

▶ Finding a user list of people who share a common interest

▶ Becoming a member of an interest group

• •

*T*his chapter explains how to spread your tentacles — wings, that is — into the ICQ community and make new friends. ICQ offers a bunch of different ways to branch out. This chapter focuses on four of them: searching the White Pages, reading and posting messages on the Message Board, visiting a user list, and becoming the member of an interest group.

And because every evening at the movie theatre should start with a "preview of coming attractions" to whet your appetite, this chapter starts with a survey of all the ways to find new friends in ICQ.

Surveying the Ways to Find Like-Minded People

Sometimes ICQ resembles a labyrinth more than it does a computer program. ICQ members have been known to wander inside the program for years before discovering all the ways to find like-minded people. To keep you from going astray, Table 7-1 describes how to seek people whose interests are the same or nearly the same as yours.

Plotting a course through the ICQ PeopleSpace Directory

To get a sweeping (and we mean sweeping) survey of all the different ways to find like-minded people, try starting from the ICQ People Navigator. To get there, click the Add Users button, and, in the Find/Add Users to Your List dialog box, click the Topic Directories tab. Then click the People Navigator hyperlink. Shortly, you land at the People Navigator page (www.icq.com/people/topic.html), where you will find a comprehensive list of all the categories in the PeopleSpace Directory for which ICQ maintains chat rooms, user lists, interest groups, message boards, and more.

To find out if others are interested in a topic and whether a chat room, message board, or whatnot can be found for the topic, scroll down the list and click on a general area subject or category. That takes you to another page, where you can select subcategories. Eventually, you arrive at the topic you're looking for (Alien Abductions in this illustration). Next to the topic are several letters: L (User Lists), C (Chat Rooms), G (Interest Groups), and so on. Click a letter to go to a user list, chat room, interest group, or whatnot that pertains to the topic. The legend tells you what the letters mean and where you'll go when you click a letter.

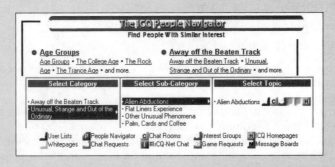

Table 7-1	Ways to Find Like-Minded People in ICQ
Seek Technique	*Description*
Chat Request page	Find someone to chat with on the Chat Request page. You can also put out a request to chat with others. See Chapter 5.
Chat room	Find and join a chat room. ICQ members can also create chat rooms of their own. See Chapter 5.
Interest group	Find and join an interest group, a page on the ICQ Website where the names of people who share common interests are listed. See "Looking for Kindred Spirits in an Interest Group" in this chapter.

Seek Technique	Description
Message Board	Go to the Message Board, read messages, reply to messages, and post messages of your own for others to read and reply to. See "Reading and Posting Messages on the Message Board" in this chapter.
User list	Find a user list, a list of ICQ members who share the same interests. Users lists are not kept on the ICQ Website, but are maintained by ICQ members on their Websites. See "Finding Friends in the User Lists" in this chapter.
White Pages	Search for ICQ members who are interested in the same things you are interested in, live in your town, have the same occupation as you, or are affiliated with the same institutions you are. See "Searching in the White Pages for People with Similar Interests" in this chapter.

Searching for a Specific Someone

As long as you know someone's nickname, first name, last name, e-mail address, or ICQ number, you can look them up in the White Pages very quickly. And after you find a name in the White Pages, you can right-click it and do a number of pleasant things from the drop-down menu, as Figure 7-1 shows.

Everyone who has registered with ICQ is listed in the White Pages. Follow these steps to search for someone you know or suspect is listed there:

1. **Click the ICQ button.**

2. **Choose Find/Add Users⇨Find User — Add To List.**

   You see the ICQ Global Directory dialog box (refer to Figure 7-1). To start with, the dialog box is in Wizard mode, but you can operate out of Classic mode as well by clicking the Classic Mode button (click the Wizard Mode button to switch back to Wizard mode).

   We recommend clicking the Classic Mode button to search in Classic mode. In Wizard mode, you can only enter one search condition at a time: the person's e-mail address, names (nickname, first, and last), or ICQ number. But in Classic mode you can enter all three conditions. Entering two or three conditions increases the chances of finding the person you're looking for.

3. **Enter what you know about the person on the three tabs (in Classic mode) or a text box (in Wizard mode).**

Wizard mode   Classic mode

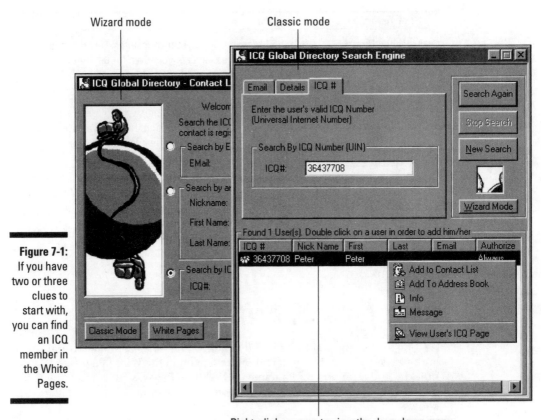

Figure 7-1:
If you have
two or three
clues to
start with,
you can find
an ICQ
member in
the White
Pages.

Right-click a name to view the drop-down menu.

In Classic mode, you enter what you know about the person on the three tabs in the dialog box: Email, Details, and ICQ #. Only enter what you know about the person. Don't fill out all three tabs because, like Mt. Everest, they are there.

In Wizard mode, you enter what you know about the person by clicking an option button and making an entry in a text box (or three text boxes if you enter the person's names).

4. Click the Search button (Classic mode) or Next button (Wizard mode).

As long as the clues you gave were good ones and the person you're looking for is in the White Pages, you see his or her ICQ number and names below the dialog box (refer to Figure 7-1).

By the way, if you have trouble reading an ICQ number or name on the bottom of the dialog box, drag a division marker between the column headings — ICQ #, Nick Name, First, and so on — to the right to make more room for the column. The pointer turns into double-arrows when you move it over a division marker. Click and start dragging when you see the double-arrows to change the width of a column.

After you've found your quarry, you can double-click his or her name to place it on the Contact List. Or you can right-click the name and choose an option from the drop-down menu to razz the person another way.

Suppose your search turns up a blank or turns up too many names to be of any use? If you are in Classic mode, either change the search conditions and click the Search Again button or click the New Search button and start all over. In Wizard mode, click the Back button and try entering a different search condition.

Of course, you can also try another technique for finding people on the ICQ network: You can search the White Pages for people whose interests are similar to yours. Keep reading.

Searching in the White Pages for People with Similar Interests

When you sign on with ICQ, you enter a bunch of information about yourself in the Registration Wizard dialog box. You enter your nickname and maybe your first and last name. Most people record their address, or at least the city and state they live in. And most people also declare their age, interests, and affiliations.

The information that members give ICQ when they register is kept in the White Pages (Chapter 9 explains how to update or change your profile in the White Pages). Think of the White Pages as the Grand Social Registry of ICQ. The White Pages are the repository of every bit of information that ICQ members care to reveal about themselves.

By searching the White Pages, you can find people who share your interests, or grew up in the same town as you, or ply the same trade as you, or pursue the same obsessions as you, or are members of the same organizations, to name only a few attributes you can look for. More than 30 million people are registered with ICQ. Chances are very good you can find someone who shares your interests in the White Pages.

Figure 7-2 shows the results of a search in the White Pages for people who live in St. Louis, are in their 40s, and like the blues. If you were planning a trip to St. Louis and happened to be a blues fan, you could conduct a search like this one to find blues fans in St. Louis. You could seek their help in finding a good blues club in the city. Along the way, you could make friends with blues fans in St. Louis and arrange to carouse with them during your trip to that fair city, the Gateway to the Mississippi.

Check to search only for people who are online.

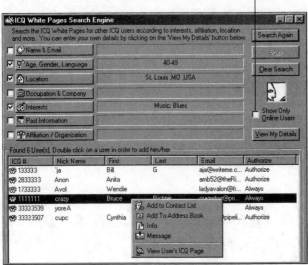

Follow these steps to track down people in the White Pages who share your interests:

1. **Click the ICQ button.**

2. **Choose Find/Add Users⇨White Pages.**

   You see the ICQ White Pages Search Engine dialog box, as shown in Figure 7-2. In the figure, the search conditions have been entered, and you can see them in the boxes in the middle of the dialog box.

3. **Check or uncheck the Show Only Online Users check box.**

   When the box is checked, your search uncovers only people who are connected at present to ICQ. That's good if you want to start chatting right away, but bad if you want to conduct a thorough search, because your search will only turn up people who are online, probably a small portion of all ICQ members who meet the search conditions you will enter.

4. **Enter the search conditions that describe the people you want to find in the White Pages.**

   To enter a search condition, click one of the seven buttons (or check boxes) on the left side of the dialog box. Then describe what you want to search for in the dialog box as that appears. Search conditions are listed in the White Pages Search Engine dialog box as you enter them.

   In the case of the first four attribute buttons, entering search conditions is pretty easy. All you have to do is enter a condition or make a simple choice from a drop-down menu in a dialog box.

But entering the Interests, Past Information, and Affiliation/Organization search conditions is a little harder. Follow these steps:

1. **Click one of the last three buttons — Interests, Past Information, or Affiliation/Organization — and you see a dialog box with a Topic drop-down, as shown in Figure 7-3.**

   When ICQ members describe themselves to the White Pages, they use these same drop-down menus.

Figure 7-3: Clicking the Interests, Past Information, or Affiliation/ Organization button brings up a dialog box like this one for describing a search keyword.

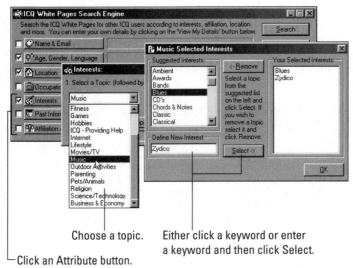

Choose a topic.

Either click a keyword or enter a keyword and then click Select.

Click an Attribute button.

2. **Choose a topic from the drop-down menu that describes who you are looking for and then click the Click To Select/Edit Topic's Keywords button.**

   You see the *Keyword* dialog box, which in Figure 7-3 is called Music Selected Interests. In this dialog box, you can choose keywords that describe who you're looking for:

   - **Choose a word from the list:** Select a word from the Suggested Interests list, and then click the Select button. The word lands in the box on the right side of the dialog box.

   - **Enter a keyword:** Type the word in the Define New Interest dialog box and then click the Select button. The word appears on the right side of the dialog box.

3. **Enter as many keywords as you need to enter (you can select a word and click the Remove button to remove it from the list).**

4. **Click OK to close the Keyword dialog box and OK again to close the Topic dialog box.**

The topic and keywords you selected appear in the White Pages Search Engine dialog box.

5. **Click the Search button in the White Pages Search Engine dialog box to search the White Pages for the people you described.**

The bottom of the dialog box opens and a bunch of names appear if your search is a success (refer to Figure 7-2). You can double-click a name to add it to your Contact List. Right-click a name and you get a menu for doing a number of different things. We suggest choosing the Info command to open the Global Directory and find out more about the person you right-clicked.

As often as not, however, a search of the White Pages yields either too many names or none at all. When that happens, click the Clear Search button to empty out the dialog box and start all over, or else narrow or widen the search:

- ✔ **Narrowing the search:** If too many names come up, enter more search conditions to pinpoint exactly who you're looking for. Then click the Search Again button.

- ✔ **Widening the search:** If too few names or no names come up, uncheck one or two of the check boxes on the left side of the dialog box. By unchecking boxes, you exclude conditions from the search but leave them intact in case you want to check them off and call on them again. Of course, you can also click a button and re-enter or remove search conditions that way. Click the Search Again button to start the search.

By the way, you can click the View My Details button to open the Global Directory dialog box and see what is known about you in the White Pages. Chapter 9 explains how to change or update your profile in the White Pages.

Reading and Posting Messages on the Message Board

The ICQ Message Board is like one of those bulletin boards in a student union or town center with hundreds of messages tacked to it. The difference between a bulletin board and the ICQ Message Board, however, is that the Message Board offers thousands upon thousands of messages from people from all walks of life.

Keep reading to find out how to read messages on the Message Board and contribute to discussions. You will also find advice for finding messages that pertain to a certain topic and discover how to mark messages and discussions so you can return to them over and over again.

Reading messages and participating in discussions

In ICQ-speak, a *discussion* is a collection of messages from ICQ members that pertain to the same topic. The ICQ Message Board offers hundreds and hundreds of discussions on many different topics. These pages explain how to find a discussion that interests you, contribute to discussion, and propose a new topic for discussion.

Burrowing into the Message Board to find discussions of interest

Figure 7-4 demonstrates how to burrow into the Message Board and read messages about a topic that is close to your heart. To begin, click the System Menu button and choose Message Boards on the pop-up menu. Your browser opens to the Message Boards Directory (www.icq.com/boards), where you'll find about two dozen message categories. Click a category that seems promising, and click a subcategory in that category — well, keep clicking. (Chapter 12 explains how to get around in the PeopleSpace Directory if you need advice for getting around there.) Eventually you come to a list of discussions, as shown at the bottom of Figure 7-4.

Discussion subjects are arranged in alphabetical order. If anyone has contributed a message to a discussion, the number of messages is listed next to the discussion subject.

Figure 7-4: Starting from the Message Boards Directory, you can dig down and find discussions about topics that interest you.

Click the subject of a discussion if you would like to read the messages that others have posted. The messages in the discussion appear on a new Web page. To begin with, messages appear in date order, and not all messages appear onscreen if there are more than a handful in the discussion. Click these buttons to tell ICQ how to display messages on your screen:

- ✔ **To Top:** Takes you to the oldest messages that were posted in the discussion.

- ✔ **Previous:** Lists the next eldest batch of messages — the ones previous to the batch you see when you open the discussion group. Click the Recent button to return to the newer batch of messages. You can find the Recent button along with the More button at the bottom of the Web page. Click the More button to see the following batch of messages.

- ✔ **All Messages:** Lists all the messages in the discussion, no matter how many there are.

- ✔ **Outline:** Shows only the first line of all the messages in the discussion. Click a first line to read a message in full.

Searching for messages about a certain topic

Looking for messages in discussions on the Message Board can be like searching for a needle in a haystack. One way to make searches go faster is to click the Search button. You can find this button at the bottom of most pages where discussion topics are listed and messages are posted. Follow these steps to conduct a search of the Message Board for messages of a certain kind:

Search

1. **Click the Search button.**

   You go to the Search page, as shown at the top of Figure 7-5.

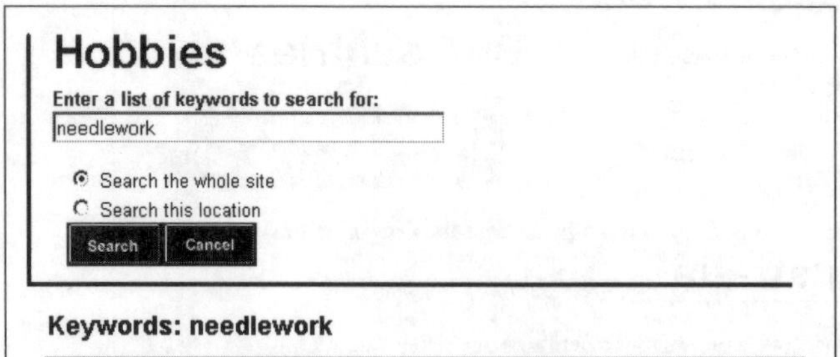

Figure 7-5:
Besides
clicking
categories
and subcat-
egories to
search the
Message
Board, you
can run a
keyword
search like
this one.

Hobbies

Enter a list of keywords to search for:

needlework

⦿ Search the whole site
○ Search this location

Search   Cancel

Keywords: needlework

❑   Jan 19, 1999 10:50 pm
Hi There I have just started up a craft group at my daughters primary school and I am after new ideas for the craft stalls for the school. In my spare time I enjoy lots of craft, needlework,crochet & tricot,Dried Flowers, Woolen Blankets, Beading etc....and alot more. I like to try everything...

2. **Enter keywords that describe what you're searching for in the text box.**

   ICQ will search for and list all messages that include the word you enter.

   If you enter more than one word, put a blank space between the words, not a comma and a blank space. Searches you make of the Message Board are "And" searches: If you enter more than one word, a message has to include both words, not either word, to turn up in the search. Entering more than one word narrows the number of messages you'll find.

   Enter your own name in the text box to find all the messages you posted on the Message Board. For that matter, enter someone else's name to find all the messages he or she posted.

3. **Click a Search option button: Search the Whole Site or Search This Location.**

   Search the whole site if you want to search all the messages on the Message Board. Search this location to look in the category or subcategory area listed at the top of the Search page ("Hobbies" in Figure 7-5).

4. **Click the Search button.**

   As shown at the bottom of Figure 7-5, you see a list of messages that include the word or words you entered in Step 2. Above each message is the subject, the name of the person who posted the message, and the date and time the message was posted. Usually, not all the message fit on a single Web page, and the Search button appears at the bottom of the page so you can click it and see another set of messages.

While the search results are onscreen and staring you in the face, you can do the following:

- ✔ Click the message subject to go to the discussion where the message is posted. There, you can read messages and maybe write a message of your own. (Click the Back button in your browser to return to the search results page.)
- ✔ Click the writer's name to go to a page with links where you can send the writer an e-mail message, go to his or her Personal Communication Center page and leave a message there, add the writer to your Contact List, or see what the White Pages have to say about the writer.

Contributing to a discussion

Suppose you want to contribute to a discussion by posting a message? ICQ offers two ways of doing that:

The first time you post a message . . .

Before you can post a message on the Message Board for the first time, you have to register and obtain a password. Passwords prevent people from submitting messages under others' names. Whenever you post a message, you have to supply your password.

To register, click the Register button (you can find it on most Message Board screens). On the New User Registration screen, enter your name, password, e-mail address, and ICQ number. Don't forget the password you enter, because you'll need it whenever you post a message or reply to a message. To spare yourself the trouble of remembering two passwords, you might as well use your ICQ password as the Message Board password.

✔ **Replying directly to the person who wrote the message:** Click the writer's name (you will find it directly above the message itself). You go to a new Web page with hyperlinks that you can click to send an e-mail message to the writer or go to the writer's Personal Communication Center page and leave a message there. You can also click links to add the writer to your Contact List or get more information about the writer from the White Pages directory. Click OK at the bottom of the page (or click the Back button on your browser) to return to the message.

`Post My Message`

✔ **Contributing to the discussion:** To enter a message of your own for all who visit the discussion to see, scroll toward the bottom of the page, where you see boxes for entering the title of your message, your ICQ number, and the message itself. Fill in the boxes and click the Post My Message button. Then enter your name and password, and click the Login button. (See the "The first time you post a message..." sidebar if this is the first time you have tried to post a message or reply on the Message Board.)

After you click OK to finalize your message, you return to the discussion page, where you can see the message you just wrote. Be sure to click the Bookmark button if you want to return to this discussion someday (see "Subscribing to discussions and bookmarking messages" later in this chapter).

Starting a new discussion on the Message Board

Besides contributing to others' discussions, you can submit a topic of your own for others to write messages about. Your discussion topic will appear on the subcategory page along with the other discussion topics. Follow these steps to start a new discussion:

1. **Go to the subcategory where your subject of discussion rightfully belongs.**

   Choose a subcategory very carefully. If you spend any time whatsoever on the Message Board, you soon find out that many messages have been entered in the wrong category or wrong discussion.

2. **Click the Add Discussion button.**

   You can find this button below the discussion topics at the bottom of the page. If the button isn't there, you can't start a new discussion from the page you're on. You see the Adding a Discussion to screen after you click the Add Discussion button.

3. **In the New Discussion Title box, enter the subject of the discussion.**

   Discussions appear by alphabetical order, so many people put a punctuation mark or number at the start of the discussion name to push their discussion to the top of the list. We suggest writing a good description instead. The more descriptive you can make the subject of your discussion, the more likely you are to attract contributors.

4. **Enter a description of the discussion you propose having in the text box.**

   Write a description that invites others to contribute. You must have noticed by now that the Message Board is filled with bland and sometimes boorish discussion topics that don't encourage people to participate.

5. **Uncheck the Show Your Name in the Discussion Heading check box if you want all contributions to appear the Message Board, not in your mailbox.**

   If your name appears beside the discussion topic, others can click your name and go to a Web page where links to your e-mail address and Personal Communication Center page are located. From there, they can click a link and reply to you personally. Uncheck the check box if you prefer not to be bothered personally by people who contribute to your discussion.

6. **Click the Add Discussion button.**

7. **Enter your name and password in the following dialog box; then click the Login button.**

   (Click the Register button, not the Login button, and read the sidebar "The first time you post a message . . ." if you have not posted a message before.)

   A screen shows you exactly what your discussion topic will look like when it is posted on the Message Board. Now is your chance to click the Edit button and change the message if it needs changing. You can also click the Delete button if you decide not to start a new discussion after all. These buttons — Edit and Delete — remain on the discussion page for a half-hour. You have that long to change your mind about the discussion.

8. Click the Add Discussion button yet again.

Tiresome, isn't it, clicking that button all the time?

The page you see next is the actual page on the Message Board on which your new discussion is displayed. Others will come to this page when they want to contribute to the discussion.

Before you leave this Web page, we recommend clicking the Bookmark button so you can come back here later and see if anyone has contributed. Keep reading to discover what bookmarks are.

Subscribing to discussions and bookmarking messages

When you post a message on the Message Board, you get the opportunity to bookmark the message and subscribe to the discussion in which you posted the message. Bookmark a message when you want to be able to return to it quickly. Unless you're a bloodhound, the only way to find a message on the crowded Message Board is to bookmark it. Subscribe to a discussion when you want to follow it closely and find out when new messages have been posted. Read on to find out how to bookmark a message and subscribe to a discussion.

Bookmarking a message

After you contribute to a discussion, the Bookmark button appears on the discussion page. Be sure to click that button if you expect to return to the discussion page again.

As long as you click the Bookmark button after you post a message, you can get back to the discussion page where the message was posted. After you click the Bookmark button, the discussion page you bookmarked is entered on your list of bookmarks, as shown in Figure 7-6.

To see the list of bookmarks, click the Bookmarks button. You can find this button at the bottom of discussion pages and subcategory pages. The top of the list of bookmarks shows new messages that were posted on the discussion pages you bookmarked. Scroll farther down the page and you see the bookmarks.

Take note of the following things that you can do from the list of bookmarks:

- ✔ **Visit a bookmarked page:** Click the name of a page to go to it straightaway. You can write comments about bookmarks to help distinguish one from another. Be sure to click the Set button after you enter a comment.

✔ **Delete a bookmark:** Click the Delete button beside the bookmark that needs removing.

✔ **Change how the bookmarks are displayed:** Uncheck the Show New Messages in This Page check box to keep new messages from appearing at the top of the page. If you change this or another setting, be sure to click the Change Settings button.

Click a page to visit it.

Figure 7-6:
After you bookmark a discussion page, you can go back to it very quickly by clicking the page's name on the list of bookmarks.

Bookmarks

Title	Last Mod.	Author	Comment		
Aliens	09 May 1999	Peter Wev	Crazy stuff	Set	Delete
The Clash	30 Nov 1998	Peter Wev	Rock the Casbah	Set	Delete
Halie Salassie	09 May 1999	Peter Wev		Set	Delete

Message Center Settings

☑ **Show new messages in this page**
☑ **Beep when the new-message list changes**
☑ **Show bookmark list in this page**
Refresh this page every `10` **minutes.** (Use 0 for no refresh.)

[Change Settings]   [Cancel]

Subscribing to a discussion

After you post a message, the Subscribe button appears on the discussion page where you posted it. As long as you click that button (and click OK when ICQ tells you it has processed your subscription), you can return to the discussion whenever you want. Subscribe to a discussion when you want to find out when others have made contributions to it and what those contributions are.

We cannot warn you strongly enough: *Do not* subscribe to a page that lists folders (you can tell which pages are folder pages because minifolder icons appear beside the folders' names). If you subscribe to a page with folders, you subscribe to every discussion group in the folder! Most folders include at least a dozen discussion groups, so merely by clicking the Subscribe button on a folder page, you subscribe to a dozen or more discussions. If you make the mistake of subscribing to a folder page, go back to the page and click the Cancel Subscripts button.

To visit a discussion page you subscribe to, click the Check Messages button. You can find this button at the bottom of discussion pages and pages where discussion topics are listed. After you click the button, enter your name and password, and click the Login button. A discussion page you subscribe to appears. Actually, the page appears only if new messages have been placed on it. After you've reviewed the page and read the new messages, if there are any, click the Check Messages button again to see the next page you subscribe to.

The Cancel Subscripts button appears on pages that you subscribe to. If you decide not to describe to a discussion anymore, click the Cancel Subscripts button and then click OK when ICQ informs you that your subscription is being canceled.

Finding Friends in the User Lists

A *user list*, also known as a *user created list,* is a list of ICQ members who are interested in the same topic. The lists are not kept on the ICQ Website, but on members' Websites. Members can submit the names of their user lists to ICQ, and ICQ puts the names in the User Created Lists Directory, as shown in Figure 7-7.

Starting from the User Created Lists Directory, you can find a list that interests you and go there by clicking the View List button. Soon you arrive at the Website where the list is found. There, you see the names of ICQ members who are interested in the same topic. You can ask the list master — the person who maintains the list — to put your name on his or her user list.

Follow these steps to find and pay a visit to a user list with the names of ICQ members who share the same passion or preoccupation:

Figure 7-7:
After you've found a user list in the User Created Lists Directory, click the View List button to go to the Website where the list is maintained.

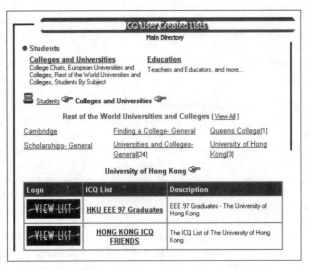

1. **Click the ICQ button and choose Find/Add Users⇨Users' Lists.**

   Your browser opens to the ICQ User Created Lists Directory (`www.icq.com/icqlist`), as shown in Figure 7-7.

2. **Scroll through the category names and click the name of a category that piques your interest.**

   You see a list of subcategories. Underneath the subcategory names are the names of the sub-subcategories where the user lists are found. (Chapter 12 explains how to find your way around the User Created Lists Directory and other parts of the PeopleSpace Directory.)

   User lists aren't found in all the sub-subcategories. To tell which sub-subcategory names are worth clicking, look beside the names for a bracketed number. The number in brackets tells you how many user lists are found in the sub-subcategory. A sub-subcategory name without a bracketed number isn't worth clicking because no user lists are found there.

   You can click the View All hyperlink to see the names of all the user lists in the subcategory.

3. **Click a sub-subcategory name to see the names of user lists in the sub-subcategory.**

   At last — you see the names of user lists.

4. **Click the View List button or the name of a list to go to the Website where the list is maintained.**

   All user lists are different, but on most you will find a roll call of names and ICQ numbers in case you want to get in touch with someone on the list. Look around and you'll find instructions for submitting your name to the list, too.

Looking for Kindred Spirits in an Interest Group

An *interest group* is a cadre of like-minded people whose interests are the same. Visit an interest group and you can see a list of its members, send them messages, or chat with them. By joining an interest group, you put your name on the list of people whom others may send messages to or chat with.

If you read the last few pages in this chapter about user lists, you're probably wondering what the difference is between an interest group and a user list. Both present the names of ICQ members who are interested in a particular topic. However, communicating with the people in an interest group is easier than communicating with the members of a user list, because interest group

Web pages offer buttons that you can click to send messages to or learn more about members, as Figure 7-8 shows. ICQ calls these buttons the *Action panel* (which leads us to believe that the creators of ICQ have seen too many Jean-Claude Van Damme movies).

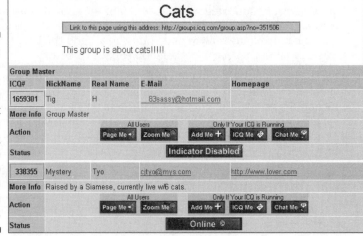

Figure 7-8: The members list in the Cats interest group. You can click the Action buttons to get in touch with a member.

Another difference between interest groups and user lists is that interest groups are more exclusive. You have to submit your password and ICQ number to join an interest group. Sometimes you have to join before you can see the names of the people in the group. A so-called group master presides over every interest group. The group master sets the rules about who can and can't join.

These pages explain how to cruise the Groups Directory to find a group that is worth investigating or joining. You also find out how to join an interest group, get in touch with other members, and quit an interest group that no longer arouses your interest.

Finding an interest group that tickles your fancy

Keeping in mind Groucho Marx's dictum, "I don't care to belong to any club that will have me as a member," follow these steps to go the Groups Directory and find an interest group that tickles your fancy:

1. **Click the Add Users button.**

   The Find/Add Users to Your List dialog box appears.

2. Click the Topic Directories tab.

3. Click the Interest Groups hyperlink.

Your browser opens to the ICQ Interest Groups page (http://groups.
icq.com). This is the starting point for doing whatever you want to do
with interest groups — find one to join, see a list of groups you've
already joined, or create an interest group of your own.

Notice the 100 Largest Groups hyperlink on the right side of the screen.
Click that link and you can see a list of the most popular interest groups.
Some of them have as many as 5,000 members.

4. Click the Select a Topic hyperlink.

Your browser takes you to the Directory of Topics page (http://groups.
icq.com/category.html). On this page is the list of general categories
and categories in which ICQ organizes its interest groups, chat rooms, and
message boards, among other things. By clicking a category, you can start
the search for an interest group. (Chapter 12 explains how to find your
way around the Directory of Topics page and other pages in the
PeopleSpace Directory.)

5. Click the name of a category that strikes you as interesting.

As shown at the top of Figure 7-9, you see a list of subcategories. For the
figure, we clicked, under Family, the Pets subcategory.

Choose a category.

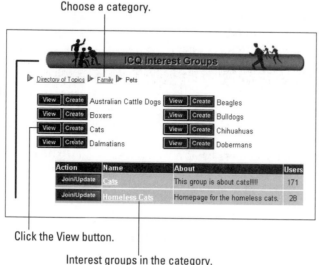

Figure 7-9:
Searching
for an
interest
group in the
Directory of
Topics.

Click the View button.

Interest groups in the category.

View

6. **Scroll to a topic you're interested in, and click the View button beside the topic's name.**

   You see a list of interest groups similar to the one at the bottom of Figure 7-9. Beside each name is a description of the group. The Users column tells you how many members are in the group. Interest groups on the list are arranged from the group with the most members to the group with the fewest.

7. **Click an interest group name to see (maybe) the list of its members.**

   Interest group names are hyperlinks. When you click a name, you go to the Web page where the members of the group are listed (refer to Figure 7-8).

   You have to scroll down the page a bit to see the members' names. At the top of the list is the name of the group master, the person who is in charge of maintaining the interest group. Then come the members' names and contact information. Members are listed in numerical order by ICQ number. Some groups do not make their membership lists public and you have to be a member to view the list.

Click a button on the Action panel to get in touch with or learn more about the member of an interest group:

- ✔ **Page Me:** Takes you to the person's Personal Communication Center, where you can leave a message.
- ✔ **Zoom Me:** Opens a page where you can see what is known about the person in the White Pages.
- ✔ **Add Me:** Puts the name of the person on your Contact List.
- ✔ **ICQ Me:** Opens the Send Message dialog box so you can send a message.
- ✔ **Chat Me:** Opens the Send Online Chat Request dialog box so you can invite the person for a chat. It goes without saying, but you can engage the person in a chat only if he or she is online.

An interest group members list is a Web page. As such, you can bookmark it in your browser and in so doing be able to visit it later without having to go to the ICQ Interest Group page first.

Joining an interest group

After you've found an interest group that is worth joining and you can see its name in the Topics Directory, follow these steps to join it:

Join/Update

1. **Click the Join/Update button.**

   The button is located to the left of the group's name. You see the Login screen after you click the button.

The first time you join an interest group . . .

The first time you click the Join/Update button and attempt to join an interest group, you see the Login screen and then the Personal Details screen, which asks for your nickname and the usual stuff. We're not sure why ICQ needs this information a second time, because you already entered most of it either when you registered or when you updated your profile in the White Pages (see Chapter 9).

Anyhow, you have to enter the information again in the Personal Details screen. The information you enter will be available to anyone who clicks the Zoom Me button below your name on an interest group list (refer to Figure 7-8). What you enter on the User Details screen, incidentally,

has nothing to do with what is entered in the White Pages. The information about you that is filed away in the White Pages stays the same no matter how you describe yourself on the User Details screen.

Later, if you decide to change the description you entered in the User Details screen, start from the ICQ Interest Groups page and click the Update Member button. Then enter your ICQ number and password in the Login Screen and click the Login button. You land on the Members Information screen, where you can click the Update Personal Details link and do just that — change your self-description on the User Details screen.

2. **Enter your ICQ number and password; then click the Login button.**

3. **In the User Details screen, introduce yourself; then click the Save My Group Message/Info button.**

   What you enter will appear beside your name on the membership list. Enter a line or two that encourages others to get in touch with you.

   If this is the first time you've tried to join an interest group, you see the Personal Details screen, not the Users Details screen. See the sidebar "The first time you join an interest group..." to find out what to do next.

   To join some groups, you need special authorization. If that is the case, you see the Reason To Join Group box as well as the Personal Info box on the User Details screen. Write a compelling reason why you need to join the interest group in the box. If the group master gives you the go ahead to join, you will find out in the Member's Information screen (see the next section in this chapter).

4. **Click OK in the message box that says the description you entered has been saved successfully.**

   You return to the Topics Directory. Congratulations — you're in the group. You're in with the In Crowd.

Visiting an interest group of which you are a member

To visit an interest group that you've joined and see what the group is up to, follow these steps:

1. **Go to the ICQ Interest Groups page** (http://groups.icq.com).

   To get there, type the page address in your browser's address bar or click the Add Users button, go to the Topic Directories tab in the Find/Add Users to Your List dialog box, and click the Interest Groups hyperlink.

2. **Click the Update Member hyperlink.**

3. **On the Login Screen, enter your ICQ number and password; then click the Login button.**

   The Member's Information screen appears with a list of the interest groups you've joined, as shown in Figure 7-10.

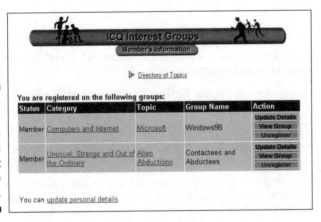

Figure 7-10: Click the View Group button to see the list of group members.

4. **Click the View Group button.**

   You see the list of members in the group. Click the Back button in your browser if you need to return to the Member's Information screen.

The Member's Information screen also offers the Update Details button. Clicking that button takes you to the User Details screen, where you can change the description that appears next to your name on the membership list.

Quitting an interest group

It didn't work out. You wanted to be a member of the group, but it didn't work out. You didn't fit in. All the time you were with the group, you felt like a square peg in a round hole. And now you want to remove your name from the interest group's membership list.

To do so, go to the ICQ Interest Groups page (`http://groups.icq.com`) and click the Update Member hyperlink. Then negotiate the Login screen. When you arrive at the Member's Information screen (refer to Figure 7-10), click the Unregister button next to the name of the group you want to quit. Then click Yes when ICQ asks if you really want to quit the group. There, you quit the group. You're on your own. You're free as a bird.

Chapter 8

Sending and Receiving Messages, Files, and Other Items

. . . .

In This Chapter

▶ The basics of sending and receiving items over ICQ

▶ Sending the same item to more than one person

▶ Sending and receiving messages

▶ Sending e-mail to and getting e-mail from addresses outside ICQ

▶ Sending and playing sound files and recorded messages

▶ Sending and receiving files over ICQ

. . . .

*T*his chapter delves into a subject area dear to the hearts of all ICQ members: It explains some of the most popular ways to communicate with other members. In this chapter, you discover the fine points of sending and receiving messages, files, sound files, recorded messages, and greeting cards.

ICQ offers about a hundred different ways to communicate with others. Well, not a hundred ways, but sometimes it seems like that many. To give you a clear picture of the avenues of communication in ICQ, this chapter starts with a survey of all the ways to communicate.

All the Ways to Communicate in ICQ

Table 8-1 describes the different ways to communicate with other ICQ members. Sometimes both parties have to be online before the lines of communication can open and gossip or valuable information can be exchanged. Table 8-1 notes whether both parties need to be online and declares where in this book each communication technique is explained.

Icon	Technique/Description	Both Parties Online?
Table 8-1	**Ways to Communicate in ICQ**	
	Chatting with others in real time. See Chapters 4 and 5.	Yes
	Sending files to others. See "Sending and Receiving Files."	Yes
	Sending greeting cards. See "Sending a Greeting Card to Someone Else."	No
	Sending Email Express messages to and receiving them from people outside the ICQ network. See "Sending E-mail to and Getting E-mail from Mailboxes Outside ICQ."	No
	Sending messages. See "Sending Messages to and Receiving Messages from Other ICQ Members."	No
	Obtaining someone's phone number. See Chapter 9.	Yes
	Obtaining someone's photo. See Chapter 9.	Yes
	Using telephony applications. See Chapter 16.	Yes
	Exchanging voice messages. See "Sending and Receiving Recorded Messages."	Yes
	Sending Web page addresses. See Chapter 10.	No

The Basics: Sending and Receiving Items

No matter what you want to send over ICQ — a message, a file, a Web page address, a lock of digital hair — the procedure for sending the thing is basically the same. And the procedures for receiving items are basically the same, too. These pages explain the nuts and bolts of sending and receiving items over the ICQ network. You'll also find instructions here for forwarding items and sending the same item to more than one person.

Sending items (now or later)

To send an item to someone, click his or her name on your Contact List. Or, if you found the person in the White Pages or some other place where ICQ members flock together, click (or right-click) the person's name there (be careful not to double-click unless you want to open the Send Message dialog box). You see a pop-up menu like the one in Figure 8-1. Choose a command from the menu to send the person a message, a Web page address, a file, or whatever. As shown in Figure 8-1, a dialog box appears so you can send the item. Figure 8-1 shows the dialog box for sending Web page addresses to other people.

Click the person's name.

Choose what you want to send.

Figure 8-1:
Click Send
to send the
item — or
click the
More button
and choose
a Send Later
option to
postpone
sending it.

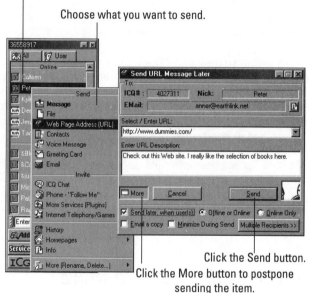

Click the Send button.

Click the More button to postpone
sending the item.

Click the Send button in the dialog box to send the item. When the recipient gets the item depends on whether you're online, whether the recipient is online, and whether you want to postpone sending the message:

✔ **You're online and so is the recipient:** The item is sent right away and the recipient receives it momentarily. However, you can postpone sending the message.

✔ **You're online, and you want to postpone sending the message:** Before clicking the Send button, click the More button. You see options for sending the item later (refer to Figure 8-1). Check the Send Later When Recipient(s) check box and then click an option button to postpone sending the item:

- **Offline or Online:** The other party receives the item next time he or she connects to ICQ.

- **Online Only:** The other party receives the item the next time he or she connects to ICQ and you're also online and connected.

✔ **You're online, but the recipient is offline:** The message is sent to the ICQ servers. The other party will receive it the next time he or she connects to ICQ. If you want to postpone sending the message until you and the other party are online simultaneously, click the More button, check the Send Later When Recipient(s) check box, and click the Online Only option button.

✔ **You're offline:** The item is sent the next time you connect to ICQ. When you're offline and attempt to send an item, the More button in the Send dialog box is pressed down automatically (refer to Figure 8-1). To postpone sending the message until the next time you and the recipient are online simultaneously, check the Send Later When Recipient(s) check box, and click the Online Only option button.

As long as you're set up to do so and the recipient has listed his or her e-mail address with ICQ, you can send a copy of the item to the recipient's e-mail account. To do so, check the Email a Copy check box before clicking the Send button in the Send dialog box. (Later in this chapter, "Sending Items to and Receiving Items from Non-ICQ Accounts" explains how to send messages to someone's private e-mail account.)

You can tell if the recipient has listed his or her e-mail address with ICQ by glancing in the Email box to see if an address is listed there. Why send a second copy of an item? For the same reason that some men wear suspenders and a belt — to make doubly sure, in this case that the message gets there.

Sending the same item to more than one person

Figure 8-2 demonstrates how you can send the same message to several different people — as long as the people to whom you are sending the item are on your Contact List. You're the captain of the softball team? Tell your players to register with ICQ, and instead of laboriously typing the team schedule, photo-copying the schedule, and distributing it to team members, put team members' names on your Contact List and send out the schedule all at once on ICQ.

Messages, Web page addresses, and e-mail can be sent to more than one person at a time. Follow these steps to send the same item to more than one person:

The OutBox: Canceling messages before they are sent

Items that you send to people who are not connected to ICQ or that you postponed sending are kept in the OutBox. Until the targets of these messages go online, the messages remain in the OutBox, where you can visit them, send them forthwith, or eradicate them.

To go to the OutBox, double-click the System Menu button or click the button and choose History and OutBox. The History Of Events dialog box appears. Click the OutBox tab to see the list of unsent items. The list tells you what type of items are waiting to be sent, when they are to be sent (Online Only or Online or Offline), who they are meant for, when you created them, and, in the Info column, what they are.

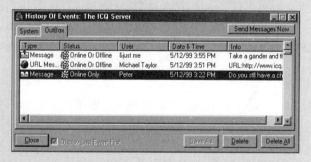

Follow these instructions to send or delete an item in the OutBox:

✔ **Sending items:** Click the Send Messages Now button. Items with Online or Offline status are sent right away. Others are sent as soon as the people to whom they're addressed connect to ICQ.

✔ **Deleting Items:** Click an item and then click the Delete button. Click Delete All to erase all the items in the OutBox.

1. **Click the name of one of the people you want to send the item to.**

2. **On the pop-up menu, choose the item you want to send.**

   A dialog box appears for sending the item.

3. **Enter the message or the Web page address, and then click the More button.**

   A handful of extra options appear at the bottom of the dialog box. Notice the Multiple Recipients button on the right side.

4. **Click the Multiple Recipients button.**

   As shown in Figure 8-2, the Select Recipients list appears. On the list are the names of people on your Contact List.

You can display names by group.

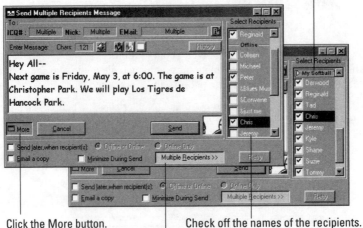

Figure 8-2:
Click the
Multiple
Recipients
button and
check off
names to
send an
item to more
than one
person.

Click the More button.   Check off the names of the recipients.
Click the Multiple Recipients button.

If all the people you want to send the item to are in the same group on your Contact List, you can send the item to everyone in the group very quickly (Chapter 6 explains what groups are). To do so, click the group's name on the Contact List, choose a Send command (Send Message To, Send URL To, or Send Email To), and then choose Entire Group on the submenu. As Figure 8-2 shows, the Send Multiple Recipients dialog box appears with the names of the people in the group already checked off.

5. **In the Select Recipients list, check the names of people you want to send the message to.**

6. **Click the Send button.**

   Your messages are sent. Who would have guessed that junk-mailing is this easy?

Receiving an item

You know when someone has sent you an item because a blinking icon appears in the lower-right corner of the screen. And if the sender's name is on your Contact List, the icon appears there as well. Table 8-2 explains what the different icons mean. Getting acquainted with the icons doesn't take long. Pretty soon you get used to reading these modern-day hieroglyphs.

Doing your part to prevent junk mail

On the subject of multiple items, some people don't like receiving items that were sent to more than one person. A message that is sent to 20 or more people, for example, probably qualifies as junk mail — and who wants junk mail. To keep from getting items that aren't meant especially for you, follow these steps:

1. **Click the ICQ button and choose Security & Privacy on the pop-up menu.**

2. **In the Security For dialog box, click the Ignore List tab.**

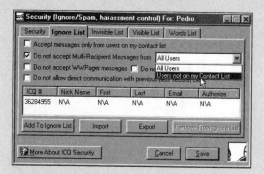

3. **Check the Do Not Accept Multi-Recipient Messages From check box.**

4. **From the drop-down list, choose Users Not on My Contact List if you want to receive multiple items from people on your Contact List but not from others.**

5. **Click the Save button.**

Table 8-2	Communication Icons	
Icon	*Name*	*You Have Been Sent . . .*
	Message	A message. See "Sending Messages to and Receiving Messages from Other ICQ Members."
	File	A file. See "Sending and Receiving Files."
	Web Page Address	A Web page address. See Chapter 10.
	Contacts	Names from someone's Contact List. See Chapter 6.
	Voice message	A recorded message or sound file. See "Sending and Receiving Recorded Messages and Sound Files."

(continued)

Table 8-2 *(continued)*

Icon	Name	You Have Been Sent . . .
	Greeting card	A greeting card. See "Sending a Greeting Card to Someone Else."
	Email Express	An e-mail message from outside of ICQ. See "Sending E-mail to and Getting E-mail from Mailboxes Outside ICQ."
	Chat request	An invitation to chat. See Chapter 4.
	Phone	A request for your phone number. See Chapter 9.
	Externals	A request for a game or chat on a telephony application. See Chapter 16.
	Photo request	A request for your photograph. See Chapter 9.
	Outside e-mail	A notice that e-mail has arrived at your Internet service provider. See "Being alerted when your private e-mail account has received mail."
	System announcement	A system announcement that someone has put you on his or her Contact List. See Chapter 6.
	System message	A message from ICQ or a notice that someone wants to put your name on his or her Contact List. See Chapter 6.

To view an item that was sent to you, double-click its icon or, if the icon appears on the Contact List, click it and choose Receive on the pop-up menu. A dialog box appears so you can read the item.

Occasionally you open ICQ and discover that more than one item has been sent your way. In that case, the Read Next button appears in the dialog box. The button tells how many items require your attention. Keep clicking the button until you have read all incoming items.

Notice the More Function button in dialog boxes where incoming items are announced. Click that button, and you see a list of commands for archiving the item, adding it to the To Do list, and fashioning a reminder note out of it. Chapter 15 describes these functions.

Forwarding an item to someone else

Suppose someone sends you a delightful item that begs to be seen by others. To send it on its merry way, click the Forward button. The Send Multiple Recipients dialog box appears (refer to Figure 8-2) so you can forward the item to not one, not two, but to all the people on your Contact List if you want to. On the Select Recipients list, click the names of the people who deserve to see the item. Then click the Send button.

Sending Messages to and Receiving Messages from Other ICQ Members

 After chatting, the most common way that ICQ members communicate is by smoke signals. That's not true, although we wouldn't put it past some of the people we have met on ICQ. No, the most popular way to communicate outside of chatting is to send messages back and forth.

Sending messages isn't very different from chatting, because the messages fly back and forth so quickly. ICQ messages travel much faster than conventional e-mail messages.

To send a message, either double-click the soon-to-be recipient's name, or click the name and choose Message on the pop-up menu. You see the Send Message dialog box shown at the top of Figure 8-3. Messages cannot exceed 450 characters; the Chars box tells how many characters have been entered in case you come close to the 450 limit. Enter your message and click the Send button. Or, before you click Send, take advantage of these nifty buttons in the Send Message dialog box:

 ✔ **Info button:** Click to open the White Pages and find out more about the person to whom you're sending the message.

 ✔ **Sound On/Off button:** Click this button to keep the "Message has arrived" sound from playing when the message reaches its destination.

 ✔ **Font:** Click to choose a new font for your message.

 ✔ **Font Color:** Click to choose a color for the letters.

 ✔ **Background Color:** Click to choose the background color.

 ✔ **History:** Click to open the message archive and read messages you sent to this person previously.

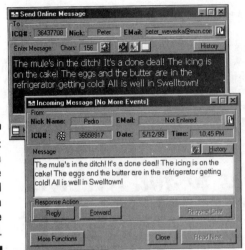

Figure 8-3:
Sending a
message
(top) and
receiving a
message
(bottom).

The message arrives on the other end in the Incoming Message dialog box, as
shown at the bottom of Figure 8-3. This dialog box also offers the History
button, which you can click to read messages you received from the sender
in the past. Click the Close button when you're finished reading the message
or the Reply button to offer up a reply.

In the Incoming Message dialog box, you can click the Reset Font & Color
button to override the sender's color scheme with a simple black-and-white
scheme, as was done in Figure 8-3.

Sending E-Mail to and Getting E-Mail from Mailboxes Outside ICQ

The Message command isn't the only way to send messages to people on
your Contact List. You can send messages to the private e-mail accounts of
people on the Contact List as well. For example, if Johnny keeps a mailbox
with the Earthlink Internet service provider, you can send a message to
Johnny at Earthlink. Not only that, you can send, with a single command, the
same message to Johnny's Earthlink mailbox and his ICQ mailbox.

These pages explain how to send e-mail to the private accounts of people on
your Contact List. You also find out how people who are not registered with
ICQ can send e-mail to you in ICQ. And, to add wealth to riches, you also discover a neat little trick: How to be informed in ICQ when mail has arrived in
your outside mailbox. Excited, are you? Better keep reading.

Registering your e-mail address with ICQ

In order to send e-mail, the person you want to send the mail to must have submitted his or her e-mail address to the ICQ White Pages. If the person's e-mail address isn't on file, the Send Email and Send Email + Notify By ICQ options are grayed out on the submenu when you try to send an e-mail message.

Follow these steps to register an e-mail address with the ICQ White Pages so that others can send e-mail to your e-mail account outside of ICQ:

1. **Click the ICQ button and choose Add/Change Current User↓View/Change My Details.**

2. **On the Main tab of the ICQ Global Directory dialog box, enter your e-mail address in the Primary Email text box.**

3. **Uncheck the Don't Publish My Primary Email address check box as well. If you** check that box, your e-mail address remains private, and others won't be able to send e-mail to your e-mail account outside of ICQ.

4. **Click the Save button.**

5. **Click the Done button.**

If someone to whom you want to send e-mail has recently registered his address but the Send Email and Send Email + Notify By ICQ options are still grayed out, do the following to retrieve the person's address from the White Pages directory: Click the person's name on your Contact List, click the Info button, and, in the ICQ Global Directory dialog box, click the Retrieve button to get the most up-to-date information from the White Pages. If no address still appears, the person hasn't registered his or her e-mail address with ICQ.

Sending e-mail to addresses outside of ICQ

As long as a person on your Contact List has registered his or her e-mail address with ICQ, you can send e-mail messages to him or her. A quick way to tell if someone has registered an e-mail address with ICQ is to click the person's name on the Contact List, choose Message, and note in the Send Message dialog box whether an e-mail address is listed. If no address appears in the Email box, you can't send an address to the person at his or her Internet service provider — at least not by way of ICQ.

Besides the other person's e-mail address being registered with ICQ, you must visit the Owner Prefs For dialog box and tell ICQ which e-mail program you'll use to send e-mail to others. How to do that and how to send e-mail are the subjects of the next few pages.

Telling ICQ to send e-mail with your default e-mail program

ICQ offers one simple option and two baffling options for sending e-mail to outside addresses. We suggest ignoring the baffling options and sticking with the simple one. With the simple option, messages you send to outside mailboxes are sent with your e-mail program, not with ICQ. To be exact, the messages are sent with your default e-mail program, the one that leaps onscreen when you click an e-mail link on a Web page, for example. With the simple option, your e-mail program starts whenever you give the command to send e-mail to an outside address.

(Users of the Windows 95 and 98 operating systems can find out what their default e-mail program is, and perhaps change default programs, by clicking the Start button, choosing Settings⇨Control Panel, double-clicking the Internet Options icon, clicking the Programs tab in the Internet Properties dialog box, and choosing a new program from the E-mail drop-down menu. The menu lists all e-mail programs that are installed on your computer.)

Follow these steps to tell ICQ to use your default e-mail program to send e-mail to outside parties:

1. **Click the Services button.**

2. **Choose Email⇨"Send Email" Setup.**

   You see the Email tab of the Owner Prefs For dialog box.

3. **Click the Use Current Registered Windows Email Client option button under Select the Default ICQ Email Client.**

   Congratulations. You just told ICQ to hand over the job of sending e-mail to outside addresses to the e-mail program you normally use.

   See those other two options, Use ICQ Email Client and Use Specified Email Client? Those are the baffling options we told you about. With the first you have to know the address of the SMTP server through which your e-mail is delivered. With the second you have to list the path to the e-mail program you use. If the Use Current Registered Windows Email Client option doesn't work out for you and you want to try out one of the baffling options, do the following to get help: Click any name on your Contact List and choose Email⇨Email Center. Your browser opens to the ICQ E-mail Integration page (www.icq.com/email). From there, click the Configure button to go to instructions for configuring your e-mailer (www.icq.com/email/#configuring).

4. **Click OK.**

   Now that ICQ knows which e-mail program you can use, you can start your e-mail program from ICQ by clicking the Services button and choosing Email⇨Send Email.

Sending e-mail to the outside address

You'll be delighted to know that sending e-mail to the outside address of someone on your Contact List is easy after you've done the setup work. Follow these steps to send an e-mail message to an outside address and to the person's ICQ mailbox as well, if you so choose:

1. **Click the person's name on your Contact List.**

2. **Choose Email on the pop-up menu.**

   You see a submenu of e-mail options. If the first two options, Send Email and Send Email + Notify By ICQ, are grayed out, the person has not registered his or her e-mail address with ICQ.

3. **Choose Send Email or Send Email + Notify By ICQ.**

   Which option you choose depends on whether you want to send a second copy of the e-mail message to the recipient's mailbox in ICQ. Choose Send Email + Notify By ICQ to send the message twice, once to the recipient's private mailbox and once to his or her ICQ mailbox.

   As shown in Figure 8-4, your e-mail program opens so you can write the message. Notice the address or addresses in the To box. In Figure 8-4, a message is being sent to a private address and an ICQ address, so two addresses appear in the To box. For the purposes of sending e-mail to you from outside the ICQ network, your e-mail address consists of your ICQ number followed by @pager.mirabilis.com.

A message sent to an ICQ member from outside ICQ. . .

. . .looks like this when it arrives.

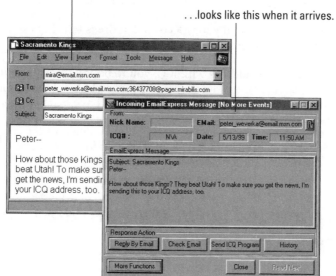

Figure 8-4:
Sending an
e-mail mes-
sage to an
outside
address as
well as an
ICQ mailbox.

4. **Write the message and then click the Send button or choose the Send command in your e-mail program to send the message or messages.**

   That's all there is to it. Your e-mail program handles the delivery of the mail.

A message sent to an ICQ member from outside the ICQ network is called an Email Express message. The Email Express icon appears next to the sender's name on your Contact List after the message arrives. And when you open the message, you see the Incoming Email Express Message dialog box shown in Figure 8-4. Click the Reply By Email button to open your default e-mail program, compose a reply, and send it.

Receiving e-mail from people who aren't on ICQ

Anybody with an ICQ number — and that includes everybody who is registered with ICQ — can receive e-mail messages from outside the ICQ network. Tell the people who want to send e-mail to your ICQ mailbox to send it to YourICQ#@pager.mirabilis.com. For example, if your ICQ number is 11223344, your friends can send e-mail to you in ICQ by addressing their messages as follows: 11223344@pager.mirabilis.com.

The messages show up on your Contact List as Email Express messages under the heading Web Message. Open them, and they appear in the Incoming Email Express Message dialog box (refer to Figure 8-4). Chapter 9 explains how you can send your ICQ e-mail address to others so they know how to reach you in ICQ.

 If you list your e-mail address with ICQ, you're bound to receive junk mail from outside advertisers. Advertisers find it easy to blanket ICQ members whose addresses are listed; computer programs have been designed for doing just that. To keep from receiving junk-mail messages from outside ICQ, you can refuse to receive messages from outside. Click the ICQ button and choose Security & Privacy. In the Security For dialog box, click the Ignore List tab, and then check the Do Not Accept Email Express Message check box.

Being alerted when your private e-mail account has received mail

 ICQ is addicting. Many an ICQ member, bug-eyed and stoop-shouldered, spend hour after hour chatting on ICQ. For people like that, ICQ offers the opportunity to be alerted when your e-mail account — not your ICQ account, but the private account you keep with an Internet service provider — has received new mail. When the alert comes in, you know to leave ICQ for a minute and collect the mail.

Configuring ICQ to check for private mail

Unfortunately, to be alerted, you have to configure ICQ, and as part of configuring, you have to know the Web address of something called your POP3 server. POP (Post Office Protocol) is the rule that governs where e-mail is retrieved from the Internet service provider so it can be delivered over the Internet to a user's computer. To find out the address of your POP3 server, try calling your Internet service provider. You can also get instructions from ICQ for finding the POP3 address by clicking the Services button and choosing Email⇨Email Center. Doing so takes you to the ICQ E-mail Integration page (www.icq.com/email). From there, click the Configure button and then click the Getting Your POP3 and SMTP Account information hyperlink, which takes you to a page with instructions for finding POP3 addresses on popular e-mail programs (www.icq.com/email/#pop3). Write down the address — you will need it shortly.

Follow these steps to tell ICQ to check for e-mail sent to your private e-mail account and alert you when mail arrives:

1. **Click the Services button.**

2. **Choose Email⇨"Check Email" Setup.**

   You land on the Check Email tab of the Owner Prefs For dialog box, as shown in Figure 8-5.

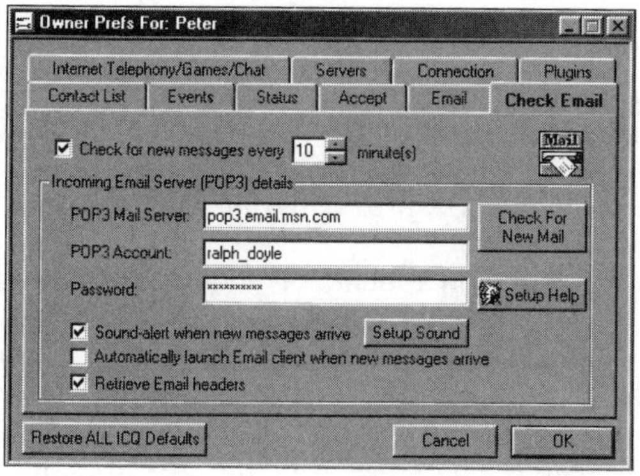

Figure 8-5:
Doing the setup work so you can be alerted when mail has arrived at your private mailbox.

3. **Check the Check for New Message Every button and enter the number of minutes between times that ICQ should check for incoming mail.**

   Unless you check the box, ICQ won't look for mail on its own, and you will have to click the Services button and choose Email⇨Check New Email to see if new mail has arrived.

4. **Fill in the Incoming Email Server (POP3) Details boxes.**

   In the POP3 Account box, enter the part of your e-mail address that is to the left of the at symbol (@). If your e-mail address is myself@ remain.com, for example, enter **myself**.

5. **Uncheck the Sound-Alert When New Messages Arrive if you're the kind who doesn't like to be startled.**

   But if you'd like to be startled in a certain way, click the Setup Sound button, choose a sound file in the Sounds Schemes Settings dialog box, and click OK.

6. **Check the Automatically Launch Email Client When New Messages Arrive if your messages need to be answered right away.**

   If you check the button, your e-mail program opens whenever you're alerted that new messages have arrived.

7. **Be sure to leave the checkmark in the Retrieve Email Headers check box.**

   As long as this box is checked, ICQ lists the message headers — the subjects of the messages that tell you what the messages are all about — when it alerts you that new messages have arrived.

8. **Click the OK button.**

   And not a moment too soon, either.

Checking to see if you received private mail

Every ten minutes (or however many minutes you asked for), ICQ checks to see if a new batch of e-mail has arrived. But if you're anxiously awaiting e-mail and you can't hold out for ten minutes, click the Services button and choose Email⇨Check New Email (or press Ctrl+Shift+C).

 Either way, the Outside E-mail icon appears on your Contact List if mail is waiting. Double-click the icon, or click it and choose Receive on the pop-up menu, to see a list of waiting e-mail messages like the one in Figure 8-6. The list tells who the mail is from, the subjects of the messages, and when they were sent. Sorry, you can't open the messages from the Incoming Email Message dialog box. To read the messages, you have to go to the e-mail program you normally use.

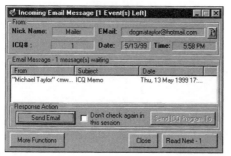

Figure 8-6:
Seeing the
list of e-mail
messages
that were
sent to your
Internet
service
provider, not
to ICQ.

Sending and Receiving Recorded Messages and Sound Files

Click the name of someone on the Contact List who is online and you'll see a command called Voice Message. The command's name is kind of misleading, because you can send sound files as well as recorded messages with the Voice Message command. You can send recorded messages and sound files, that is, as long as they are not longer than 15 seconds. Of course, your computer has to be equipped to play sounds and record them as well if you want to send recorded messages. And the people who receive the voice messages you send need sophisticated computers, too.

Read on to find out how to record and send a message to someone, send a sound file to someone, and play recorded messages and sound files that others have sent you. The sender and receiver have to be online and connected to ICQ before recorded messages and sound files can be sent.

Recording and sending a recorded message or sound file

Whether you want to send a recorded message or a sound file, follow these basic steps:

1. **On your Contact List, click the name of the person you want to send the voice message to.**

    The person must be online and connected to ICQ.

2. **Click the Voice Mail command on the pop-up menu. You see the Send Online Voice Message dialog box, as shown in Figure 8-7.**

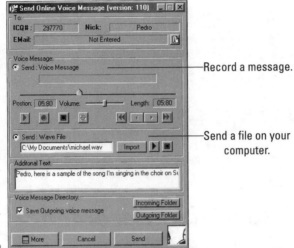

Record a message.

Send a file on your computer.

Figure 8-7:
From this
dialog box,
you can
send a
recorded
message or
sound file to
someone on
your
Contact List.

3. **In the Additional Text box, enter a word or two that describes why you're sending the recorded message or sound file.**

   The message you write will accompany your sound file when you send it.

4. **Choose one of the option buttons, Send: Voice Message or Send: Wave File, and keep reading.**

   Make a choice to tell ICQ what kind of file you want to send:

   • **Send: Voice Message:** Click to record a message to send to your ICQ buddy. See "Recording a message" later in this chapter to find out how to record your voice.

   • **Send: Wave File:** Click to send your ICQ buddy a sound file that has already been recorded and is stored on your computer. See "Sending a sound file" later in this chapter to choose which sound file to send.

5. **Check the Save Outgoing Voice Message check box if you want to save a copy of the sound file you are sending in the Outgoing folder.**

   By keeping a copy of the file in the Outgoing folder, you can send it again. However, if you're sending a sound file, don't bother keeping a copy in the Outgoing folder, because a copy of the file is already stored on your computer.

6. **Click the Send button.**

   The sound file isn't sent right away. The person to whom you addressed the sound file may decide not to hear your plea. If you get turned down, either a message box tells you why or nothing happens because the other party has simply ignored your lonely cry in the wilderness.

A quick way to send sound files

Sound files that others send you are kept in the C:\Program Files\ICQ\Plugins\VoiceMessage\Incoming folder and its subfolders. As long as you check the Save Outgoing Voice Message check box, sound files that you send to others are kept in the C:\Program Files\ICQ\Plugins\VoiceMessage\Outgoing folder and its subfolders. The subfolders are named after the people to whom you send files and from whom you receive files.

To quickly send a sound file in the Outgoing or Incoming folder to someone who is online and on your Contact List, choose the Voice Message command and click the Incoming Folder or Outgoing Folder button in the Send Online Voice Message dialog box (refer to Figure 8-7). The My Computer Program opens and you see the folder you chose. In the subfolders, find the sound file you want to send and right-click it. On the shortcut menu, choose ICQ – Send to User and the person's name. Then, in the Send Online File Request dialog box, write a description of the sound file and click the Send button.

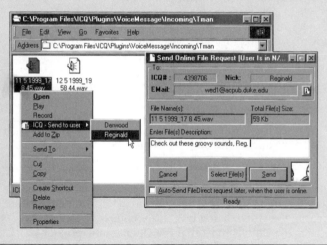

Recording a message

It goes without saying, but you need a microphone and sound card to record a message. With your microphone ready, follow these steps to start recording:

1. **Click the Send: Voice Message option button.**

2. **Click the Record button.**

   You can also press Ctrl+R to start recording.

3. **Speak into your computer's microphone.**

   Speak with a mellifluous voice, if you can. (Mellifluous: from the Latin *mellifluus*; *mel* honey + *fluere* to flow.) Your message can't be longer than 15 seconds.

4. Click the Stop button when you are finished recording.

You can also press Ctrl+S to stop recording.

 Click the Play button to play back the recording you made. You can drag the Volume slider left or right to change the volume. To play the sound over and over, click the Play Loop button.

If your recording needs to be edited, click a Move Step button or drag the slider until you come to the point where you want to record additional sound. Then click the Record button and start recording again.

Sending a sound (.wav) file

Besides sending a recorded message, start from the Send Online Voice Message dialog box to send someone a .wav file. Only .wav sound files can be sent from the dialog box. If you want to send another kind of sound file, follow the procedure for sending files, not .wav files (see "Sending and Receiving Files" later in this chapter).

Follow these steps to send a .wav sound file starting from the Send Online Voice Message dialog box (refer to Figure 8-7):

1. Click the Send: Wave File option button.

 2. Click the Import button.

You see the Open dialog box, the same dialog box you see when you want to open a file on your computer.

3. Locate the .wav file on your computer, select it, and click the Open button.

 A .wav file, of course, has the .wav file extension. If file extensions do not appear in the Open dialog box and you need to know whether a file is a .wav file, click the Details button in the Open dialog box. Then look in the Type column for the words Wave Sound.

The name of the file you chose, as well as the path to the file on your computer, appears in the text box after you click the Open button.

 Now you can send the .wav file, although you may decide to click the Play button and hear the file before you send it.

Playing recorded messages and sound files when they arrive

You know someone wants to send you a sound file when the Voice Message icon appears beside a name on your Contact List. When you double-click the icon or click it and choose Receive, you see the Incoming Voice Message dialog box, as shown in Figure 8-8.

Figure 8-8: Read the description of the sound file, and click the Accept button if you want to hear it.

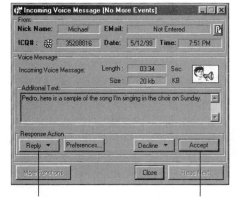

Click Reply to reply with a standard message.

Click Accept to hear the sound.

Read the message to see if you want to hear the file. If you want to hear it, click the Accept button. However, you can click the Reply button to send a message to the sender first, or you can decline by clicking the Decline button and choosing a decline message or entering a message of your own.

As soon as you click Accept, the Voice Message dialog box, as shown in Figure 8-9, appears and the sound file starts arriving on your computer. The file transfer takes but a second. After the sound file arrives, click these buttons in the Voice Message dialog box to hear it:

✔ **Play:** Plays the sound file.

✔ **Play Loop:** Plays the file continuously.

✔ **Stop:** Stops playing the file.

✔ **Seek to Start/End:** Goes to the beginning or end of the file.

✔ **Move Step:** These buttons take you second by second backward or forward through the file. As you click the Voice Message slider moves. You can also move backward or forward through a file by dragging the slider.

Figure 8-9:
Playing a
sound file
someone
has sent to
you.

As long as the Save Incoming Voice Message check box is checked, a sound file someone has sent you is stored in the C:\Program Files\ICQ\Plugins\ VoiceMessage\Incoming folder. However, you can store the file in a different folder by clicking the Save To File button and negotiating the Save As dialog box.

Sending and Receiving Files

 As long as both parties are online and connected to ICQ, they can sling files at each other like there's no tomorrow. ICQ makes sending and receiving files pretty easy. What's more, you can decide for yourself where to store the files on your computer *before* they arrive. In conventional e-mail programs, the files always land in the same folder, whether you like it or not.

These pages explain how to send a file to someone else and what to do to accept or reject a file that has been sent to you. You also discover how to store a file in a specific folder and automatically decline files to keep them from ever being sent to you.

 Computer files are a little like candy: You should be careful about accepting them from strangers. Files can carry viruses. Most people are not malicious enough to deliberately infect someone's computer with a virus, but it happens. If you suspect a file of being tainted, copy it to a floppy disk and open it there. That way, your hard disk is not as likely to be damaged if the file carries a virus.

Sending a file to someone else

You can send files only to people whose names are on your Contact List. To send a file, click a name on the list and choose File from the pop-up menu. You see the Send File Request dialog box — but only momentarily. Right away, the Open dialog box appears so you can select the file you want to send. In the dialog box, find and select the file, and then click the Open button.

As shown on the left side of Figure 8-10, the Send File Request dialog box comes onscreen. The name of the file you selected appears in the File Name(s) box (the box lists the number of files to send if you chose to send more than one file). The Total File(s) Size box lists, in kilobytes, how much data is to be sent.

Sending a file

Receiving a request to
send a file

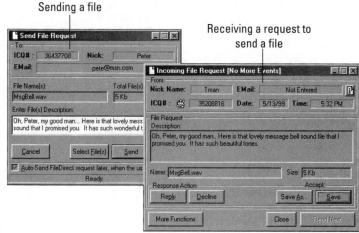

Figure 8-10:
Sending a
file to
someone
else.

You can send more than one file at a time, but to do so, all the files have to be in the same folder on your computer. To send more than one file, Ctrl+click the files. Hold down the Ctrl key and click each file you want to send. You can click the Select Files(s) button in the Send File Request dialog box to see the Open dialog box and choose a different file or set of files to send.

Click the Send button when you're ready to send your file or files. On the other side, the person to whom you sent the file sees the Incoming File Request dialog box shown on the right side of Figure 8-10. But the file isn't sent right away. No, it isn't. The other person can turn down your offer of a free file. Better keep reading.

Choosing how you want to receive files

Some people prefer not to get files over ICQ; others accept all incoming files. To decide for yourself how to handle files, click the ICQ button and choose Preferences to open the Owner Prefs For dialog box. Then click the Events tab and choose File Transfer from the Select Event to Configure drop-down menu. You see a bunch of different options for handling file transfers:

✔ **Yea or Nay files when they arrive:** Make sure the Show File Request Response Dialog option button is clicked.

✔ **Accept all files:** Click the Auto Receive Files option button. If you check the And Minimize check box as well, the files arrive without the Receiving Files From dialog box appearing (refer to Figure 8-11).

✔ **Accept files only from people on your Contact List:** Check the Auto Decline From People Not On My Contact List check box.

✔ **Reject all files:** Click the Auto Decline option button.

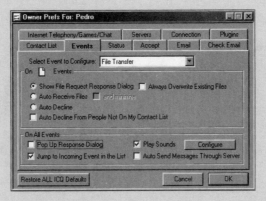

Receiving a file from someone else

You see the File icon next to the name of a person on your Contact List when someone wants to send you a file. Double-click the File icon or click it and choose Receive to open the Incoming File Request dialog box and find out what's up (refer to Figure 8-10). The dialog box tells you the name of the file and how large it is. With any luck, the Description box explains what kind of file you're dealing with and why the file is being sent.

If the file doesn't interest you at all, click the Decline button and either choose a reason for declining the file from the drop-down menu or choose an option for entering a reason of your own. You can also click the Reply button to send a message to the sender and inquire about the file.

To start downloading the file to your computer, click the Save As or Save button:

> ✔ **Choose where to save the file:** Click the Save <u>A</u>s button. The Open dialog box appears so you can choose which folder to save the file in.

> ✔ **Save the file in the default folder for incoming files:** Files that others send you land in your computer in subfolders of the C:\Program Files\ICQ\Received Files folder. In the Received Files folder is a sub-folder named after each person who has sent you files.

> (You can choose a different default folder for incoming files: Click the ICQ button and choose Preferences. In the Owner Prefs For dialog box, click the Accept tab. Then, under Default Incoming File(s) Path, click the folder button and choose a new default folder in the Select Directory dialog box.)

As soon as you either click the Save button or finish choosing which folder to save the file in, you see the Receiving Files From dialog box, which is shown in Figure 8-11.

How long the file takes to download depends on how big it is. The File and Batch graphs tell you how much of the file has been transferred, and you supposedly can click the Speed slider to increase the speed of the transfer, but we haven't noticed a marked difference in speed by moving the slider. If you lose patience and decide not to download the file, click the Abort button. Click the Skip File button if more than one file is being sent and you don't care to download the file whose name is shown in the FileName box.

Eventually, the ICQ File Transfer Completed Successfully dialog box, as shown at the bottom of Figure 8-11, appears. Click OK in this dialog box, unless you want to open the file or open it in My Computer:

> ✔ **Open the file:** Click the Open button. If your computer is capable of opening the file, it opens in the program for which it was designed.

> ✔ **Go to the folder where the file is stored:** Click the Goto Dir button. The My Computer utility opens, and you see the file there.

Sending a Greeting Card to Someone Else

 Greeting cards are colorful messages that you can send to other ICQ members. When you receive a greeting card notice, you're invited to click the Click Here to See the Card in Your Web Browser button. When you click the button, you go to a Web page, where the card is displayed. Figure 8-12 shows an example of a greeting card. The cards are signed by the people who send them and include a little message. They're colorful and fun!

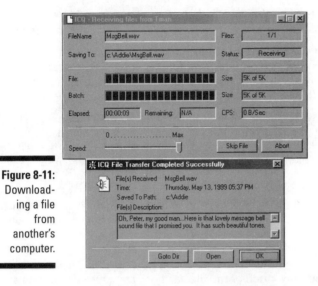

Figure 8-11:
Download-
ing a file
from
another's
computer.

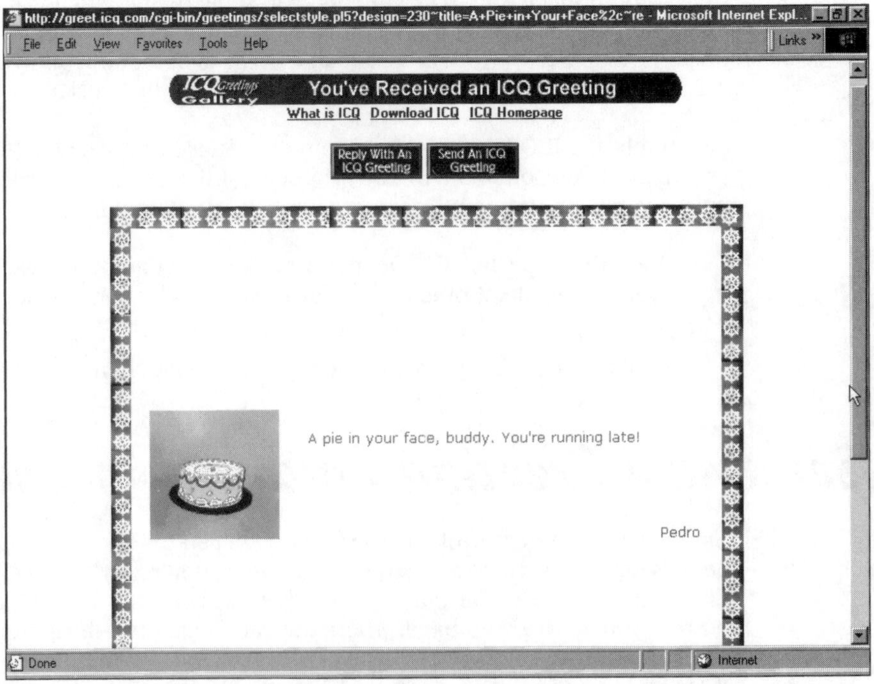

Figure 8-12:
A greeting
card. Click
the Replay
With An ICQ
Greeting
button to
reply to one
greeting
card with
another.

To send a greeting card, click a person's name on the Contact List and choose Greeting Card. You see the Send Greeting Card dialog box. To construct your card, make choices in the dialog boxes — you have three choices — and keep clicking Next:

1. **Choose a theme and title for your card.**

   In Step 2, you'll get the chance to enter a title of your own, in case you don't like the titles shown in the dialog box.

2. **Enter the message that will accompany the card and change the title if you want to.**

   While you're at it, you can change the receiver's name and the sender's name — that's you — by entering pet names in the Receiver and Sender text boxes.

3. **Click the Send button.**

   Or, before clicking Send, click the Preview The Card On Your Browser button to see precisely what the card will look like when the other person gets it.

If you're the artistic type, it's raining outside, and you have nothing better to do, you can create your own greeting cards. Click the Create Your Own Card option button and then the Click to Create button in the Send Greeting Card dialog box. That takes you to the ICQ Greetings Gallery (`http://greet.icq.com/greetings/create.html`), where you're invited to follow the directions and make your own greeting card.

Chapter 9

Publicizing Yourself on ICQ and the Internet

In This Chapter

▶ Entering new information about yourself in the White Pages

▶ Visiting your Personal Communication Center on the Web

▶ Alerting others to your ICQ addresses

▶ Sending out invitations to join ICQ

▶ Making your photo available for others to download

▶ Letting others obtain your telephone number

This chapter explains how to make your presence known inside and outside the ICQ community. We want you to obtain a degree of notoriety. We want your fame to spread near and far on the ICQ network. We want your reputation to precede you.

In this chapter, you find out how to update your profile in the White Pages, the place in ICQ where information about all the members is kept. You also find out what the Personal Communication Center is and how you can invite people to visit it — even people who aren't registered with ICQ. This chapter also describes how to make your photo available to others, find out what other ICQ members look like, and obtain the telephone numbers of ICQ members.

Updating Your Profile in the White Pages

When you signed on with ICQ, you volunteered a bunch of information about yourself. You listed your name, perhaps the city you live in, and other intimate details. The information you entered was recorded in the White Pages.

As Chapter 7 explains, ICQ members can go to the White Pages to search for people whose interests are similar to their own. In other words, people can go to the White Pages to find you!

Because others are looking for you, we suggest going to the White Pages from time to time and updating your profile there so that others can find you easily. You may have moved to a new city. You may have undergone a massive spiritual transformation. Perhaps you learned how to spell better. No matter, your profile in the White Pages needs to be up to date.

Follow these steps to go to the White Pages and describe yourself there:

1. **Click the Services button and choose ICQ White Pages⇨Publicize in White Pages.**

   You can also click the ICQ button and choose Add/Change Current User⇨Publicize in White Pages. Either way, you see the Global Directory – My Details dialog box, shown at the top of Figure 9-1.

Figure 9-1:
The information you enter in the Global Directory – My Details dialog box (top) is available to everyone who clicks the Info button to open the Global Directory – User Info On dialog box (bottom).

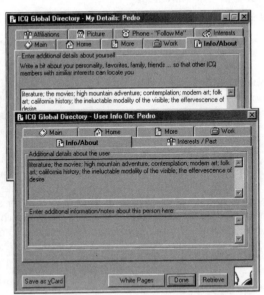

The information you enter in this dialog box is stored in the White Pages for all to see. As we point out far too often in this book, anybody can click the Info button or choose the Info command to open the Global Directory – User Info On dialog box, shown at the bottom of Figure 9-1. Message dialog boxes, Chat Request dialog boxes, and numerous other dialog boxes offer the Info button.

What's more, as Chapter 7 points out, people can search the White Pages by keyword. By entering *jazz* as one of your interests on the Interests tab, for example, you make yourself available to other jazz lovers for chats and messages.

2. **Visit each tab in the Global Directory – My Details dialog box and describe yourself.**

   We suggest being as thorough as possible. Not that you should list your street address or phone number, but you should describe yourself as best you can.

   (Don't worry about the Picture and Phone tabs for now. We explain how they work later in this chapter.)

3. **Click the Save button when you are finished.**

   Clicking Save enters your self-description in the ICQ member database so that others can look you up.

4. **Click the Done button.**

   The deed is done.

The only tab in the Global Directory – My Details dialog box that might give you any trouble is the Interests tab, shown at the top of Figure 9-2. When others search the White Pages, they see what you enter on the Interests tab on the Interest/Past tab of the Global Directory – User Info On dialog box, as shown at the bottom of Figure 9-2.

Follow these steps to describe your Interests on the Interests tab:

1. **Check a check box, open a Selected Categories drop-down menu, and choose a category.**

   Choose a category carefully. When others search for people of similar interests in the White Pages, they search by category. Choose a category that others are likely to search in when they go looking for someone like you.

2. **Click the Edit button.**

   You see the Selected Interests dialog box, shown in the middle of Figure 9-2.

3. **Describe your interests by making entries in the Your Select Interests box.**

   You can make the entries in either of two ways:

   • **Choose an interest from the list:** Click a subject in the Suggested Interests box and then click the Select-> button.

   • **Describe an interest yourself:** Type a subject in the Define New Interest box and click the Select-> button.

1. Click a check box and choose a category.

2. Click the Edit button.

3. Select or enter an interest.

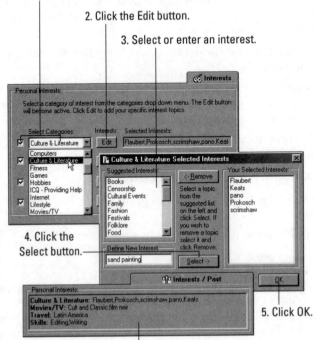

4. Click the Select button.

5. Click OK.

Figure 9-2: Describing your interests to other ICQ members.

How others read your interest.

We suggest describing your interests by entering them in the Define New Interest box instead of choosing them from the list. The interests on the list are kind of vague. Describe your interests yourself and you are sure to attract like-minded people.

4. **Repeat Step 3 to describe all your interests in the category and then click OK.**

To remove a subject from the Your Selected Interest box, click it and then click the <-Remove button.

5. **Back on the Interests tab, click another check box and select another category, if you so desire.**

The more ways you describe your interests, the more likely you are to connect with like-minded ICQ members.

Telling Others How They Can Reach You in ICQ

ICQ members know how to reach you. They can search the White Pages for you. They can look you up in the Global Directory, as Chapter 7 explains. They can put your name on their Contact Lists and tell when you are online. You can run, but you can't hide from other ICQ members — and that's good. You joined ICQ to be a part of the ICQ community.

It might interest you to know as well that people who are not ICQ members can contact you. They can look you up, find out if you are connected to ICQ, and send you messages or chat with you. People outside ICQ can go to your Personal Communication Center, a place on the Internet for you and you alone. After they get there, they can contact you.

These pages explain how the Personal Communication Center works. You will also find advice here for telling others how to get to your Personal Communication Center and how to send out invitations to join ICQ.

Visiting your Personal Communication Center

The next section in this chapter explains how to tell others how to get to your Personal Communication Center. But before you invite anyone to your Personal Communication Center, we think you should visit it yourself. The place might need tidying up. The dishes might need washing. Better make sure the place is in good shape before guests arrive.

Figure 9-3 shows the Personal Communication Center. As you can see, "Personal Communication Center" is way too fancy a name. The thing is just a Web page, not the NASA headquarters. This page is available day or night and can be visited by anyone who is connected to the Internet.

Everybody who registers with ICQ gets a Personal Communication Center. The Web address of your Personal Communication Center is `http://wwp.icq.com/Your ICQ#` (notice the *wwp*, not *www*). For example, if your ICQ number is 11223344, the Web address of your Personal Communication Center is `http://wwp.icq.com/11223344`. (Personal Communication Center addresses are also maintained at `http://wwp.mirabilis.com/Your ICQ#`. When you send someone the address of your Personal Communication Center with the "four addresses" command — the subject of the next section in this chapter — the mirabilis.com address, not the icq.com address, is sent.)

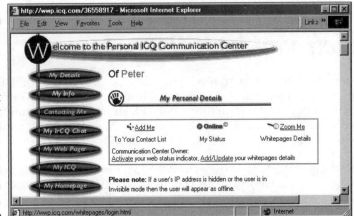

Figure 9-3:
People who
are not reg-
istered with
ICQ can visit
your
Personal
Communi-
cation
Center and
get in touch
with you.

Here's how to get to your own or someone else's Personal Communication Center:

- **Not a member of ICQ:** People who aren't members of ICQ can visit someone's Personal Communication Center by entering its address in their Web browser.

- **The person's name is on your Contact List:** Click the name and choose Homepages⇨Goto User's Communication Center.

- **Going to your own Personal Communication Center:** Click the System Menu button and choose View My Communication Center. You can also click the Services button and choose My ICQ Page⇨My Communication Center.

The Personal Communication Center is really for people who are not members of ICQ. While they are visiting, they can click a cigar-shaped hyperlink and go to these parts of the Center:

- **My Details:** The description you entered of yourself in the White Pages.

- **My Info:** The description you entered on the Info/About tab in the Global Directory dialog box (see Figure 9-1).

- **Contacting Me:** Instructions for getting in touch with you.

- **My IrCQ Chat:** A mini-chat room where the visitor can engage you in a chat.

- **My Web Pager:** The so-called World-Wide Pager, a form that visitors can fill out to send you an e-mail message.

- **My ICQ:** Links visitors can click (if they are ICQ members) to add you to their Contact Lists, invite you for a chat, and learn about you in the White Pages.

✔ **My Homepage:** A link visitors can click to go to your homepage (if you created a homepage and it can be displayed because you are online — Chapter 11 explains how to create a homepage).

✔ **My Email Express:** Links for sending you e-mail either to your ICQ address or to you Internet service provider address.

✔ **Phone Callback**: A place where visitors can send you their phone numbers.

Sending your "four addresses" to others

ICQ offers a special command for e-mailing the "four addresses" to someone. As Figure 9-4 shows, people who receive a four-addresses e-mail are informed that you've joined ICQ and that you can be reached various ways. What are the four addresses? Here, count 'em on your fingers:

Figure 9-4:
Click the System Menu button and choose Send My ICQ Four Addresses to send an e-mail message that explains how you can be reached in ICQ.

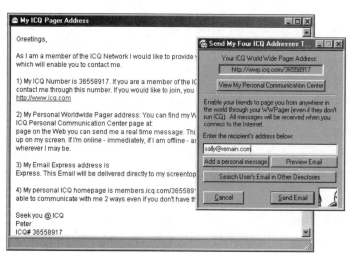

✔ **The address of ICQ:** The e-mail invites others to go to the ICQ home-page (`www.icq.com`) and download the program.

✔ **Your World-Wide Pager address**: The form on your Personal Communication Center page (`wwp.mirablis.com/Your ICQ#`), for writing an e-mail message (see the previous section in this chapter).

✔ **Your Email Express address:** The address to which others can address e-mail messages that are sent to you in ICQ (`Your ICQ#@pager.mirabilis.com`).

Publicizing your Personal Communication Center on popular search engines

In effect, your Personal Communication Center is a Web page — and a free one to boot, since you don't have to pay rent for keeping it on the Internet. Now that you have your own Web page (if you didn't have one already), you can submit its address to popular search engines. That way, a long-lost friend can find you at your Personal Communication Center page, write you a note, and get in touch with you after all these years.

To see about submitting your Personal Communication Center address to popular search engines such as Yahoo! and Excite, do the following: Click the ICQ button and choose Add/Change Current User➪Publicize in Web-Directories. You go to the Web Directories publicize page (`www.icq.com/sitecreator/pageme-distribute.html`), where you can get advice for submitting your address. Also on the page are hyperlinks to popular search engines so you can submit your address and get "found" when others look for you.

✔ **The address of your homepage:** Your homepage address (`http://members.icq.com/Your ICQ#`). Not everyone has a homepage. Chapter 11 explains how to create one.

People who receive the "four addresses" e-mail message can click hyperlinks to go to the addresses and see what all the fuss is about. We suggest sending a "four addresses" e-mail to yourself to find out if you want to send it to others.

Take note of the e-mail address of the person to whom you want to send the four addresses, and follow these steps to send them:

1. **Click the System Menu button and choose Send My ICQ Four Addresses.**

   As shown in Figure 9-4, you see the Send My Four ICQ Addresses dialog box.

2. **In the text box, enter the recipients' e-mail addresses.**

3. **Click the Add a Personal Message button, write a note in the Personalized Message dialog box, and click OK.**

   The words you write will appear at the top of the e-mail message.

4. **Click the Send Email button.**

   The Preview dialog box shows the message you are about to send. If you change your mind about sending it, click the No button.

5. Click the Send Invitation button.

The message is sent and you see the mysteriously named ICQ WWPager Address Sent dialog box. Hey, weren't you supposed to be sending four messages? The dialog box asks if you want to send the message you just sent to anyone else.

6. Click Yes or No.

If you click No, you're done with it. Click Yes and the Send My Four ICQ Addresses dialog box stays onscreen so you can send another message.

If you enclosed a personal message along with the four addresses, the same personal message goes to the next person you send it to unless you click the Add a Personal Message button again and either delete the personalized message or write another one to the next recipient. If your personalized message is very personal, be careful not to send it to more than one person.

Sending someone an invitation to join ICQ

You long to chat or exchange messages with someone on ICQ but that someone isn't a member? Don't despair. ICQ offers a command for inviting someone to join. What's more, the name of the person you invite is added to your Contact List automatically if the person joins. Sorry, ICQ doesn't give discount coupons for signing up new members, but you do get the satisfaction of introducing someone new to the wonders of ICQ.

To send someone an invitation to join, start by jotting down his or her e-mail address. Then follow these steps to send the invitation:

1. Click the System Menu button and choose Invitation to Join ICQ.

You see the Invitation to Join ICQ dialog box.

2. In the text box, enter the e-mail address of the person to whom you want to extend the invitation.

3. Click the Add a Personal Message button, scribble a note in the Personalized Message dialog box, and click OK.

ICQ has written a note for you: "Want to get in touch with me. Here's the fastest way. Check it out." Of course, you can erase that and try for something a little more to the point. How about, "Here's that weird ICQ thing I've been telling you about. You can click the link in this message to join up."

4. Click the Send Invitation button.

The Preview dialog shows you precisely what the invitation says. You can click the No button if you balk at sending it.

The invitation explains where to go on the Internet to download ICQ. It also lists your "four addresses" (the previous section in this chapter explains what those are).

5. **Click the S̲end Invitation button in the Preview dialog box.**

As long as the person accepts your invitation to join, registers with ICQ, and lists an e-mail address identical to the one you entered in the Invitation to Join ICQ dialog box, the person's name will be placed automatically on your Contact List.

Sending and Obtaining Photos

Believe it or not, you can break the anonymity barrier and show other ICQ members what you look like (or what you wished you looked like). As long as you are online and connected to ICQ, others who have put your name on their Contact Lists can download your photograph (or a photograph). And you can see photographs of people whose names are on your Contact List as well.

Of course, you have to make a photograph available before others can see what you look like. To be specific, you have to make a .jpg or .bmp digital photograph available, since conventional photographs do not travel well over telephone lines. These pages explain how to make a photograph available for others, give others permission to view your photograph, and obtain other people's photographs.

Exhibiting yourself on the ICQ network

No one can see what you look like until you make a photograph available. To do that, take note of where on your computer the .jpg or .bmp picture you want to show others is located. Then follow these steps to point the way to the picture:

1. **Click the ICQ button.**

2. **Choose Add/Change Current User➪View/Change My Details.**

You see the Global Directory dialog box.

3. **Click the Picture tab.**

Figure 9-5 shows the Picture tab.

4. **Click the Browse button.**

The Open dialog box appears. Use the dialog box to locate your photo file.

Click options to give others permission to download your photo.

Click to tell ICQ where your photo file is located.

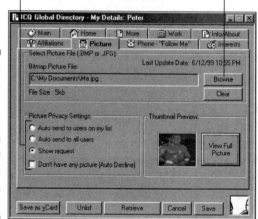

Figure 9-5:
On the
Picture tab,
you can
make a pho-
tograph of
yourself
available to
other ICQ
members.

5. **Locate the photo file on your computer, select it, and click the ICQ Open button.**

Of the two file types, .jpg files are better than .bmp files. Bitmap (.bmp) files take longer to download. Someone who tries to obtain your photograph has to wait longer for a .bmp file than a .jpg file.

Your photo appears under the words *Thumbnail Preview* in the Global Directory dialog box. You can click the View Full Picture button to get a better look at yourself in your browser window. My, are you good-looking!

Read on to find out how to enable others to see your photograph.

Giving others permission to view your photo

Your photograph resides on your computer, not on the ICQ computers. Therefore, to exhibit yourself on ICQ, you have to be online and connected to the network. To obtain your photograph, someone who has put your name on his Contact List downloads it from your computer. You can distribute your photograph to all and sundry or require others to ask for permission before they can see what you look like in the flesh.

After you have told ICQ where your photo file is located, follow these steps to tell ICQ how or whether you want to make your photograph available to others:

1. **Go to the Picture tab of the Global Directory dialog box (refer to Figure 9-5).**

   To get there, click the ICQ button, choose Add/Change Current User➪View/Change My Details, and click the Picture tab.

2. **Under Picture Privacy Settings, choose how or whether you want to make your photograph available.**

   The Picture tab offers these options for exhibiting yourself:

   - **Auto Send to Users on My List:** Allows people whose names are on your Contact List to get your photo whenever you are online. They don't need your permission first.

   - **Auto Send to All Users:** Allows people who have put your name on their Contact Lists to download your photo while you are online. They don't need permission.

   - **Show Request:** Requires everyone to ask permission to obtain your photo. When someone wants to see it, the Photo request icon appears in the lower-right corner of the screen. Double-click the icon and you see the Incoming Picture dialog box. Click the <u>S</u>end Picture button to send the picture.

   - **Don't Have Any Picture (Auto Decline):** When the box is checked, it makes your photo unavailable but retains your picture settings in case you want to make your photo available again. To make your photo available again, uncheck the box.

3. **Click the Save button.**

4. **Click the Done button.**

   How do others obtain or try to obtain your photograph? Read on to find out.

Obtaining someone's photograph

You can only get photos of people whose names are on your Contact List. How readily you can get the photos depends on whether you need permission to obtain them.

Whether you need permission or not, start by clicking the person's name on your Contact list and choosing Info on the pop-up menu. You see the User Info On dialog box. And if you click the Picture tab in the dialog box, you see commands for downloading someone's picture, as shown in Figure 9-6.

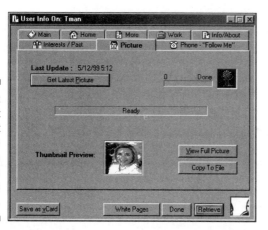

Figure 9-6:
Click the Get
Latest
Picture
button to
obtain
someone's
picture.

Click the Get Latest Picture button to obtain the photo. If it is obtainable, if the other person is online, and if you don't need permission, the picture soon arrives on your computer and you can see it in the Thumbnail Preview box. Click the View Full Picture button to see a bigger version of the photo on your browser. Click the Copy To File button to copy of the photo file to a new location on your computer.

If you need permission to get the photo, you might see the Picture Request dialog box when you try to obtain the photo. You see that dialog box if the other person refuses your request. But if the other person gives you permission, the photo appears shortly.

Sending and Obtaining Others' Telephone Numbers

You can list your telephone number in the White Pages, but we don't recommend doing it because every Tom, Dick, and Harry can find it there. A better way to handle phone numbers is to wait until you know someone well enough and then offer your phone number. And if someone wants your phone number or you want his or her phone number, ask for it. "I want to speak with you in person, so can I have your phone number?" isn't a hard question to ask, if you think about it.

But in keeping with the computer tradition of automating absolutely everything, ICQ offers a means of letting others obtain your phone number without asking. These pages explain how to make your phone number available to others, obtain others' phone numbers, and put in a request to call someone or have someone call you.

The techniques that we describe in the following pages for making your phone number available do not list your phone number in the White Pages. No way! Only people who have put your name on their Contact Lists can get your phone number with the techniques we describe here. What's more, you have to be online for people to get it.

Listing your phone numbers

The first step in making your phone number available to others is to list it. Follow these steps to tell others where they can reach you:

1. **Click the Services button.**

2. **Choose Phone – "Follow Me"**⇨**Update/Add Current Phone#.**

   The Phone – "Follow Me" tab of the Global Directory dialog box opens, as shown in Figure 9-7.

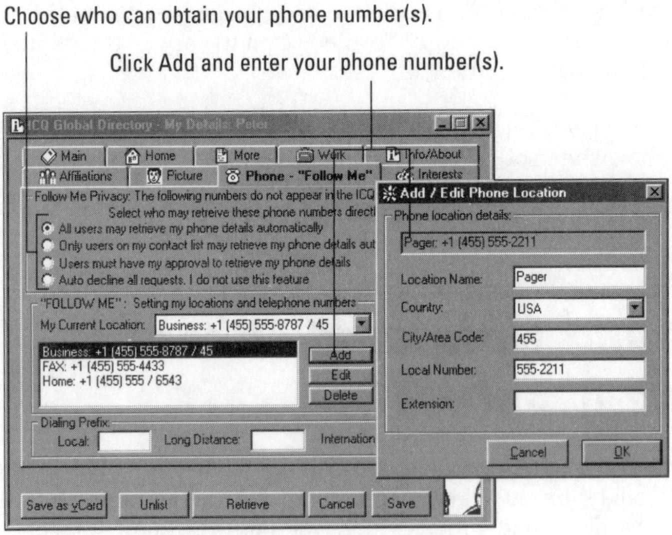

Choose who can obtain your phone number(s).

Click Add and enter your phone number(s).

Figure 9-7: Making your phone number(s) available to people who have put your name on their Contact Lists.

3. **Click the Add button.**

   You see the Add/Edit Phone Location dialog box, also shown in Figure 9-7.

4. **Enter a name for the phone number you are about to list.**

   For example, you can enter **Home**, **Business**, **Fax**, or **Pager**. The name you enter will appear on the Phone – "Follow Me" tab.

5. **Enter the area code, the phone number itself, and the extension if there is one, and then click <u>O</u>K.**

   You return to the Phone – "Follow Me" tab. If you entered the phone number incorrectly, select it and click the Edit button to change it.

6. **Repeat Steps 3 to 5 to enter more phone numbers, if you want to.**

7. **Click the Save button.**

8. **Click the Done button.**

   Your phone numbers are listed and are ready for others to cadge.

Go back to the Phone – "Follow Me" tab, select a phone number, and click the Edit or Delete button to change or remove it. Meanwhile, read on to find out how to tell ICQ exactly who can get your phone numbers.

Deciding who can obtain your phone number

The Phone – "Follow Me" tab is also where you tell ICQ who can and can't obtain your phone number. To get to the Phone – "Follow Me" tab (refer to Figure 9-7), click the Services button and choose Phone – "Follow Me"⇨ Update/Add Current Phone#. Then choose one of these options, click the Save button, and click the Done button:

✔ **All Users May Retrieve My Phone Details Automatically:** Anybody can click the Info button or choose the Info command, go to the Phone — "Follow Me" tab in the User Info On dialog box, and get your phone number by clicking the Update From User button.

✔ **Only Users on My Contact List May Retrieve My Phone Details Automatically:** Only people whose names are on your Contact List can get your phone number.

✔ **Users Must Have My Approval To Retrieve My Phone Details:** Anyone who wants to call you has to request your phone number.

✔ **Auto Decline All Requests. I Do Not Use This Feature:** You don't want to give out your phone number under any circumstances and no one can obtain it.

Obtaining someone else's phone number

To obtain someone else's telephone number without asking directly, click his or her name on the Contact List and choose Info. Then, in the User Info On dialog box, click the Phone – "Follow Me" tab, and click the Update From User button. The person's phone number(s) appear on the Phone – "Follow Me" tab.

They appear there unless you need permission in order to obtain them. In that case, if permission is denied, you might receive a message box that informs you that your request was denied.

Asking someone to call you

To ask someone to call you, send a message and plead your case. Write, "Hey, buddy, call me, would you?" Barring that technique, you can try out the ICQ command that was designed to help you ask someone for his or her phone number: Click his or her name on the Contact List and choose Phone – "Follow Me"⇨Send Phone Call Request. In the Send Phone "Follow Me" dialog box, click the May I Call You or Please Call Me option button, describe why you want the phone call, and click the Send button.

Part III
ICQ and the Internet

The 5th Wave   By Rich Tennant

"QUICK KIDS! YOUR MOTHER'S FLAMING SOMEONE ON THE INTERNET!"

In this part . . .

In Part III, you stake out a little corner of the Internet as your own. No fooling — Part III explains how you can become a mini-Web site developer. And you don't have to be some kind of Web expert to do it, either.

This part tells how to create an ICQ homepage, a little Web site that others can visit whenever you are online. You also discover how to search the Internet without leaving ICQ, send the addresses of your favorite Web sites to ICQ friends, and travel deep into the PeopleSpace Directory without getting lost or encountering wolves and goblins.

Chapter 10

Searching the Internet from ICQ

· ·

In This Chapter

▶ Sending someone a Web page address

▶ Bookmarking Web page addresses that others send you

▶ Visiting Web pages that you bookmarked

▶ Searching for information with ICQ iT!, the search engine of ICQ

▶ Searching for lost people on the Internet

· ·

*T*his chapter explains how to turn ICQ into a surfboard and surf the Internet. Most people don't realize it, but lurking right in the middle of the ICQ window is a search engine for trolling the Internet. Can you find it? Finding it is almost as hard as finding Waldo in a picture book.

Besides searching the Internet with ICQ iT!, the ICQ search engine, this chapter explains how to send a Web page address to someone else and bookmark a Web page address that someone has sent you.

Collaborative Surfing: Sending and Receiving Web Page Addresses

Before you find out how to surf the Internet, we want to tell you about one of the best things going in ICQ: collaborative surfing. Normally, you send someone an e-mail message to tell him or her about a great Website you discovered, the other person gets the message, and then all is forgotten. But in ICQ you can send a Web page address like the one shown in Figure 10-1.

Invitation to visit the Website

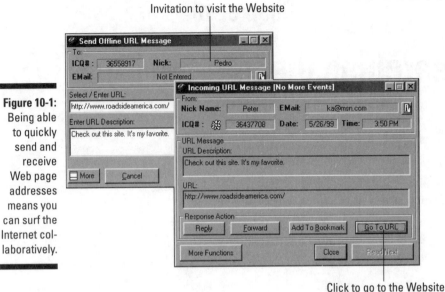

Figure 10-1:
Being able
to quickly
send and
receive
Web page
addresses
means you
can surf the
Internet col-
laboratively.

Click to go to the Website

As soon as the other person receives it, he or she can click the Go To URL button and go straight to the Website. In this way, by sending and receiving Web page addresses, you can surf the Internet with someone else. You can go from Web page to Web page along with your partner and make surfing the Internet a collaborative activity.

What's more, bookmarking a site someone has recommended to you is easy. All you have to do is click the Add To Bookmark button in the Incoming URL Message dialog box (later in this chapter, "Visiting a Web Page You've Bookmarked" explains how to revisit pages). *Bookmarking* means to mark down the address of a Web page so you can visit it again. These pages explain how to send and receive Web page addresses.

Sending someone a Web page address

Follow these steps to send someone a Web page address:

1. **Click the person's name on your Contact List and choose Web Page Address (URL).**

   You see the Send URL Message dialog box (refer to Figure 10-1). The address of the Website you're visiting appears in the Select/Enter URL box. The Enter URL Description box lists the Website's official name.

2. **If necessary, enter the address you want to send in the Select/Enter URL box.**

   You don't have to enter anything if the Web page address you want to send happens to be the page you're visiting. But if it's not the page you are visiting, either type the address in the box or open the drop-down menu and choose an address. The addresses on the menu are the same ones you will find on the Address bar of your Web browser.

3. **Enter a word or two about the site in the Enter URL description box.**

   You might say what is so special about the site. Or you can simply leave the Website's name in the box.

4. **Click the Send button.**

   The Webpage address is sent on its merry way.

Receiving a Web page address

 You know when you have received a Web page address because the Web page icon appears in the lower-right corner of your screen and on your Contact List. Looks like a drop of grease, doesn't it? We've peered closely at the icon, and we think it's meant to be a little globe.

Anyhow, after you have opened the Web page address message, you see the Incoming URL Message dialog box (refer to Figure 10-1). From there, you can visit the Web page, bookmark it, and also reply to the person who sent it to you:

✔ **Visit the Web Page:** Click the Go To URL button to pay a visit to the Web page.

✔ **Bookmark the Web page:** Click the Add To Bookmark button to bookmark the site and be able to visit it later. As the next section in this chapter explains, you can click the System Menu button and choose Incoming Bookmarks to go to a list of people who have sent you bookmarks, click a name, and then see a list of the Websites you bookmarked. From there, you can click the address of a Web page to visit the page.

   After you click the Go To URL button, a drop-down list appears. Choose Open in Current Browser Window to go from the Web page you're looking at to the Web page whose address was sent you; choose Open in New Browser Window to open a second window on the Web page.

✔ **Reply to the Sender:** Click the Reply button and write a reply in the Send Message dialog box.

Choosing how you want to handle Web page addresses

ICQ offers a couple of commands for handling Web page addresses as they arrive. To decide how to handle Web page addresses, click the ICQ button and choose Preferences. In the Owner Prefs For dialog box, click the Events tab, and then choose Web Page Address (URL) from the Events drop-down menu. You see these options for handling Web page addresses:

✔ **Show URL Response dialog:** The standard way of receiving Web page addresses. You see the Incoming URL Message dialog box (refer to Figure 10-1) and get the opportunity to visit the Web page and bookmark it.

✔ **Auto Add URL to Bookmarks**: Web page addresses that are sent to you are bookmarked automatically.

✔ **Auto Decline:** All Web page addresses that are sent to you are refused. Choose this option if you get tired of receiving junk-mail Web page addresses.

✔ **Auto Open URL in Browser:** When a Web page address is sent to you, the Web page it refers to is opened automatically in your browser window.

Visiting a Web Page You've Bookmarked

Visiting the Web page addresses that others sent to you and you bookmarked is easy. (Too bad you can't bookmark Web pages on your own, but it appears that the makers of ICQ decided to leave that job to the commands and buttons in the browser.) To bookmark a site means to mark it so you can visit it later.

ICQ offers two ways to visit a site you bookmarked by clicking the Add To Bookmark button in the Incoming URL Message dialog box (refer to Figure 10-1):

✔ **If you know the name of the person who sent you the Web page address:** If you know the name of the person who sent you the Web page address you're looking for, you can click the person's name on the Contact List and choose History⇨Incoming Bookmarks. Doing so takes you to the Incoming Bookmarks From page shown in Figure 10-2, where you see a list of Web page addresses. Click an address to go to a Web page.

✔ **If you don't know the name of the person:** Click the System Menu button and choose Incoming Bookmarks. You go to the Incoming Bookmarks page, where the names of people who sent you Web page addresses are listed. Click a name to go to the Incoming Bookmarks From page (refer to Figure 10-2) and click a Web page address to go to a Web page. If the address you're looking for isn't listed, click the Back button in your browser and start all over.

Figure 10-2:
The addresses and descriptions of Web pages whose addresses you bookmarked appear in the Incoming Bookmarks From page on your computer.

Click an address to visit a page.

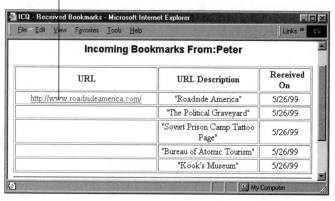

Incoming Bookmarks From:Peter

URL	URL Description	Received On
http://www.roadsideamerica.com/	"Roadside America"	5/26/99
	"The Political Graveyard"	5/26/99
	"Soviet Prison Camp Tattoo Page"	5/26/99
	"Bureau of Atomic Tourism"	5/26/99
	"Kook's Museum"	5/26/99

By the way, the Incoming Bookmarks and Incoming Bookmarks From pages are not on the Web, although it seems that way because the pages open in your browser. Those pages are located inside your computer in the C:\Program Files\ICQ\Bookmarks folder. Appendix B explains how to back up the pages you bookmarked by way of ICQ.

If you're running Internet Explorer, you can make an ICQ bookmark available in Internet Explorer as well. To do so, right-click a Web page address on the Incoming Bookmarks From page and choose Add to Favorites. Then, in the Add Favorite dialog box, click the Links folder to open it, enter a descriptive name in the Name text box, and click OK.

ICQ iT!: Searching the Internet for Information

You wouldn't know by looking, but ICQ offers its very own search engine for scavenging information from the Internet. And as long as you're in Advanced mode (click the To Advanced Mode button if you're not there), you can start searching right away. Believe it or not, the ICQ iT! search engine is right there in the ICQ window. You might have to beat the bushes a couple of times to make it come out, but it's there.

The fastest way to conduct a search with ICQ iT! is to enter a keyword in the Enter Search Keyword box and click the GO button. Do that and you go to a Results page at the ICQ iT! Website (`www.icqit.com`), where Web pages that fulfill your search conditions are listed, as shown in Figure 10-3.

The Results page also shows if ICQ interest groups, user lists, or group directory topics match your search.

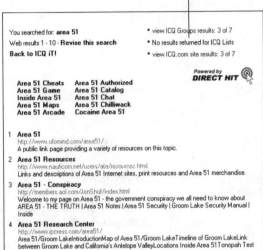

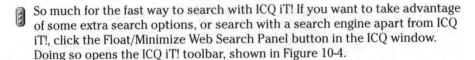

Figure 10-3: The ICQ iT! Most Popular Results page lists Web pages as well as ICQ interest groups and lists that meet your search conditions.

For each Web page found in the search, you'll find a description. Sites are listed by "keyword density," or the proximity of the keywords you entered to the top of the Web pages. Besides Web pages, you're notified if your keywords pertain to any ICQ interest groups, user lists, or directory topics. You know the routine: Click the name of a page to go visit it.

So much for the fast way to search with ICQ iT! If you want to take advantage of some extra search options, or search with a search engine apart from ICQ iT!, click the Float/Minimize Web Search Panel button in the ICQ window. Doing so opens the ICQ iT! toolbar, shown in Figure 10-4.

The middle menu on the toolbar, the Select Search Engine menu, doesn't appear until you choose an "Other Services" option on the Select Search Group drop-down menu. Table 10-1 describes the options in the Select Search Group drop-down menu. After you choose an "Other Service" option, choose a search engine with which to do your searching from the Select Search Engine drop-down menu.

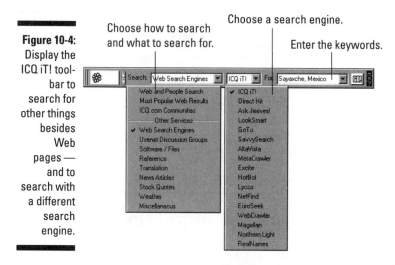

Choose how to search
and what to search for.

Choose a search engine.

Enter the keywords.

Figure 10-4:
Display the
ICQ iT! tool-
bar to
search for
other things
besides
Web
pages —
and to
search with
a different
search
engine.

Click the GO! Button or press the Enter key when you have chosen a search
group and entered the keywords for the search in the Enter Search Keyword
box. To start a new search, click the ICQ iT! button and choose New Search
from the drop-down menu.

Table 10-1   Select Search Group Menu Options

Option	*What It Finds*
Web and People Search	Information and people by name on the Internet
Most Popular Web Results	Websites that are most popular with ICQ members
ICQ.com Communities	ICQ chat rooms, interest groups, user lists, and message boards
Web Search Engines	Web pages in the Search engine you choose
Usenet Discussion Groups	Discussion groups AltaVista, Usenet, RemarQ, DejaNews, or HotBot Usenet
Software/Files	Software programs
Reference	Various reference works, including Merriam-Webster Online and Roget's Thesaurus
Translation	Online translation services
News Articles	Articles from various news services

(continued)

Table 10-1 *(continued)*

Option	What It Finds
Stock Quotes	Stock quotes from different financial reporting services
Weather	Weather from different weather reporting services
Miscellaneous	People finder and movie databases

Techniques for handling the ICQ iT! toolbar

The ICQ iT! toolbar can get in the way of your other work. One way to get around the problem of the toolbar always getting in the way is to "dock" the toolbar to the top or bottom of the browser window. To do so, click the ICQ iT! button (the leftmost button on the toolbar) and choose Docking To Browser⇨Docking To Top or Docking To Browser⇨Docking To Bottom from the submenu. Doing so makes the ICQ iT! toolbar adhere to the top or bottom of the browser window.

Of course, you can also minimize the ICQ iT! toolbar by clicking its Minimize button or by clicking the ICQ iT! button and choosing Minimize from the pop-up menu. After you minimize the toolbar, the iT! icon appears on the right side of the taskbar. Double-click the icon to see the toolbar again.

Believe it or not, you can do everything you can do with the ICQ iT! toolbar without ever displaying the toolbar. To see what we mean, click the arrow to the right of the GO button. A pop-up menu with all the options on the ICQ iT! toolbar appears. By clicking these options and the options on the submenus, you can do everything that you can do in the ICQ iT! toolbar.

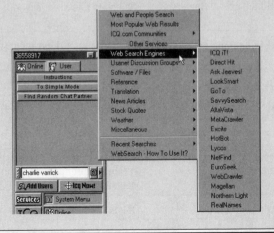

Searching for People on the Internet

Information isn't the only thing you can look up on the Internet. You can also get ICQ's help to find old friends, prom dates, and rock musicians from yesteryear. Make sure you're connected to the Internet and follow these steps to search for people online:

1. **Click the ICQ button.**

2. **Choose Find/Add Users⇨Search Other Directories.**

   You see the Looking For dialog box, as shown in Figure 10-5.

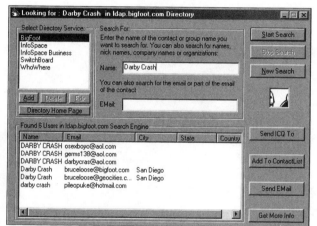

Figure 10-5: Looking up someone on the Internet.

3. **Choose a search service in the Select Directory Service box.**

   If you often search for people on the Internet, you soon find which service works best for you. You are hereby invited to experiment with the different services.

4. **Enter a name in the Name box, and, if you know the person's e-mail address, enter it as well in the Email box.**

5. **Click the Start Search button.**

   If the search turns up any names, the names appear at the bottom of the dialog box.

Notice the buttons in the Looking For dialog box. By clicking a name on the list and clicking a button, you can send someone an invitation to join ICQ, add a name to your Contact List, or send someone an e-mail message.

Chapter 11

Creating and Designing an ICQ Homepage

. . . .

In This Chapter

▶ Understanding how a homepage works

▶ Starting the Homepage Factory application

▶ Creating the different pages on the homepage

▶ Choosing a homepage heading and status indicator

▶ Selecting a predesigned color scheme for the homepage

▶ Choosing fonts and colors for the homepage and frame

▶ Registering your homepage in the White Pages

▶ Activating your homepage

. . . .

*T*his chapter explains how, within the scope of ICQ, you can become a Website developer! That's right — a Website developer.

As the start of this chapter explains, an ICQ homepage is something like a Website. However, you don't have to know a lot about coding or Web pages to create an ICQ homepage. ICQ offers a special program for developing homepages. This chapter explains how to use the special program, called the Homepage Factory, to put together a professional-looking homepage that other ICQ members can enjoy.

How ICQ Homepages Work

An *ICQ homepage* is something like a Website. Really, what ICQ calls a homepage can comprise several different Web pages. Anyone, registered with ICQ or not, can visit your homepage. ICQ members can visit your Web page by clicking your name on the Contact List and choosing Homepage➪User's ICQ Homepage; others can visit your homepage by entering its Web page address in their browser. Like Web pages, ICQ homepages are HTML (hypertext markup language) files. Browsers read and display homepages the same way that they read and display Web pages.

However, the difference between a Web page and a homepage is that others can visit your homepage only when you're online. A Web page, by contrast, resides on a computer that is maintained by an Internet service provider (ISP). Because the ISP is always up and running and always connected to the Internet, Web surfers can get to a Web page any time of day or night. But an ICQ homepage is only available when the person to whom it belongs is online.

Creating an ICQ homepage is considerably easier than creating Web pages because ICQ provides special templates and tools for creating homepages. To create a homepage, you visit the Homepage Factory, a special program designed to help ICQ members construct their homepages. This chapter explains the Homepage Factory in detail. The Homepage Factory offers many opportunities for making a homepage that is distinctly your own. People who venture onto your homepage can chat with you, send messages to you, learn more about you, see your picture if you posted a picture, and even download files from the hard disk on your computer.

After you're finished creating a homepage, the next step is to activate your homepage so that others know you have one. People who have put your name on their Contact Lists can visit your homepage (when you're online, of course) by clicking your name and choosing Homepage⇨User's ICQ Homepage. When you're online, the Homepage icon, a little house, appears next to your name on others' Contact Lists. The Homepage icon means you have created a homepage that others can visit. Anybody can visit your home-page (while you're connected to ICQ) by entering this address in their browser: `http://members.icq.com/Your ICQ Number`. For example, if your ICQ number is 4433221, someone can visit your homepage at this address: `http://members.icq.com/4433221`.

Another thing you ought to know about homepages: While your homepage is available on the Internet, others can view your IP (Internet protocol) address. And a devious hacker who learns your IP address can invade your computer and wreck havoc. Don't be alarmed, because your chances of being hacked are slim, but it can happen, and we feel obliged to tell you that. (See Chapter 14 for a detailed explanation of IP addresses.)

Getting Started in the Homepage Factory

The Homepage Factory is a separate ICQ application whose purpose is to help you create the several Web pages that make up a homepage. Depending on the homepage you want, the Homepage Factory can be difficult or easy to manage. For a generic homepage with a white background and the bare basics, you can simply go with the default options that you get when you open the Homepage Factory. But if you want a one-of-a-kind homepage with fancy colors and gizmos, explore all the amenities that the Homepage Factory offers.

Follow these steps to visit the Homepage Factory and start creating your homepage:

1. **Click the Services button.**

   You can't see the button if you're not in Advanced mode. If necessary, click the To Advanced Mode button in the ICQ window to switch from Simple mode to Advanced mode.

2. **Choose My ICQ Page⇨Make My ICQ Homepage on the pop-up menu.**

   The ICQ Homepage Factory dialog box, shown in Figure 11-1, appears. Now you're ready to get going. The Homepage Factory offers three tabs: Main, Design, and Advanced. To create a homepage, you visit the tabs and tell ICQ what you want on your homepage.

Click to see different pages.

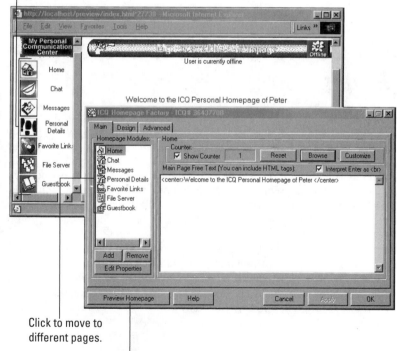

Figure 11-1: As you create your homepage, click the Preview Homepage button from time to time to see how your home-page is shaping up.

Click to move to different pages.

Click the Preview Homepage button to see what your homepage looks like.

As you create your homepage, no matter how far along you are or which tab you're working in, you can click the Preview Homepage button to see precisely what your homepage looks like. As Figure 11-1 shows, your homepage appears in the browser window when you click the Preview Homepage button. Keep an eye on the browser window to see how your homepage is shaping up.

While the browser window is open, click the icons in the frame on the left: Home, Chat, Messages, Personal Details, Favorite Links, File Server, and Guestbook. Each time you click, your browser takes you to another page. People who visit your homepage will click the same icons and go to the same pages. Notice, on the Main tab of the ICQ Factory dialog box (refer to Figure 11-1), that the homepage modules are also named Home, Chat, and so on. In the next section of this chapter, you find out how to visit the different modules and in so doing decorate the different pages.

Click the Apply button in the Homepage Factory dialog box to make your designs show up on the homepage. You can close the Homepage Factory dialog box, take a breather, and get back to work later on. To do so, click the OK button in the Homepage Factory dialog box. To start to work again, click the Services button and choose My ICQ Page⇨Make My ICQ Homepage.

Main Tab: Creating and Decorating the Pages

As the last part of this chapter explained, the Main tab of the ICQ Homepage Factory (refer to Figure 11-1) is where you go to put together the different pages of your homepage. For some reason, probably to keep with the computer tradition of making things as difficult to understand as possible, ICQ calls the pages *modules,* a dreary name if there ever was one. To decorate a page or change what is on it, click a module under Homepage Modules and take it from there. And remember to click the Preview Homepage button to open your browser and find out what the page looks like as you decorate it.

Read on to find out how, starting from the Main tab in the Homepage Factory dialog box, to decorate each page, remove a page, or add a page. By the way, if you only visit the Main tab, you'll create a fine little Website. But the Design and Advanced tabs aren't as intimidating as they seem at first, so don't hesitate to plunge in and try them as well.

Adding and removing pages

Table 11-1 describes the seven pages you get to start with. Everybody needs the Home page, but the File Server page isn't for everybody. Shortly, we describe how to decorate the different pages, but before you start decorating, you may as well decide which ones to keep. Take a look at Table 11-1 and decide which pages are for you. Then read on to find out how to add and remove pages.

Table 11-1	The Seven Generic Pages that the Homepage Factory Offers
Page/Module	*What's on It*
Home	The Welcome page with a message from you, the creator of the homepage, and a counter that tells how many people have visited.
Chat	A chat window that visitors can use to engage you in a chat. Visitors don't have to be ICQ members to start chatting with you.
Messages	A message form so others can write you a message. Visitors don't have to be ICQ members to send messages starting here.
Personal Details	Personal information about you from the ICQ White Pages.
Favorite Links	Links to Websites that you enjoy. Visitors can click a link to go to a Website.
File Server	Opportunities to download files directly from your computer.
Guestbook	A place where visitors can enter their names and write notes.

Removing a page

To remove a page you created yourself or one of the generic pages (you can't remove the Home page), click it under Homepage Modules in the Homepage Factory dialog box, click the Remove button, and then click Yes in the confirmation dialog box. Back in the Homepage Factory dialog box, click the Apply button.

As the confirmation dialog box notes, pages you remove are kept on hand in case you need them again. To restore a page you removed, click the Add button and, on the menu, click the name of the page you want to restore.

Adding a page

To add a page of your own, you need to know a little bit about HTML codes. Either that, or you can choose another generic page. The Homepage Factory offers generic pages for describing your family, favorite games, hobbies, pets, favorite sports, or musical tastes. The name of the page you add will appear under Homepage Modules in the Homepage Factory dialog box.

To add a page, click the Add button and choose Custom Module on the menu. You see the Create/Edit Web Page Module dialog box, as shown in Figure 11-2. Fill in the dialog box as follows:

Figure 11-2:
To create a page, choose a page from the Select/Enter Module Name drop-down menu or describe the page of your own.

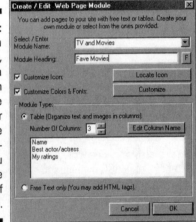

- ✔ **Select/Enter Module Name:** Choose a page from the drop-down list or enter a name of your own.

- ✔ **Module Heading:** What you enter in this box appears at the top of the page.

- ✔ **Customize Icon:** See "Choosing the icon that appears next to the page's name" later in this chapter to discover how to choose the icon that appears next to the page name in the frame on the left side of the browser window.

- ✔ **Customize Colors & Fonts:** The next section in this chapter describes how to choose a font and background color for a page.

- ✔ **Module Type:** Either click the first option button, choose how many columns you want, and click the Edit Column Name button to write descriptive names for the columns, or click the second option button and rely on your own skills at entering HTML codes to format the page.

Click the Apply button in the Homepage Factory dialog box to make your choices take effect.

Choosing a font and background color for individual pages

No matter which page you're dealing with, the techniques for choosing a font for the text on the page and a background color are the same. However, before you start decorating individual pages, be sure to read "Choosing Fonts and Colors for Your Homepage" later in this chapter. There, you'll find techniques for decorating all the pages at once and for relying on an ICQ "scheme" to decorate the pages. Those techniques are preferable to decorating the pages one at a time.

But if you want to decorate a particular page, follow these steps to do so:

1. **Under Homepage Modules in the ICQ Homepage Factory dialog box, click the name of the page you want to make over.**

2. **Click the Edit Properties button.**

   You see the Edit Homepage Module dialog box.

3. **Check the Customize Colors & Fonts check box.**

4. **Click the Customize button.**

   The Customize Colors For dialog box, shown in Figure 11-3, appears.

Click a box. . .

. . .to choose a different color.

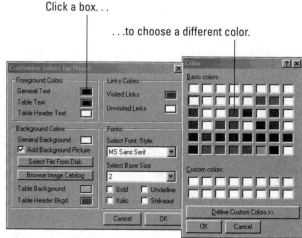

Figure 11-3: Click a color box to choose a color for part of a page.

5. **Choose options in the dialog box to choose a font and background color.**

The options are as follows:

- **Text color:** Under Foreground Colors, click the color box next to General Text, Table Text, or Table Header Text to choose a new color for text, text in tables, or text in table headers. We're not sure why the term *foreground color* describes the color of text, but it does. A table header, by the way, is the first row in a table, the row that describes what is in the rows below. As soon as you click a box, you see the Color dialog box shown on the right side of Figure 11-3. Choose a color and click OK.

- **Background color:** Click the color box next to General Background and choose a new color in the Color box.

- **Picture for the background:** For something really fancy, choose a picture for the background of the page. To do so, check the Add Background Picture check box. Then click the Browse Image Catalog button to see which images are available. Take note of the image you want, return to the Customize Colors For dialog box, and click the Select File From Disk button. In the Select Background Picture dialog box, choose a .gif file and click Open.

- **Font and font size:** Under Fonts, choose a font and base size.

6. **Click OK in the Customize Colors For dialog box and OK again in the Edit Homepage Module dialog box.**

7. **Click the Apply button in the Homepage Factory dialog box.**

   Try clicking the Preview Homepage button to see what your page looks like now.

To make the text and background color of all the pages the same, go to the Design tab of the Homepage Factory dialog box. As "Choosing Fonts and Colors for Your Homepage" explains later in this chapter, the Design tab also offers design schemes that you can apply to all the pages for a professional look.

Choosing the icon that appears next to the page's name

No matter which page visitors to your homepage go to, they see a set of icons in the frame on the left side of their browser windows (refer to Figure 11-1). By clicking one of those icons, they can go to a different page. The Homepage Factory provides icons, but that doesn't mean you can't choose an icon of your own for a page. Follow these steps to choose a new icon:

1. **Under Homepage Modules, click the page whose icon needs changing.**

2. **Click the Edit Properties button.**

   You see the Edit Homepage Module dialog box.

3. **Check the Customize Icon check box.**

4. **Click the Locate Icon button.**

   The Customize Module Icon dialog box appears. It lists which icon is in use at present.

5. **Click the Browse Pictures button. You go to a window that shows which icons are available. Note the name of the icon you like best.**

6. **Return to the Customize Module Icon dialog box (click the Homepage Factory button on the taskbar) and click the Select From Disk button.**

7. **In the Customize Icon dialog box, choose the .gif image you like and click the Open button.**

8. **Click OK in the Customize Module dialog box and OK again in the Edit Homepage Module dialog box.**

9. **Click the Apply button in the Homepage Factory dialog box.**

   If you want the original icon back, return to the Customize Module Icon dialog box and click the Set Default button.

Writing headings for the different pages

Besides the text that appears on each page (shortly we'll show you how to write the text), you can enter a heading. The Edit Homepage Module dialog box offers a command for doing just that. Headings are centered and appear at the top of pages. Follow these steps to enter a heading on one of the pages:

1. **Under Homepage Modules in the Homepage Factory dialog box, click the page that needs a secondary heading.**

2. **Click the Edit Properties button.**

   You see the Edit Homepage Module dialog box.

3. **In the Module Heading text box, enter the heading.**

4. **Click the F (for Font) button.**

   The Select Font dialog box appears.

5. **Choose a font and font size for the heading. You can also check a check box to boldface, italicize, underline, or draw a strikethrough line through it.**

6. **Click the OK button in the Select Font dialog box and OK again in the Edit Homepage Module dialog box.**

7. **Click the Apply button in the Homepage Factory dialog box.**

   We've said it before, we say it again, and we will never tire of saying it: Click the Preview Homepage button in the Homepage Factory dialog box to see exactly what your homepage looks like in the browser window.

Hand-coding your homepage

To display Web pages, browsers such as Netscape Navigator and Internet Explorer read HTML codes. The codes tell the browser how to display text and graphics onscreen.

For example, if you look at the Chat screen in the Homepage Factory dialog box (refer to Figure 11-1), you'll see HTML codes at the top of the page. The codes, `<center>` and `</center>`, tell browsers to center text across the page. HTML codes are enclosed in angle brackets (`<>`). Where text is concerned and you want to format text in a certain way, codes are entered in pairs. The first code tells the browser to start displaying the text a certain way: `<center>`. The second code, which is preceded by a forward slash (/), tells the browser to stop displaying the text a certain way: `</center>`.

If you know a bit about HTML codes, you can hand-code the different pages on your homepage. Just remember to click the Preview Homepage button in the Homepage Factory dialog box to make sure you have entered the codes correctly.

To help you along, here are a few standard HTML codes you can use on your homepage:

`<b></b>`   Boldfaces the text.

`<i></i>`   Italicizes the text.

`<u></u>`   Underlines the text.

`<br>`   Inserts a blank line (this one is done automatically as long as the Interpret Enter as `<br>` check box is checked).

Suppose you want a bulleted list like the ones in this book? The list begins and ends with the `<ul>` code, the bullet code is `<li>`, and you enter the text after the `<li>` code:

```
<ul>
<li>Text you enter.
<li>Text you enter.
<li>Text you enter.
</ul>
```

Cousin to the bulleted list is the numbered list. Numbered lists start and end with the `<ol>` code. The number code, like the bullet code, is `<li>`, but the `<ol>` code tells the browser to number the list instead of attach bullets to it. The browser numbers the items in the list as it reads the codes:

```
<ol>
<li>First item in list that you
    enter.
<li>Second item in list that
    you enter.
<li>Third item in list that you
    enter.
</ol>
```

Home Module: The Home page

The Home page is the first page that visitors see when they venture onto your ICQ homepage (sorry for the tongue-twister, but the *Home page*, the first page you see, is different from the homepage, which refers to all the pages). The Home page is where you put your best foot forward and make a special statement about who you are or what you want to discuss.

To create the Home page, click the Home icon under Homepage Modules in the Homepage Factory dialog box. The dialog box presents a box for entering text on the Home page and options for including a counter on the page (refer to Figure 11-1). No doubt you've seen counters on Web pages. A *counter* tells how many people have visited a page.

Entering the text

In the Main Page Free Text box, enter the text for the Home page. To begin with, the Homepage Factory provides a sort of dull opening message: "Welcome to the ICQ Personal Homepage of *Your Name*." We suggest something a bit more enticing. However, when you erase the generic message and replace it with one of your own, don't erase the <center> or </center> HTML tags. Those tags make sure that what you write is centered across the page.

Below the message, enter more text if you so choose. We suggest writing the text in a word processor and copying it to the Home page. To do so, cut or copy the text in the word processor, right-click in the Main Page Free Text box, and choose the Paste command on the shortcut menu. Write a two-page treatise or a single sentence. The choice is yours.

If you are proficient with HTML tags, you can include them on this and the other pages.

As long as the Interpret Enter as <br> check box is checked, a blank line appears between paragraphs when you press the Enter key.
 is the Break tag, the HTML tag that inserts a blank line on a Web page.

Setting up the counter

Uncheck the Show Counter check box if you don't care for counters. But if you want a counter, click the Customize button and choose what kind of counter you want. The menu offers five choices. To see what these choices are, choose them one at a time and click the Preview Homepage button to see what they look like in the browser window.

If the counters that the Homepage Factory dialog box offers aren't to your taste, you can click the Browse button to connect to an ICQ Web page where more counters are available.

You can reset the counter to 0 at any time by clicking on the Reset button.

Chat Module: The Chat page

Your homepage can include a chat module all its own. A visitor to your home-page can go to the Chat page and enter into a chat session with you. Visitors don't have to be ICQ members to chat with you on the Chat page. Chats take place right on the Chat page, which visitors can see on their browsers.

The Chat page includes a place for visitors to enter their names, e-mail addresses, and the reason they want to chat. After visitors fill in this information and click the Send button on the Chat page, a chat request along with the sender's name appears under the words "Web Message" on the Contact List. Open the chat request and you see the Incoming Chat Request dialog box (Chapter 4 explains how the dialog box works).

To enter the message at the top of the Chat page that invites others to chat, click the Chat icon under Homepage Modules in the Homepage Factory dialog box. You see the Chat screen, as shown at the top of Figure 11-4. If you so desire, enter a message of your own in place of the message that is already there, and then click the Apply button. You might say that you are online right now (since you have to be online for others to see your ICQ homepage) and that you welcome all opportunities to gab.

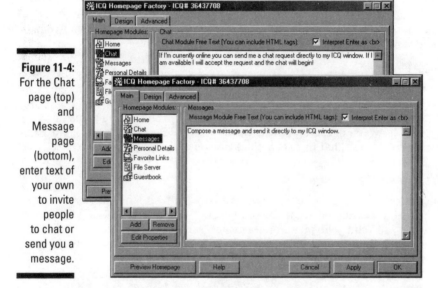

Figure 11-4: For the Chat page (top) and Message page (bottom), enter text of your own to invite people to chat or send you a message.

Message Module: The Message page

People who visit the Message page can send you a message. And they don't have to be ICQ members to do it, either. A visitor to the Message page can enter his or her name, e-mail address, and a message, and click the Send button to send the message. The message, along with the sender's name, arrives on your Contact List under the words "Web Message." When you open the message, you see the Incoming Message dialog box.

To change the generic invitation to write a message that appears at the top of the message page, click the Messages icon under Homepage Module in the Homepage Factory dialog box. You see the Messages screen shown on the bottom of Figure 11-4. Erase what is there and enter an invitation of your own to send a message. Then click the Apply button.

Personal Details Module: The Personal Details page

There's nothing new on the Personal Details page — it lists all the things you revealed about yourself in the ICQ White Pages. Click the Personal Details icon under Homepage Modules in the Homepage Factory dialog box to tinker with your details. If you click the Preview Homepage button, review the Personal Details page, and discover a detail you would like to omit or add, click the View/Change My Details button. You see the ICQ Global Directory dialog box, where you can change your personal details (the start of Chapter 9 explains the ICQ Global Directory dialog box).

You can also place a picture of yourself or anyone else for that matter on the Personal Details page. To do so, however, the picture must be a .gif file. Click the Select Picture button and locate the .gif file you want to put on the page in the Select User's Picture dialog box. After you click the Open button and then the Apply button in the Homepage Factory dialog box, the picture appears near the top of the page, directly below the "My Personal ICQ Homepage" banner.

In our humble opinion, the Personal Details page needs a heading. See "Writing headings for the different pages" earlier in this chapter to find out how to put a heading at the top of a page.

Favorite Links Module: The Favorite Links page

Most Websites include a Favorite Links page. In fact, clicking others' favorite links is the best way to surf the Web, in our opinion. If somebody else likes a Web page it must be good — or at least it must not be one of the numerous junk sites that clog the Internet.

The Favorite Links page is where you can list your favorite Websites. Visitors to your homepage merely have to click the name of a site to go there right away. Besides listing each site, you can briefly describe it.

Click the Favorite Links icon under Homepage Modules in the Homepage Factory dialog box to start listing your favorite Websites. You see the Favorite Links screen shown in Figure 11-5. Before you do anything else, write an introductory paragraph in the Links Module Free Text box so that visitors to the Favorite Links page know that they have stumbled upon a gold mine — the best sites on the World Wide Web.

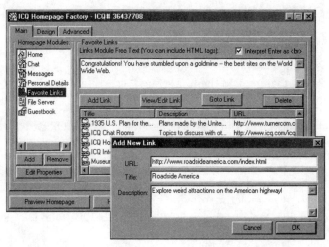

Figure 11-5:
Click the
Add Link
button and
fill in the
Add New
Link dialog
box to list a
site on your
Favorite
Links page.

Jot down the address of a site you want to list or copy its address to the Clipboard. Then follow these steps to list one of your favorite Websites:

1. **Click the Add Link button on the Favorite Links screen.**

   You see the Add New Link dialog box, shown on the bottom of Figure 11-5.

2. **Enter the Website's address in the URL text box.**

   To do that, either type it in or copy it from the Clipboard.

3. **Enter the title of the Website in the Title box.**

4. **Enter a description of the site in the Description box.**

   It doesn't have to be a long description. Visitors to the Favorite Links page can simply click the site's name to go there and see for themselves what is on the site.

5. **Click OK.**

   The site is listed along with the others on the bottom of the Favorite Links screen.

6. **Click the Apply button in the Homepage Factory dialog box.**

As soon as you add a site to the list, we suggest clicking its name on the Favorite Links screen and clicking the Goto Link button. By doing so you go directly to the site — you go to the site, that is, if you entered its address correctly in the Add New Link dialog box. If clicking the Goto Link button doesn't take you to the site, you need to change its address.

Select a link on the Favorite Links screen and follow these instructions to change it address, change its name or description, or remove it from your favorites list:

- ✔ **Correct an address:** Click the View/Edit Link button to open the View/Edit Link dialog box and enter the correct address in the URL text box.

- ✔ **Change a title or description:** Click the View/Edit Link button and change the title or description in the View/Edit Link dialog box.

- ✔ **Remove a link:** Click the Delete button and click Yes in the confirmation dialog box.

In a bit of shameless self-promotion, ICQ lists it primary sites on the Favorite Links screen. We suggest removing them. People who come to your site from ICQ already know about them and people who come from elsewhere won't care very much.

File Server Module: File Server page

If you so desire, you can allow visitors to your homepage to download files directly from the File Server page. *Download* means to transfer a file over the Internet from one place to another. The File Server page is a good place to offer files for your co-workers, graphics files, and other kinds of files that friends and family might like to have.

As shown in Figure 11-6, visitors who go to the File Server page see a list of the files that they can download. Someone who wants to download a file can click its name and take it from there.

For people who intend to offer many files, the Homepage Factory gives you the opportunity to place the files in different folders so that visitors can find them easily. You can also protect files with passwords to prevent any Tom, Dick, or Harry from scavenging them from your computer.

To make files available to others from your homepage, click the File Server icon under Homepage Modules in the Homepage Factory dialog box. You see the File Server screen, as shown in Figure 11-7. From this screen, you can create folders for files, list files for downloading, and password-protect files. Notice the Free Text box. Use this box for typing a description at the top of the page — in this case, a description of files that others can download.

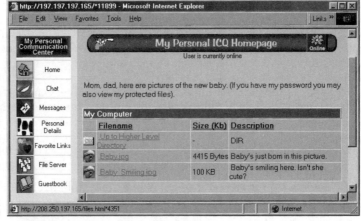

Figure 11-6:
Visitors to the File Server page see a list of files they can download.

You can check folders to help visitors find files.

Enter a description of the files that visitors can download.

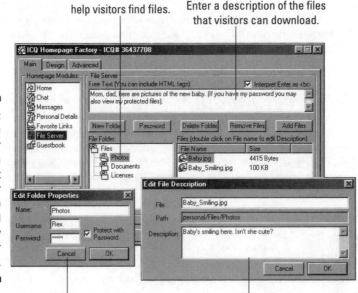

Figure 11-7:
On the File Server screen, you can make it possible for others to download files directly from your computer.

You can password-protect files.

Double-click to describe a file.

Creating folders for the files

To begin with, the Homepage Factory offers one folder — called Files, wouldn't you know it — for keeping files in. But if you want to offer a bunch of files for downloading, we suggest putting them in different folders. That way, others can find them easily. Instead of scrolling through a list of many files, visitors to the File Server page see folder names. By clicking a folder name, they can see a short list of the files in the folder they clicked.

Here's another good reason for putting files in different folders: If you intend to protect some of the files with passwords, put those files in their own folder. As we explain shortly, you can protect all the files in a folder with a password. Keep the password-protected files in the same folder so that visitors only have to enter the password when they attempt to see files that are protected by passwords.

Be sure to create your new folder correctly from the start. If you misspell its name or place it in the wrong parent folder, you can't correct your mistake without starting all over. In other words, you have to delete the folder and start anew.

Follow these steps to create a new folder for keeping files in:

1. **Make sure that the Files folder is selected in the File Folder box on the File Server screen, or else select a different parent folder.**

   If necessary, click the Files folder to select it. To create a folder inside of another folder that is already there, click the parent folder.

2. **Click the New Folder button.**

   You see the New File Folder dialog box.

3. **Enter a name for the new folder and click OK.**

   Don't worry about passwords for now. Later, we show you how to password-protect a folder. The new folder you created appears in the File Folder box (refer to Figure 11-7).

To delete a folder, click its name in the File Folder box, click the Delete Folder button, and click Yes in the confirmation box.

Making files available for downloading

Follow these steps to make a file available for downloading from the File Server page:

1. **On the File Server screen of the Homepage Factory dialog box, click the folder that you want the file to reside in.**

   Folder names appear in the File Folder box.

2. **Click the Add Files button.**

   The Open dialog box appears. This dialog box looks and works exactly like a Windows dialog box for opening a file.

3. **Locate the file you want others to be able to download, select it, and click the Open button.**

   Any file on your computer can be made available for downloading. Very likely, you have to climb the folder hierarchy to find the file you want, since the Open dialog box opens to files deep inside your computer.

The name of the file you made available for downloading is listed in the Files box, as is the size of the file.

When you make a file available for downloading, ICQ makes a copy of the file and places it in the C:\Program Files\Homepage\Root\ *Your ICQ Number*\Personal\Files folder on your computer. Not that you need to know that, necessarily, except we want you to know that a copy of the file is made. ICQ doesn't move the file. The file stays right where you usually go when you want to open it.

To remove a file from the list, click the file's name in the Files box, click the Remove Files button, and click Yes in the confirmation dialog box.

Describing files to visitors

Of course, visitors to your homepage want to know what files are before they attempt to download them. To tell visitors what's what, double-click a file name in the Files box. You see the Edit File Description dialog box (refer to Figure 11-7). Write a description of the file and click OK. Your description will appear next to the file name on the File Server page (refer to Figure 11-6).

To change the description of a file, double-click its name again in the Files box.

Protecting files with passwords

As we explained earlier, you can clamp a password on a folder and thereby prevent snoops from downloading its files. Folders for which a password is needed are marked with a circle with a line drawn through it on the File Server page. Before a visitor can open the folder and see the files inside it, he or she has to enter the correct password.

Before you consider clamping a password on a file, remember that you have to distribute the password to others.

Follow these steps to put a password on a folder and thereby prevent everybody and his brother from downloading its files:

1. **On the File Server screen, click the folder in the File Folder box whose files need protecting.**

2. **Click the Password button.**

   The Edit Folder Properties dialog box appears (refer to Figure 11-7).

3. **Check the Protect with Password check box.**

4. **In the Username box, enter the ICQ name you are registered under.**

5. **In the Password box, enter a password.**

6. **Click OK.**

7. Click the Apply button in the Homepage Factory dialog box.

In the File Folder box, a green padlock appears on the icon of folders that have been password protected.

To remove the password from a folder, click its name in the File Folder box. Then click the Password button, uncheck the Protect with Password check box, and click OK. Oh, and click the Apply button in the Homepage Factory dialog box as well.

Guestbook Module: The Guestbook page

The guestbook is becoming a standard feature on Web pages. A *guestbook* is a place where visitors to a site can enter their names, other information, and perhaps a comment or two about the site. Webmasters, the people who maintain Websites, like guestbooks because they can read the comments and find out what visitors like and don't like about their Websites.

Visitors to the Guestbook page can enter their names, e-mail addresses, and other information. They can also write a comment about your homepage or click the View My Guestbook link and read the names and comments of other visitors.

In the Homepage Factory dialog box, click the Guestbook icon under Homepage Modules to design a Guestbook page. You see the Guestbook screen, as shown in Figure 11-8. The names of people who have visited the Guestbook page and entered their names in the Guestbook appear in the dialog box.

Take advantage of these amenities on the Guestbook screen:

- ✓ **Enter an invitation to sign the Guestbook:** Be sure to enter a warm invitation to sign the Guestbook in the Homepage Module Free Text box. You want as many signers as you can get.

- ✓ **Get more information about signers:** Click a name and then click the View Guest Record button. You see the Guest Info dialog box shown in Figure 11-8.

- ✓ **Remove a name from the Guestbook:** Click a name and then click the Delete Guest Record button.

Be sure to click the Apply button in the Homepage Factory dialog box to make your changes to the Guestbook page take effect.

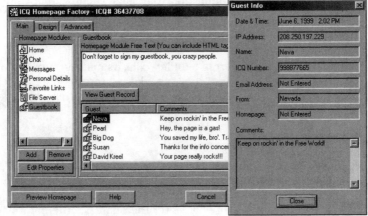

Figure 11-8:
The
Guestbook
screen lists
the names
of everyone
who has
signed your
guestbook.

Design Tab: Decorating Your Homepage

The Design Tab offers a mixed bag of options for decorating your homepage. As you fiddle with the options that are described on the next several pages, don't forget to click the Preview Homepage button in the Homepage Factory dialog box from time to time. Clicking that button opens the homepage in your browser, where you can see right away whether your design decisions were good or bad.

On the Design tab, you can do the following to spruce up your homepage:

- ✔ Change the Homepage heading, the banner that appears across the top of all the pages.

- ✔ Change the online status icon, the icon that appears to the right of the Homepage heading and tells visitors what your online status is.

- ✔ Change the background color, color of text, and text font of all the pages in the homepage.

- ✔ Change the link colors, the color of hyperlinks that have been clicked and are yet to be clicked.

- ✔ Change the background color, color of text, and text font of the *frame,* the panel that appears on the left side of the homepage.

To get to the Design tab of the Homepage Factory dialog box, click the Services button and choose My ICQ Page⇨Make My ICQ Homepage. Then click the Design tab in the Homepage Factory dialog box.

Later in this chapter, "Choosing Fonts and Colors for Your Homepage" explains a technique for letting ICQ make all the design choices for you: Relying on an ICQ Homepage Factory scheme. You can save a lot of time by choosing an ICQ Homepage Factory scheme.

Choosing a Homepage heading

The *Homepage heading* is the banner that appears across the top of all the pages. To begin with, you see the "purple seeker" heading, but you can choose one of the homepage headings shown in Figure 11-9 as well as another heading. The heading you choose appears atop all the pages, so choose carefully.

Figure 11-9: You can choose a Homepage heading of your own.

 A status indicator icon appears to the right of the Homepage heading. If you choose a new Homepage heading, you also have to choose a new status indicator that matches the color of the Homepage heading you chose. The next section in this chapter explains how to choose a status indicator. Unfortunately, choosing a new indicator for all the different types of status — Online, Free for Chat, Away, and so on — takes a bit of time.

Follow these steps to choose a Homepage heading:

1. **On the Design tab, make sure the Add ICQ Homepage Heading check box is checked.**

   And check it, if necessary.

2. **Click the Customize ICQ Homepage Heading button.**

   You see the Select Homepage Heading dialog box.

3. **Click the Browse Pictures button.**

   You go to an HTML page on your computer where the headings are shown (refer to Figure 11-9). Study them closely and decide which one you like.

Take note of the color of the Homepage heading you chose. You might need to choose a status indicator that matches it.

4. **Back in the Select Homepage Heading dialog box, click the Select From Disk button.**

   The Select Homepage Heading dialog box appears. You see the names of the different Homepage headings. To return to the Select Homepage Heading dialog box, click the Homepage Factory button on the taskbar.

5. **Click the heading you want and click Open.**

6. **Click OK in the Select Homepage Heading dialog box and then Apply in the Homepage Factory dialog box to put your new heading to work.**

   Too bad you can't choose a Web page banner or something original in the Select Homepage Heading dialog box. You just can't. You can't because the Homepage heading you choose has to fit and match the status indicator icon. Keep reading.

If you choose a new Homepage heading or status indicator and regret making the change, click the Customize ICQ Homepage Heading button or Customize Online Status Icons button, and, in the dialog box that appears, click the Set Default button. You'll get the original Homepage heading and status indicators back.

Choosing new status indicator icons

Whether you notice or not, a status indicator appears to the right of the Homepage heading (Chapter 3 explains the status indicators). The problem with status indicators, as we noted in the previous section, is that they have to match the color of the Homepage heading. So if you chose a different Homepage heading, you likely have to choose seven new status indicators as well!

The status indicator tells visitors to your homepage whether your are on- or offline, away, occupied, or free to chat. To choose a new status indicator for the different kinds of status, click the Customize Online Status Icons button on the Design tab of the Homepage Factory dialog box. You see the Customize Status Icons dialog box, shown in Figure 11-10.

For each type of status, do the following to choose a status indicator that matches the style and color of your Homepage heading:

1. **Click the Browse button.**

   You go to a Web page that shows what the status indicators look like. Note that a folder name as well as a file name appear next to each indicator. Take note of the folder and name of the indicator that you prefer.

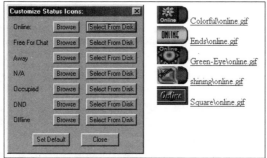

Figure 11-10:
Take note of
the status
indicator
you like, and
then click
the Select
From Disk
button to
choose it.

2. **In the Customize Status Icons dialog box (click the Homepage Factory button on the Taskbar to see it again), click the Select From Disk button.**

   The Customize Online Status Icon dialog box appears.

3. **Find the indicator you want by double-clicking a folder, selecting a file, and clicking the Open button.**

   To keep from mismatching Homepage headers and status indicators, repeat these steps for each type of status indicator, and don't get a hernia while you're at it.

Be sure to select indicators from the same folder to create a coherent design scheme.

Choosing fonts and colors for your homepage

To choose the fonts and colors for the different pages that make up the homepage, you can go about it in three different ways. Hold out your left hand and count the ways on your fingers as you read the following:

🖝 **Rely on an ICQ Homepage Factory Scheme:** If you're in a hurry, we highly recommend this technique. Choose a scheme and ICQ does all the work for you. You get a Homepage heading, status indicators, background colors, and fonts. You get a professional-looking though somewhat slick design.

🖝 **Customize the fonts and colors on your own:** Apply a text color, background color, and font to all the pages. This technique requires some work, but you get an original, one-of-a-kind homepage with a uniform presentation.

✓ **Customize the fonts and colors on each individual page:** We don't recommend this technique at all. This way, you have to do a lot of work, because you decorate each page individually. And when you're done, each page looks different, which doesn't create a good impression. See "Choosing a font and background color for individual pages" earlier in this chapter.

Relying on a Homepage Factory scheme

Before you investigate any techniques for decorating your homepage, see if you can find a Homepage Factory scheme that does the job. Figure 11-11 shows the UFO scheme. Compare this figure to Figure 11-6 to see how a Homepage Factory scheme and self-designed page compare.

ICQ offers no less than four schemes (eight if you download them from the ICQ Website), each designed by a pro. It takes but a minute to apply a scheme, so you can pick and choose among schemes until you find a suitable one. The only drawback to using a Homepage Factory scheme is that your homepage won't be a complete original. Somewhere, someplace, someone else is using the scheme you choose.

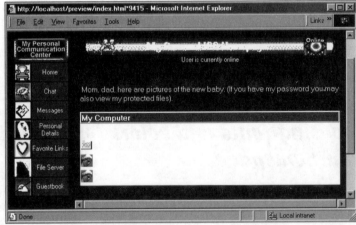

Figure 11-11:
The UFO
Homepage
Factory
scheme.
Compare
this figure to
Figure 11-6.

TIP

Before you choose a Homepage Factory scheme, save the design changes you've already made under a new scheme name. That way, you won't lose the work you already did on your homepage. To save the designs you've made thus far, click the Save As button on the Design tab of the Homepage Factory dialog box. In the Save Scheme dialog box, enter a name and click OK. The name you entered appears on the Scheme menu, where you can choose it again.

Follow these steps to choose a Homepage Factory scheme for your homepage:

1. **On the Design tab, click the down arrow to open the Scheme drop-down menu and choose a scheme.**

2. **Click the Apply button.**

3. **Click the Preview Homepage button to see whether or not you like the scheme.**

   If you don't like it, you can always choose another.

To get more schemes from the Internet, click the Click Here For More Schemes button on the Design tab. Your browser opens to the My Personal ICQ Homepage page on the Internet (www.icq.com/hpf). From there, click the Download hyperlink. You land on the Download Homepage Factory Scheme page (www.icq.com/hpf/down.html). The page offers four extra schemes: Warm Glow, Home Scheme, Greenery, and Skies. Click a scheme to download it and be able to select it on the Scheme drop-down menu.

Customizing the fonts and colors

If you're the do-it-yourself type, you can click the Customize Homepage Main Section Colors and Customize Homepage Side Frame Colors buttons on the Design tab and go to work on your own. The *side frame* is the frame on the left side of the homepage where the Home, Chat, and other hyperlinks are located.

No matter which button you click, you see a dialog box like the one in Figure 11-12 (the Set Homepage Common Colors or Customize Colors for Left Frame dialog box). The dialog boxes offer options for changing the elements of the homepage or side frame. As Figure 11-12 shows, clicking a color box button brings up the Color dialog box, where you can pick a color for part of your Web page.

The Foreground Colors options determine what color the text is. Click a color box button to choose a color for text in the Color dialog box.

- **General Text:** The color of text apart from the text in tables, if any tables are on your homepage.

- **Table Text:** The text in the tables, but not the table headers.

- **Table Header Text:** The text in the table headers, the row at the top of the table that describes what is in the columns below.

The Background Colors options determine which color or image appears in the background:

- **General Background:** The background color. Be sure to choose a different color for the side frame and homepage background.

✔ **Add Background Picture:** Choose this option to put an image instead of color behind the Web page. Check the Add Background Picture check box and choose Browse Image Catalog. Your browser opens to a page where you can see image samples. Note which image you like and then click the Homepage Factory button to return to the dialog box. Next, click the Select File From Disk button, select the image you want in the Select Background Picture dialog box, and click the Open button.

✔ **Table Background:** For the background of tables, if your homepage includes any tables.

✔ **Table Header Bkgd:** For the background of table headers, the first row in tables.

The Links Colors options determine what clicked and unclicked hyperlinks look like:

✔ **Visited Links:** By tradition, hyperlinks that have been clicked and visited are red, but you can choose a different color.

✔ **Unvisited Links:** Hyperlinks that haven't been clicked are blue by convention, but you can choose a different color.

The Fonts options determine what the text looks like:

✔ **Select Font Style:** Choose a new font from the drop-down list.

✔ **Select Base Size:** The *base size* is the common denominator by which text on the page is measured. Choose a number to decrease or increase all the text proportionally.

✔ **Bold, Underline, Italic, Strikeout:** Choose one of these character styles if you want.

To change the width of the side frame, you have to go to the Advanced tab of the Homepage Factory dialog box. On that tab, drag the Frame Width slider to make the side frame narrower or wider.

Be sure to click the Preview Homepage button early and often as you construct your homepage. Clicking the button shows what your homepage will look like to visitors who will see it in their browser windows.

Click a color box...

...to see the Color display box and choose a color there.

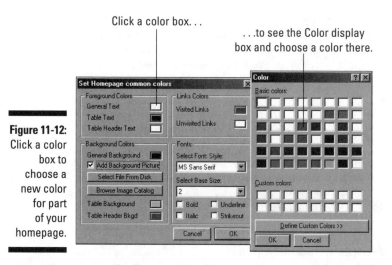

Figure 11-12:
Click a color box to choose a new color for part of your homepage.

Advanced Tab: Putting on the Finishing Touches

You're almost finished creating your homepage. At this point, you could give up the ghost and call it a day, if you wanted. The thing is done, unless you want to add a few finishing touches on the Advanced tab of the Homepage Factory dialog box, shown in Figure 11-13.

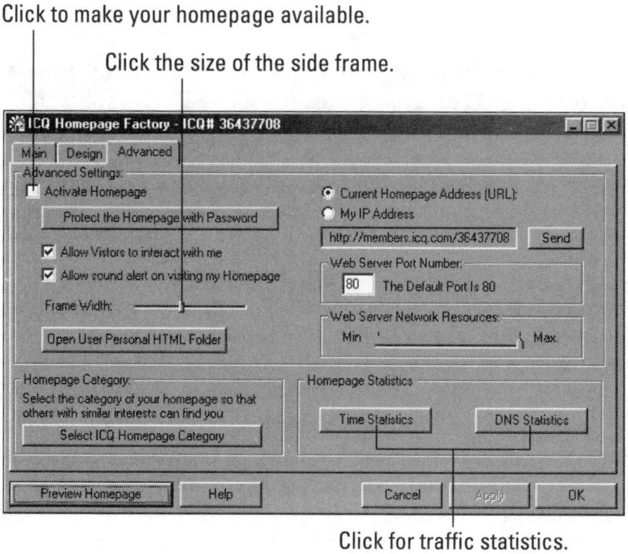

Click to make your homepage available.

Click the size of the side frame.

Figure 11-13:
The Advanced tab offers miscella-neous options for handling your homepage.

Click for traffic statistics.

On the Advanced tab of the Homepage Factory are options for activating your homepage, being alerted when visitors come, and clamping a password on a homepage. You can also send a notice that tells others you have a homepage, enter your homepage in the White Pages so that people who find you there can go to your homepage, and view traffic statistics. Better read on.

Making your homepage come alive

In the classic monster movie *Frankenstein,* Dr. Frankenstein brings his monster to life by pulling a lever and juicing the monster with electricity. Bringing a homepage to life is considerably easier. All you have to do is click the Activate Homepage check box on the Advanced tab.

 Next time you go online, or if you are online already, the Homepage icon — a tiny house — appears beside your name on others' Contact Lists. Others know you have a homepage and that it can be visited by clicking your name and choosing Homepages⇨User's ICQ Homepage. Anybody can visit your homepage (while you are online and connected to ICQ) by entering this address in their browser: `http://members.icq.com/Your ICQ Number`. For example, if your ICQ number is 1122334, someone can visit your homepage at this address: `http://members.icq.com/1122334`.

You can activate or deactivate your homepage at any time without having to go to the Advanced tab of the Homepage Factory dialog box. To do so, click the Service button in the ICQ window and choose My ICQ Page⇨Activate Homepage.

The Advanced tab also offers these options for handling visitors to your homepage:

- **Allow Visitors to Interact with Me:** Check this check box so others can chat with you and send messages from the Chat page or Messages page.
- **Allow Sound Alert on Visiting My Homepage:** Check this box to hear a doorbell sound whenever someone visits your homepage.

Registering your homepage in the White Pages

 As you know if you read Chapter 9, ICQ members can go to the White Pages and learn all about you. In the Global Directory dialog box, they can find out where you live, what your interests are, and even see your picture. And if you play your cards right, people who look you up in the White Pages can also go to the More tab of the ICQ Global Directory dialog box and click the Homepage button to go to your homepage. Figure 11-14 shows where the

Homepage button is located. After you register your homepage, the Web address of your homepage appears on the More tab as well. What's more, others can click the Homepage Category button to see a description of your homepage, as Figure 11-14 also shows.

Follow these steps to register your homepage in the White Pages:

1. **On the Advanced tab of the Homepage Factory dialog box, click the Select ICQ Homepage Category button.**

   You see, very briefly, the Global Directory dialog box, and then the HomePage Information dialog box (refer to Figure 11-14).

2. **In the Homepage Address text box, type the Web address of your homepage if it isn't already there.**

   Your Web address is `http://members.icq.com/Your ICQ Number.`

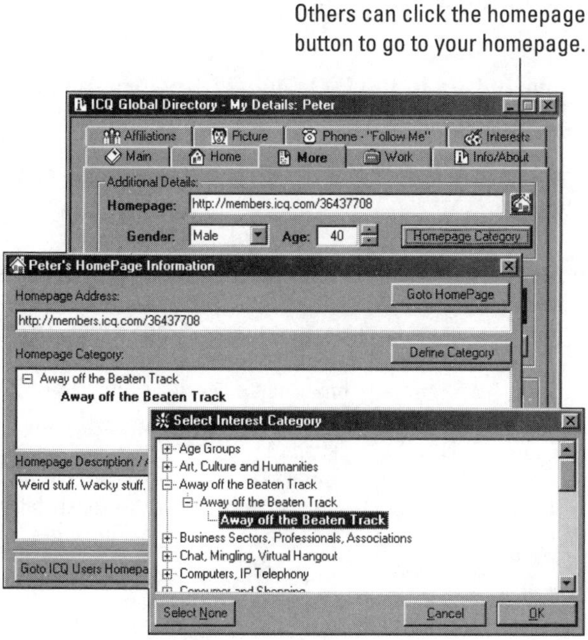

Others can click the homepage button to go to your homepage.

Figure 11-14: Register your homepage in the White Pages to make finding your homepage easier.

3. **Click the Define Category button.**

   The Select Interest Category dialog box, shown in Figure 11-14, appears.

The categories in this dialog box are described in Chapter 12. Your job now, if you choose to accept it, is to find a category for your homepage. After you choose a category, your homepage is entered in the PeopleSpace Directory. ICQ members looking by category in the People Navigator for homepages will find your homepage in the category you choose when you're online and connected to ICQ.

4. **Keep clicking plus signs next to category and subcategory names until you arrive at the subcategory you want; then, with the subcategory name selected, click the OK button.**

The subcategory you chose, as well as its parent category or categories, appears in the HomePage Information dialog box.

5. **In the Homepage Description/About box, enter a brief description of your homepage.**

People who click the Homepage Category button in the ICQ Global Directory dialog box (refer to Figure 11-14) will read the description you enter, so enter a good description.

6. **Click OK.**

7. **Click the Save button in the ICQ Global Directory dialog box.**

8. **Click the Done button.**

Now your homepage is registered with the White Pages and the PeopleSpace Directory.

Announcing your new homepage to the world

The Advanced tab offers a means of telling your ICQ friends that you have given birth to a homepage. To make the announcement, click the Send button on the Advanced tab. You see the Send Multiple Recipients URL Message dialog box. Chapter 8 explains how to send a message to more than one person. The Send Recipients list shows the names of all the people on your Contact List. Click the box next to each person you want to alert and then click the Send button.

Protecting your homepage with a password

To make your homepage a "members only" homepage, you can clamp a password on it. Only people with the password will be able to see your homepage.

To protect your homepage with a password, click the Protect the Homepage with Password button on the Advanced tab of the Homepage Factory dialog box. Then, in the Edit Folder Properties dialog box, click the Protect with Password check box, enter your user name, enter a password, and click the OK button.

Want to remove the password? Click the Protect the Homepage with Password button, remove the checkmark from the Protect with Password check box, and click OK.

Caring for and Feeding Your Homepage

After your homepage is up and running, you still have to care for and feed it. A homepage is like a furry animal in that it demands your attention now and then. Follow these instructions to make sure your homepage is in good working order:

- ✔ **Make sure your homepage is online (or offline):** The computer runs slower when someone is viewing your homepage. You might decide to render your homepage inactive to make your computer run faster. To do so, click the Service button in the ICQ window and choose My ICQ Page⇨ Activate Homepage to remove the checkmark next to the command name. Choose the command again to make the homepage active again.

- ✔ **Tinker with the design:** As any Website designer can tell you, every Web page is a work in progress. To go back and tinker with your homepage, click the Services button and choose My ICQ Page⇨Make My ICQ Homepage. You see the Homepage Factory dialog box, where you can tinker and tinker some more.

- ✔ **Remove names, if necessary, from the guestbook:** From time to time, examine the guestbook to make sure no one has written an obscenity or signed in under a ridiculous pseudonym. You might have to remove a name from the guestbook. "Guestbook Module: The Guestbook page" earlier in this chapter explains how.

- ✔ **Remove the files that aren't needed:** If your File Server page offers files for others to download, periodically remove the files you no longer want to offer to others.

✔ **Add links to the Favorite Links page:** The more links on the Favorite Links page, the better. If you work at it, your homepage can become one of those places Web surfers go when they want to find something interesting on the Internet ("3 million channels and nothing's on!").

✔ **Check the traffic statistics:** On the Advanced tab of the Homepage Factory dialog box, click the Time Statistics button to see when people visit your homepage. As shown in Figure 11-15, the Homepage Time Statistics dialog box tells you what day of the week and what time people visited. (Click the DNS Statistics button to see the IP addresses of visitors, if that means anything to you.)

Figure 11-15:
Study the
Homepage
Time
Statistics
dialog box
to find out
when
people
come to
your
homepage.

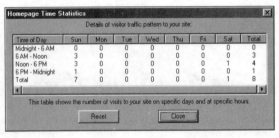

Homepage Time Statistics

Details of visitor traffic pattern to your site:

Time of Day	Sun	Mon	Tue	Wed	Thu	Fri	Sat	Total
Midnight - 6 AM	0	0	0	0	0	0	0	0
6 AM - Noon	3	0	0	0	0	0	0	3
Noon - 6 PM	3	0	0	0	0	0	1	4
6 PM - Midnight	1	0	0	0	0	0	0	1
Total	7	0	0	0	0	0	1	8

This table shows the number of visits to your site on specific days and at specific hours.

Reset   Close

Chapter 12

Getting Around
the PeopleSpace Directory

● ●

In This Chapter

▶ Finding your way around the PeopleSpace Directory

▶ Searching for a topic that interests you in the PeopleSpace Directory

▶ Surveying the general areas and categories in the PeopleSpace Directory

● ●

*T*his brief chapter takes a look at the PeopleSpace Directory, ICQ's attempt to impose order on chaos. When you go searching for people whose interests are similar to yours, you search in the PeopleSpace Directory. This chapter explains how to search there and surveys the general areas and categories in the directory.

Navigating the PeopleSpace Directory

The *PeopleSpace Directory* is ICQ's way of organizing all its user lists, message boards, chat rooms, and interest groups. When you search for a user list, message board, or whatnot, you have to start with the general areas of the PeopleSpace Directory.

From there, you start clicking — first a general area, then a category, and then a subcategory. Finally, with a little luck, you pinpoint the topic you are looking for. (Later in this chapter, "General Areas in ICQ PeopleSpace Directory" briefly describes the general areas.)

The important thing to remember as you search the PeopleSpace Directory is that retracing your steps or going forward to a screen you saw in the course of your search is easy. Follow these instructions to navigate the PeopleSpace Directory:

- ✔ **Click the Back and Forward buttons in your browser:** By clicking the Back or Forward button, or by opening the Back and Forward drop-down menus, you can move backward or forward through the PeopleSpace screens you've visited.

- ✔ **Click the navigation links:** As you burrow into the PeopleSpace Directory to find a topic, ICQ places navigation links at the top of the page for each page you visit. To retrace your steps, click a navigation link.

Figure 12-1 shows a search through User Created Lists pages in the PeopleSpace Directory. Here, we are looking for lists that pertain to quilting. For each page that we visited in the course of the search, a navigation link appears near the top of the page. You can click a navigation link or use the Back or Forward drop-down menus in your browser to get around in the PeopleSpace Directory.

Click the back or forward button. . .

. . .or click a navigation link.

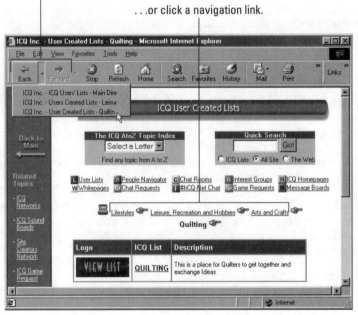

Figure 12-1: To get around in the PeopleSpace Directory, use the buttons in your browser or click a navigation link.

People Navigator: Searching by Topic in the PeopleSpace Directory

No matter what you're looking for in the PeopleSpace Directory — a chat room, interest group, message board, or user list — you can find it by looking in the People Navigator. The People Navigator offers a means of searching by topic in the general category areas of the PeopleSpace Directory. In the People Navigator, you search for a topic, and then you find out if any chat rooms, interest groups, message boards, or user lists in a topic are ready to receive visitors.

Follow these steps to use the People Navigator to search for a chat room, interest group, message board, or user list where a particular topic is discussed:

1. **Click the Add Users button.**

   You see the Find/Add Users to Your List dialog box.

2. **Click the Topic Directories tab.**

3. **Click the People Navigator hyperlink.**

   Soon you land at the People Navigator page (`www.icq.com/people/topic.html`). Here, you find the standard general interest categories. Your next step is to find a topic that interests you.

4. **Scroll down the screen and click a general area or a category.**

   You see a screen similar to the one in Figure 12-2. On the right side of the screen are topics (click a subcategory, if necessary to see the topics). And next to the topics are buttons you can click to go to user lists, chat rooms, interest groups, message boards, and other things that pertain to the topic.

Click to see user lists,
message boards, and more.

Choose a category.

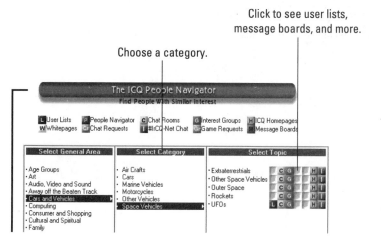

Figure 12-2:
Searching
the People-
Space
Directory by
way of the
ICQ People
Navigator.

5. **Click a button to go a chat room, message board, or whatever, where the topic in question in mulled over and discussed.**

Unfortunately, the People Navigator doesn't offer the navigation links that the PeopleSpace Directory does. You have to click the Back and Forward buttons on your browser to retrace your steps in the People Navigator.

Searching for Chat Rooms, Message Boards, and More in the PeopleSpace Directory

Now that you know your way around the PeopleSpace Directory, you can search for chat rooms, message boards, interest groups, and user lists. Table 12-1 explains where to start looking for those items in the PeopleSpace Directory.

Table 12-1	Searching the PeopleSpace Directory	
Item	*How to Get There*	*Web Address*
Chat rooms	Click the Add Users button, click the Chat tab, and click the Chat Room Directory hyperlink.	`www.icq.com/icqchat`
Interest groups	Click the Add Users button, click the Topic Directories tab, click the Interest Groups hyperlink, and click the Select a Topic hyperlink.	`http://groups.icq .com/category.html`
Message boards	Click the System Menu button and choose Message Boards.	`www.icq.com/boards`
User lists	Click the ICQ button and choose Find/Add Users⇨Users' Lists.	`www.icq.com/icqlist`

General Areas in the ICQ PeopleSpace Directory

According to ICQ, every topic under the sun falls into one of the general areas in the PeopleSpace Directory. Look for a user group, chat room, message board, or interest group and you have to start with one of the general areas in Table 12-2. From there, you click one of the categories in Table 12-2. And from there? Who knows what you will find at the end of the rainbow?

Table 12-2	General Areas in the PeopleSpace Directory
General Area	*Categories*
Age Groups	Age Groups, The College Age, The Rock Age, The Trance Age
Art	Animation, Art General, Artists Talk, Fine Arts, Literature and Poetry, Museums
Audio, Video, and Sound	Audio, Video, Sound
Away Off the Beaten Track	Away Off the Beaten Track, Unusual and Out of the Ordinary
Cars and Vehicles	Air Crafts, Cars, Marine Vehicles, Motorcycles, Other Vehicles, Space Vehicles
Computing	Computer Hardware Users, Computer Industry, Computer Related User to User Help, Computer Software Users, Other Computer Issues, Web Master's and Site Owner's
Consumer and Shopping	Audio, Video and Stereo, Cellular, Phones and Services, Computer Hardware, Computer Software, Consumer Electronics, Home Equipment
Cultural and Spiritual	Christian Groups, Cultures, Islamic Groups, Jewish Groups, Other Groups
Family	Friends and Family, Genealogy, Parenting, Pets
Games	Board Games, Card Games, Collecting Trade and Exchange, Computer Games A to Z, Computer Games by Company, Console Games, Arcades and Emulations
Health and Medicine	Health and Medicine, Nutrition

(continued)

Table 12-2 *(continued)*

General Area	*Categories*
Internet	Administrators Newsgroups Networks, Apache Server, BBSs Newsgroups and Usenet, GNU, IRC, ISP
Internet Telephony Voice and Chat	CUseeME, Conferencing, IBM Internet Connection Phone, ICUII, Intel Internet Video Phone, Microsoft NetMeeting
Lifestyles	Gathering for Events, Leisure Recreation and Hobbies, Lifestyles
Living Abroad	Countries, Lost Friends and Relatives
Local	By Cities and Towns, By Countries, By Languages, International
Money and Business	Agriculture, Banking, Business-Other, Community and Social Associations, Computers and Technology, Consumer Goods
Movies and TV	Celebrities, Movies, TV Series
Our Culture Heroes	Animations Cartoons and Comics Heroes, Fine Arts Heroes, Great Creators, Leaders, More Culture Heroes, Musicians Actors and Singers
Romance	Celestial Chat, Just Friends, Looking for Love, Other Chat Issues
Science and Technology	Nature and Environment, Science Technology and Research Networks, Space and Astronomical Events
Sports	Indoor, Other Sports, Outdoor, Professionals, Sports Officials
Students	Colleges and Universities, Education, Fraternities and Sororities, High Schools Alumni, Students by Field of Study
Travel	Commuter Request, Travel Agencies and Organizations, Travel Experiences and Advice, Travel Locations, Travel Mates
Volunteer and Community Services	Clubs Social Organizations, Community Services, Emergency Rescue and Law Enforcement, Volunteer Groups
Women	Lifestyle, Marriage, Parenting Issues, Single Women, Women by Location, Women in Art and Music

Part IV
Getting More out of ICQ

The 5th Wave   By Rich Tennant

"Face it Vinnie— you're gonna have a hard time getting people to subscribe online with a credit card to a newsletter called 'Felons Interactive!'"

In this part . . .

Part IV explains how to squeeze every last bit of juice out of ICQ. We want you to use ICQ to the hilt — and this part explains how to do just that.

In Part IV, you find out how to customize ICQ so the program works exactly how you want it to work. We also describe how you can reach into every corner of ICQ and still maintain your privacy. This part explains how to store stuff in and retrieve stuff from the Message Archive, the depository for all things ICQ. Finally, you find how out to use telephony applications to video-conference and do other fancy stuff.

Chapter 13

Making ICQ Work Your Way

● ●

In This Chapter

▶ Choosing for yourself how and when to start ICQ

▶ Taking charge of the ICQ window

▶ Choosing how you are alerted to incoming communications

▶ Choosing the folder where files sent to you are stored

▶ Communicating directly with people on your Contact List

▶ Changing the ICQ keyboard shortcuts

● ●

Sprinkled throughout this book are tips and ideas for making ICQ work your way. However, because only the lucky few will read this book from start to finish, we have assembled all our advice for customizing ICQ in this chapter. In this chapter, you find out how to bend ICQ to your will.

Read on to discover how to make ICQ start your way and take charge of the ICQ window. You also find out techniques for being alerted when chat requests, messages, and other communications are sent your way. This chapter explains how to choose a folder for incoming files and how to make special considerations for people on your Contact List. Last but not least, you discover how to trade the left mouse button for the right mouse button and change the ICQ keyboard shortcuts.

Deciding How and When to Start ICQ

By design, ICQ starts whenever you open your browser and connect to the Internet. But some people prefer to be the masters of their fate and start ICQ only when they decide to start running the program. These pages explain how to decide for yourself when ICQ starts. You'll also find instructions here for bypassing the ICQ Announcements box, the one that appears whenever you start ICQ.

Choosing whether or not to start ICQ automatically

People who like to jump aboard the Internet quickly get annoyed at having to wait a moment for ICQ to start each time they connect to the Internet. They prefer to start ICQ by clicking the Start button and choosing Programs⬦Icq⬦ICQ. Follow these steps if you prefer ICQ *not* to start automatically, and you want to start ICQ on your own:

1. **Click the ICQ button and choose Preferences.**

   You see the Owner Prefs For dialog box.

2. **Click the Connection tab.**

   Figure 13-1 shows the Connection tab.

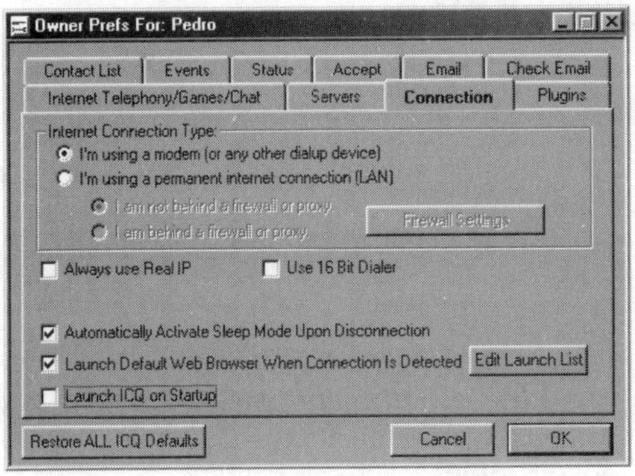

Figure 13-1:
Uncheck the
Launch ICQ
on Startup
option if you
prefer to
start ICQ on
your own.

3. **Uncheck the Launch ICQ on Startup check box.**

4. **Click the OK button.**

   Next time you open your browser and go on the Internet, ICQ won't launch automatically. When you want to start ICQ, you have to do it on your own.

In case you're curious about the other options on the Connection tab (refer to Figure 13-1), Chapter 3 explains all the details of starting ICQ and choosing how you want to start the program.

Seeing or bypassing the ICQ Announcements box

The ICQ Announcements box pokes its head onscreen each time you start ICQ. If you prefer to bypass the ICQ Announcements box when you start ICQ, click the ICQ button, choose Preferences, and click the Contact List tab in the Owner Prefs For dialog box. Then check the Don't Show Announcements check box, and click OK.

You can see the ICQ Announcements box whenever you wish by clicking the ICQ button and choosing Help➪ICQ Announcements.

Managing the ICQ Window

Unless you get out your socket wrench and start changing things around, the ICQ window appears in the middle of your screen on top of all other program windows. In other words, the ICQ window hogs screen space and gets in the way.

Fortunately for you, ICQ offers a bunch of different ways to tame the ICQ window. Chapter 3 explains the following techniques in detail. Here, in a nutshell, are all the ways to make the ICQ window more manageable:

✔ **Attach the window to a side of the screen:** To begin with, the ICQ window "floats" and you can move it wherever you please by dragging its title bar. However, you can also attach the window to the left, right, top, or bottom of the screen. To do so, click the ICQ button, choose Windows/Alerts➪Contact List Position, and choose an option: Left, Right, Top, or Bottom. Choose the Float option when you want the window to float again.

✔ **Allow the ICQ window to appear behind other windows:** Click the ICQ button and choose Windows/Alerts➪Always On Top to uncheck the Always On Top option. After you choose the option, the ICQ window works like a normal window — it yields to other windows when they appear onscreen.

✔ **Minimize the window automatically when you are not using ICQ:** You can make the ICQ window disappear from the screen after a certain amount of idle time has elapsed. To do so, click the ICQ button, choose Preferences, and click the Contact List tab in the Owner Prefs For dialog box, as shown in Figure 13-2. Then click the Auto Hide Delay check box and enter the amount of idle time you will tolerate.

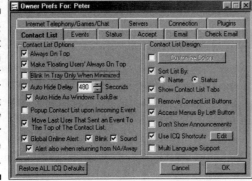

Figure 13-2:
The Contact List tab in the Owner Prefs For dialog box offers many options for handling the ICQ window.

If you set aside ICQ and work in another program for the amount of time you enter, the ICQ window is minimized. Double-click the Flower button in the lower-right corner of the screen to see the window again.

✔ **Make the window appear automatically when someone sends you a communication:** After you minimize the window (the subject of the previous bullet in this list), you can make the window pop onscreen whenever someone sends you a message, chat request, or other communication. To do so, go to the Contact List tab of the Owner Prefs dialog box (refer to Figure 13-2), and check the Popup Contact List Upon Incoming Event check box.

✔ **Reduce the window to a single button, the Status button:** With this strategy, which is strictly for people who know their way around ICQ, the ICQ window shrinks to a single button — the Status button. When you want to give a command, click the Status button, choose a command on the pop-up menu, and choose a command from a submenu.

To shrink the window to the Status button, click the ICQ button and choose Windows/Alerts➪Status "Floating" On. To remove the Status button, click it and choose "Floating" Off on the pop-up menu.

Handling Incoming Chat Requests, Messages, and Other "Events"

As you know if you've spent a minute with ICQ, an icon appears on your Contact List and in the lower-right corner of the screen when you receive what ICQ calls an *event* — a communication from someone else. Glance at the icon and you can tell if you're being sent a chat request, message, Web page address, voice message, greeting card, Email Express message, phone number request, photo request, or system announcement. Prick up your ears and you will hear when someone has sent you a so-called event.

These pages explain the various ways to decide for yourself how to be alerted when someone is trying to communicate with you. Starting from the Events tab in the Owner Prefs For dialog box, you can do a bunch of different things to make sure you stay alert to incoming communications. Figure 13-3 shows the Events tab. Follow these steps to get there:

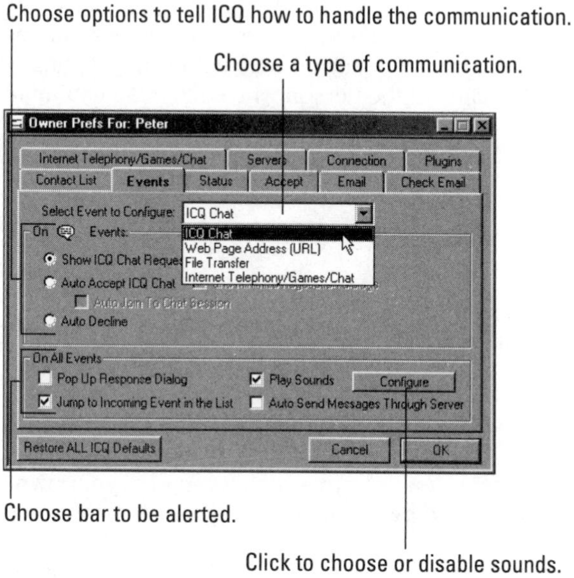

Choose options to tell ICQ how to handle the communication.

Choose a type of communication.

Figure 13-3:
On the
Events tab,
you can tell
ICQ how you
want to be
alerted to
incoming
communica-
tions.

Choose bar to be alerted.

Click to choose or disable sounds.

1. **Click the ICQ button and choose Preferences on the pop-up menu.**

   You see the Owner Prefs For dialog box.

2. **Click the Events tab.**

   There, you made it.

The On All Events options at the bottom of the dialog box are for telling ICQ how you want to be alerted to incoming communications. Choose a Select Event to Configure option to handle chat requests, Web page addresses, file transfers, and telephony requests in different ways. Click the Configure button to choose sounds for different events. Keep reading.

Choosing how you want to be alerted to incoming events

Check or uncheck On All Events check boxes at the bottom of the Events tab (refer to Figure 13-3) to tell ICQ how you want to be told when someone has sent you a communication:

✔ **See a Response dialog box as soon as the communication arrives:**
Normally when you get a communication, you double-click an icon or
click it and then click Receive to see it in a dialog box. Check the Pop Up
Response Dialog check box to make the dialog box appear as soon as
the communication arrives.

✔ **Make the Contact List scroll to the sender's name:** On a Contact List with
many names, you will have trouble seeing the name of the person who
sent you a communication unless you leave the checkmark in the Jump to
Incoming Event in the List check box. By doing so, you make the Contact
List scroll to the name of the person who sent you a communication.

✔ **Turn off the sounds:** If you prefer not to hear sounds when communications arrive, uncheck the Play Sounds check box. (The next section in
this chapter explains how to choose the sounds that are heard when
events arrive and how to disable some sounds but keep others.)

Assigning sounds to incoming events

As long as the Play Sounds check box is checked on the Events tab of the
Owner Prefs For dialog box (refer to Figure 13-3), you hear a unique sound
whenever someone sends you a communication. But suppose you don't like the
sound you hear? Suppose you want to attach a sound of your own to a communication or not be distracted by sound when certain kinds of events arrive?

You can be the master of your own fate when it comes to hearing sounds as
you use ICQ. You can disable a sound or attach a new sound to an event.
Follow these steps to decide for yourself what sounds you hear:

1. **Go to the Events tab of the Owner Prefs For dialog box.**

   To get there, click the ICQ button, choose Preferences, and click the
   Events tab.

2. **Make sure the Play Sounds check box is checked, and then click the
   Configure button.**

   You see the ICQ Sound Schemes Settings dialog box, shown at the top of
   Figure 13-4. The dialog box lists every event to which a sound can be
   attached. Click an event and click the Preview button to hear the sound
   that has been attached to it. You can attach any .wav sound file to an
   event in the list.

3. **Open the Sound Schemes drop-down menu and choose My Settings.**

   Choose My Settings so you can go back to using the ICQ sound settings
   later on, if you want to.

Click to disable a sound.

Click to select a new sound.

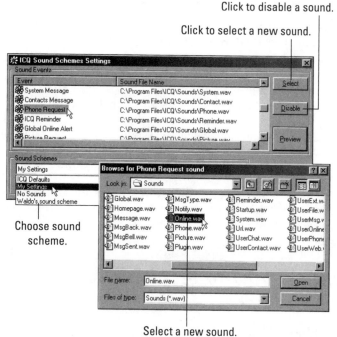

Figure 13-4:
Disabling
sounds and
selecting
new sounds
for ICQ
events.

Choose sound
scheme.

Select a new sound.

4. Scroll through the Event list and click the event whose sound you want to change.

Remember that you can click the Preview button to find out which sound is associated with the event.

5. Either select a new sound for the event or disable the sound.

Disable a sound if you want to hear no noise whatsoever when a communication arrives. Follow these steps to disable or select a new sound for an event:

- **Disable a sound:** Click the Disable button and click Yes in the dialog box that asks if you really want to stop hearing the sound.

- **Select a new sound:** Click the Select button. You see the Browse for Sound dialog box, shown at the bottom of Figure 13-4. Select a sound in this dialog box and click the Open button. If none of the sounds in the dialog box excite your ears, find another .wav file on your computer that does. To do so, rummage in the Browse for Sound dialog box until you find the .wav file and then click the Open button.

Back in the ICQ Sound Schemes Settings dialog box, the name of and path to the file you chose appears beside the event.

6. **Repeat Steps 4 and 5 to disable or select new sounds, if you so desire.**

7. **Click OK to close the ICQ Sound Schemes Settings dialog box and OK again to close the Owner Prefs For dialog box.**

   Next time a communication arrives, you'll hear the sound you want to hear. Or you will hear no sound at all if you disabled the sound.

By the way, the ICQ Sound Schemes Settings dialog box offers a means of choosing many more sound schemes for ICQ. To fashion yet another sound scheme, disable sounds and select new sounds, and then click the Save As button in the ICQ Sound Schemes Settings dialog box. In the Save Scheme As dialog box, enter a name for your scheme and click OK.

Return to the ICQ Sound Schemes Settings dialog box and choose a new scheme from the Sound Scheme drop-down menu when you want to impose one scheme or another on ICQ.

Deciding how to receive chats, Web page addresses, files, and telephony/game requests

The Events tab in the Owner Prefs For dialog box (refer to Figure 13-3) also offers a means of deciding how you want to handle chat requests, Web page addresses, incoming files, and telephony/game requests. The Events tab gives you the chance to decline these items and do various other things to them.

Choose an option from the Select Event to Configure drop-down menu and read on to tell ICQ how you want to receive chat requests, Web page addresses, files, and telephony/game requests.

Chat requests

 Normally, the Incoming Chat Request dialog box appears when someone wants to chat with you, and you either accept or decline the invitation. However, you can bypass the Incoming Chat Request dialog box and get straight to it by choosing options on the Events tab:

- ✔ **Accept all invitations to chat automatically:** Click the Auto Accept ICQ Chat option button. The Incoming Chat Request dialog box still appears when you choose this option, but you can dispense with it as well by checking the And Minimize Negotiation Dialogs check box.

- ✔ **Let third parties join your chats right away:** Chapter 4 explains how you can include third parties in a chat you are having. Check the Auto Join To Chat Session check box if you want others to be able to join in without getting your permission first.

✔ **Decline all invitations to chat:** Click the Auto Decline option button if you're not the chatting kind and you don't care to chat with anybody.

If you change your mind about automatically accepting or declining all invitations to chat, return to the Events tab and check the Show ICQ Chat Request Response dialog box check box.

Web page addresses

As Chapter 10 explains, the Incoming URL Message dialog box appears when someone sends you a Web page address. By clicking buttons in the dialog box, you can bookmark the Web page address or visit the Web page.

ICQ offers a couple of other ways to handle Web page addresses. Choose Web Page Address (URL) on the Select Event to Configure drop-down menu on the Events tab (refer to Figure 13-3) to tell ICQ how you want to handle incoming Web page addresses. Dig these options:

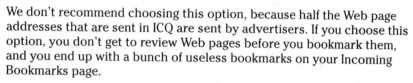

✔ **Bookmark the Web pages automatically:** Click the Auto Add URL to Bookmarks option button to place all Web page addresses that are sent to you on the Incoming Bookmarks From page. Choose this option if you want to bookmark all addresses that are sent to you without reviewing them first.

We don't recommend choosing this option, because half the Web page addresses that are sent in ICQ are sent by advertisers. If you choose this option, you don't get to review Web pages before you bookmark them, and you end up with a bunch of useless bookmarks on your Incoming Bookmarks page.

✔ **Decline all Web pages addresses:** Click the Auto Decline option button if bookmarking and viewing Web pages is not your cup of tea.

✔ **Open your browser to Web pages as their addresses are sent to you:** Check the Auto Open URL in Browser check box if you want to go straight to Web pages as their addresses arrive. Choose one of the option buttons — Open in New Browser Window and Open in Current Browser Window — to switch to the Web page in question or open a second browser window for viewing the Web page.

To go back to seeing the good-old Incoming URL Message dialog box when a Web page address arrives, click the Show URL Response dialog box option button.

File transfers

 As Chapter 8 explains, both parties have to be online and connected to ICQ before a file can be sent from one party to the other. Sending files can be kind of problematic, so the Events tab offers options to make sending files a little easier. (The next section in this chapter explains how to tell ICQ where to store incoming files.)

Go to the Events tab of the Owner Prefs For dialog box (refer to Figure 13-3), open the Select Event to Configure drop-down menu, and choose File Transfer to decide for yourself how to receive files in ICQ. Here's what you can do with files from the Events tab:

- **Receive files without being asked:** Click the Auto Receive Files option button to receive files without reviewing them first. The Incoming File Request dialog box still appears when you choose this option, but you can click the And Minimized check box if you don't care to see it, either.

- **Decline all files automatically:** Click the Auto Decline option button if you are suspicious of files and don't want to receive them.

- **Decline all files from people not on your Contact List:** Check the Auto Decline From People Not On My Contact List check box to decline all offers of files from people whose names aren't on your Contact List.

Click the Show File Request Response dialog box if you want to go back to seeing the Incoming File Request dialog box whenever someone sends you a file. If someone sends you two files of the same name, ICQ asks if you want to overwrite the first file when the second file arrives. But if you check the Always Overwrite Existing Files dialog box, the first file is erased by its namesake.

Internet telephone/games/chat

 As Chapter 16 explains, the Incoming Internet Telephony/Games dialog box appears when someone wants to engage you in a game or a telephony activity. Choose Internet Telephony/Games/Chat from the Select Event to Configure drop-down menu on the Events tab (refer to Figure 13-3) and check out these techniques for handling telephony stuff:

- **Automatically accept all telephony invitations:** Click the Auto Accept Internet Telephony/Games/Chat option button to take on all comers without seeing who's calling first.

- **Automatically decline all telephony invitations:** Click the Auto Decline option button if you want nothing to do with telephony stuff.

To go back to seeing the Incoming Internet Telephony/Games dialog box, click the Show Internet Telephony/Games/Chat Request Dialog option.

Deciding Where to Store Incoming Files

Unless you choose a different folder, files that were sent to you are kept in the C:\Program Files\ICQ\Received Files folder and its subfolders. For each person who sends you a file, ICQ creates a subfolder, places the file in the subfolder, and places the subfolder in the C:\Program Files\ICQ\Received Files folder. For example, if someone named Tex sends you a file, the file is kept in this location: C:\Program Files\ICQ\Received Files\Tex.

We respectfully submit two reasons for keeping files that were sent to you in a different folder:

✔ **To maintain your privacy:** Anyone can go to the C:\Program Files\ICQ\Received Files folder and find your files there.

✔ **To store the files with other files you receive over the Internet:** If you receive a lot of files over the Internet, you might decide to keep the ones sent by way of ICQ with the ones sent to you in your e-mail program. That way, you always know where to find a file that has been sent to you over the Internet.

Follow these steps to tell ICQ where to store incoming files:

1. **Click the ICQ button and choose Preferences.**

   You see the Owner Prefs For dialog box.

2. **Click the Accept tab.**

   Figure 13-5 shows the Accept tab. The Default Incoming File(s) Path box lists the folder where files sent to you are kept.

Click to choose a new folder.

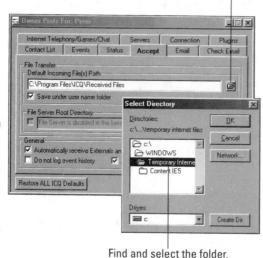

Figure 13-5: Choosing a new folder for storing incoming files.

Find and select the folder.

3. **Click the folder button to the right of the Default Incoming File(s) Path box.**

The folder button has no name, but it does look like a folder. As soon as you click the button, you see the misnamed Select Directory dialog box shown in Figure 13-5. (They're called *folders* now, not *directories*.)

4. **Locate and select the folder where you want to keep incoming files.**

If the folder is on a drive different from the one where ICQ is, open the Drives drop-down menu and select a drive. Click the Network button to store the files on the network, if you're connected to a network and want to store files there.

5. **Click the OK button.**

Back on the Accept tab, the Default Incoming Files(s) Path box lists the location of the folder you chose in Step 4.

6. **Click the OK button in the Owner Prefs For dialog box.**

Uncheck the Save Under User Name Folder check box on the Accept tab (refer to Figure 13-5) if you want all files to be stored in a single folder, not in subfolders named after the people who sent you files.

Making Special Considerations for People on Your Contact List

The names of the friends you have made on ICQ appear on your Contact List. As long as someone's name is there, you can give him or her special consideration. For example, you can tell your ICQ friend that you're online, although everyone else thinks you're offline because you chose Invisible as your online status. You can accept chat requests and files automatically, without having to negotiate a dialog box. And you can be alerted when someone on your Contact List goes online.

These pages explain all the different ways to give special consideration to someone on your Contact List. To get going, click the name of the person who deserves special consideration, choose More (Rename, Delete) on the pop-up menu, and then choose Alert/Accept Modes. You see the Alert/Accept dialog box, three tabs of which are shown in Figure 13-6. By clicking these tabs and choosing options, you can give special consideration to the person whose name you clicked:

Figure 13-6:
Click a
Contact List
name and
choose
More
(Rename,
Delete)⇨
Alert/-
Accept
Modes to
give special
considera-
tion to
someone on
your
Contact List.

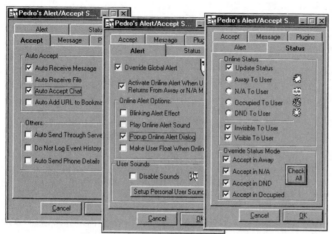

✔ **Accept tab:** Accept messages, files, chat requests, and Web page addresses automatically.

✔ **Alert tab:** Be alerted when the person goes online.

✔ **Message tab:** Write a personalized status message for the person to read.

✔ **Plugins tab:** Accept or decline telephony/game/chat requests automatically.

✔ **Status tab:** Declare your online status to the person independently of what others think your online status is.

Accept tab: Receiving items faster

On the Accept tab of the Alert/Accept dialog box (refer to Figure 13-6) are options for receiving items faster from a certain someone. Check these check boxes to tell ICQ how you want to handle items sent to you from the person whose name you clicked on your Contact List:

✔ **Auto Receive Message:** Makes the Incoming Message dialog box appear automatically when the person sends you a message. You don't have to click the Message icon and choose Receive or double-click the message icon to see the message in the dialog box.

✓ **Auto Receive File:** Accepts files sent to you from the person in question. The Incoming File Request dialog box doesn't appear first so you can accept or decline the file being sent to you. Earlier in this chapter, "Deciding Where to Store Incoming Files" explains where files are kept on your computer after they arrive.

✓ **Auto Accept Chat:** Invitations to chat from the person are accepted automatically. You don't see the Incoming Chat Request dialog box. Instead, the Chat window appears onscreen right away.

✓ **Auto Add URL to Bookmarks:** Places all Web page addresses that are sent to you from the person on the Incoming Bookmarks From page. Chapter 10 explains bookmarks.

The Accept tab also offers these options for communicating with a person on your Contact List:

✓ **Auto Send Through Server:** Sends all communications to the person through the ICQ computers, not directly from your computer to the other person's.

✓ **Do Not Log Event History:** Prevents communications to and from the person from being recorded in the Message Archive. Chapter 15 describes the Message Archive.

✓ **Auto Send Phone Details:** Permits the other person to obtain your phone number automatically. See Chapter 9.

Alert tab: Being informed when someone comes online

The options on the Alert tab in the Alert/Accept dialog box (refer to Figure 13-6) are for being informed when someone on your Contact List is online and has plugged into the ICQ network. To be able to choose an option, check the Override Global Alert check box. After you click the check box, you can choose among these options for being alerted:

✓ **Activate Online Alert When User Returns From Away or N/A Mode:** Alerts you when the person changes status from Away or N/A (Extended Away) so you can contact him or her. Chapter 3 explains how to tell others what your online status is.

✓ **Blinking Alert Effect:** Makes the person's name blink (and change color (from blue to red and back again) when the person comes online.

✓ **Play Online Alert Sound:** The words "user is online" (or another sound of your choice) are heard when the person goes online.

✔ **Popup Online Alert Dialog:** A message box appears in the middle of the screen when the person goes online. The message box informs you — guess what? — that the person is online.

✔ **Make User Float When Online:** Makes the person's name float in the form of a button while he or she is online. You can click the person's name and see the same pop-up menu that you see when you click a name on the Contact List. (To keep the menu from floating and moor it again to the Contact List, click the name and choose "Floating" Off.)

The Alert tab also offers a means of playing a sound whenever the person in question sends you an item — a message, chat request, or Web page address, for example.

To attach a sound to communications you receive from someone on your Contact List, start by clicking the Setup Personal User Sounds button on the Alert tab of the Alert/Accept dialog box. You see the Sound Config For dialog box, as shown in Figure 13-7. The dialog box offers these strategies for attaching a sound to items you receive from a person on your Contact List:

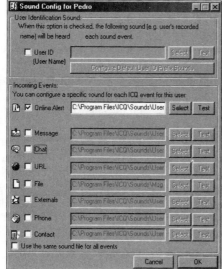

Figure 13-7:
You can
identify
communica-
tions from a
person on
your
Contact List
by sound as
well as by
sight.

✔ **Hear a specific sound as well as the sound you usually hear:** With this strategy, you hear two sounds, a sound that identifies the person in question and then the sound that identifies an incoming message, chat request, or whatever.

Click the User ID (User Name) check box, click the Select button, and choose an identifying sound in the Open dialog box. The sound you choose will identify the person who is trying to communicate with you.

✔ **Hear the same sound no matter what kind of item was sent to you from the person:** You hear a sound that identifies who the item came from. The usual sound that accompanies the message, chat request, or whatever, is not heard.

Click the Use the Same Sound File for All Events check box, click the General check box (it appears shortly), and then click the Select button and choose a sound file in the Open dialog box.

✔ **Hear a specific sound:** You hear a sound that tells you that you are receiving a message, chat request, or whatever from the person.

For each type of communication you want to identify, click a check box and then click the Select button and choose a sound file in the Open dialog box. For example, to choose a sound that identifies incoming chat requests, click the Chat check box and then the Select button beside the box that lists where the Chat sound is located on your computer.

You can always click a Test button to find out exactly what a sound is.

Message tab: Writing a Status message

As you know if you read Chapter 3, someone who sees the Free for Chat, Away, N/A, Occupied, or DND icon next to your name on his or her Contact List can click the icon, choose the Read Message option from the pop-up menu, and read a message that explains why you are incommunicado.

However, if you want to leave a personalized message from someone on your Contact List, click the Message tab in the Alert/Accept dialog box. Then check the Customize Message check box, enter the message, and click the OK button.

Plugins tab: Handling telephony stuff

The Plugins tab is for handling telephony requests, game requests, and chat requests with third-party programs from someone on your Contact List. Check the Override General Prefs check box and choose among these options:

✔ **Show Response Dialog:** Make sure the Incoming Internet Telephony/Games dialog box appears so you can accept or decline all invitations.

✔ **Auto Accept:** Accept all telephony/game/chat invitations without reviewing them first in the Incoming Internet Telephony/Games dialog box.

✔ **Auto Decline:** Automatically decline all telephony/games/chat invitations from a person on your Contact List.

Status tab: Declaring your online status

The Status tab of the Alert/Accept dialog box (refer to Figure 13-6) is for declaring your online status exclusively to someone on the Contact List. Whatever status others see, the person on your Contact List sees the status you chose on the Status tab of the Alert/Accept dialog box. (Chapter 3 explains what declaring your online status is.)

Click the Update Status check box and then click an option button to declare your online status. You can also check the Invisible To User or Visible To User check boxes. These options are for making yourself invisible or visible to a person on your Contact List. When you're invisible, the other person thinks you are offline. When you're visible, the other person knows you are online, even when you make yourself invisible to others by choosing Privacy (Invisible) on the Status menu.

Click the Override Status Mode check boxes at the bottom of the Status tab if you want to be alerted to items the person has sent to you while you are in Away, N/A, DND, or Occupied status.

ICQ for Right-Clickers

Some people prefer clicking with the right mouse button to clicking with the left mouse button. For those people, ICQ offers the opportunity of trading in the left mouse button for the right mouse button. Instead of clicking a name on the Contact List to see the pop-up menu, you right-click a name.

If you prefer right- to left-clicking, click the ICQ button and choose Preferences to open the Owner Prefs For dialog box. Then click the Contact List tab and uncheck the Access Menus By Left Button check box.

Changing the ICQ Keyboard Shortcuts

ICQ, like all computer programs, offers keyboard shortcuts for doing tasks quickly. Figure 13-8 shows what the keyboard shortcuts are. If these shortcuts don't do the job for you, you can invent keyboard shortcuts of your own.

Follow these steps to change the keyboard shortcuts:

1. **Click the ICQ button and choose Preferences.**

   You see the Owner Prefs For dialog box.

Figure 13-8:
Enter your
own
keyboard
shortcuts in
the boxes if
you aren't
happy with
the ones
ICQ
provides.

2. **Click the Contact List tab.**

3. **Click the Edit button beside the Use ICQ Shortcuts check box.**

   The System Shortcuts dialog box, shown in Figure 13-8, appears.

4. **Backspace over a keyboard shortcut you want to change, and then type the shortcut.**

   When you type the shortcut, press the actual keys. For example, if the shortcut is Ctrl+Z, press the Ctrl key and the Z key — don't type out **C-t-r-l-+-Z**.

5. **Repeat Step 4 until you've changed the keyboard shortcuts you want to change.**

6. **Click OK in the System Shortcuts dialog box and OK again in the Owner Prefs For dialog box.**

   You can always return to the System Shortcuts dialog box and click the Restore Defaults button to get the original shortcuts back.

Uncheck a check box in the System Shortcuts dialog box to neuter a shortcut. If you often find yourself pressing a keyboard shortcut combination accidentally, you can solve the problem by disabling the keyboard shortcut.

Chapter 14

Maintaining Your Privacy and Security as You Use ICQ

. . . .

In This Chapter

▶ Preventing viruses

▶ Discovering how IP addresses work

▶ Cutting off all communications with an ICQ member

▶ Making yourself invisible on the ICQ network

▶ Enabling or disabling the status indicator

▶ Clamping a password on ICQ

. . . .

*T*his chapter explains how you can be a full-fledged member of the ICQ community and still maintain your privacy, not to mention your sanity. Here, you find out how to make yourself invisible to pesky ICQ members — and expose yourself to people you want to chat or exchange messages with. This chapter explains how to prevent viruses from infecting your computer, how to keep snoops out of your ICQ stuff, and how to prevent profanity from appearing in messages and the White Pages.

Be sure to read Chapter 19 as well as this chapter if you are adamant about maintaining your privacy and security. This chapter focuses on the options in the Security For dialog box. Chapter 19 explains strategies for maintaining your privacy and security in other areas of ICQ.

Making Sure You Don't Get a Virus

Here's some good news: Your computer can't be infected with a virus by way of ICQ if you never accept files from anyone. Only a file can carry a virus. Chat exchanges, messages, Web page addresses, e-mail messages, and photo files can, under no circumstances, carry viruses.

Furthermore, not all files are capable of carrying a virus. Only these kinds of files can carry a virus: .exe files, .bat files, .com files — what are known as *executable files* — and Microsoft Office files that include macros. As long as you're careful where you get files from, who you get files from, and what kind of files you are getting, you can rest assured that your computer will never be tainted by a virus.

Here is the doctor's prescription for preventing viruses:

✔ See if the file is an executable file. In other words, find out if the file is a software file, not a data file. Only software files — that is, executable files — can carry viruses, as mentioned earlier.

✔ Find out as well if the file is a Microsoft Office file. Office files, including files made with Word and Excel, can include macros, and viruses can be hidden inside macros.

✔ Ask yourself if the person or company who sent you the file is trustworthy. You can trust software made by commercial software companies. If your pal sent you a program file that he or she cooked up, the file is probably safe. But what if your pal got the program second-hand? As Mom used to say, "Don't touch that; you don't know where it's been."

✔ Get antivirus software. Studies show, incidentally, that most viruses are passed from computer to computer on floppy disks, not by way of the Internet. But to be safe, running antivirus software on your computer doesn't hurt a bit.

To Protect (Sort of) or Not Protect Your IP Address

Without going into too much technical detail, an *IP (Internet Protocol) address* is a number that is assigned to your computer when you go on the Internet. Almost every Internet service provider assigns IP addresses dynamically to its subscribers. Unless you maintain a direct connection to the Internet and don't have to dial in to connect, your IP address changes each time you connect to the Internet. When you chat or exchange messages with another ICQ member, the chats and messages are passed back and forth between your IP address and the other person's. The communications do not pass through the ICQ computers.

So what's the big deal? The big deal — and it can be very big if your IP address gets into the hands of the wrong person — is that someone who knows your IP address can invade your computer while you're online. Someone can go into your computer and mess with the files. We emphasize, however, that you have to be online for the damage to be done. And, of course, you also have to be the target of a devious and skillful hacker.

When you register with ICQ, you're asked if you want to publish your IP address. If you answer "yes," anyone can choose the Info command or click the Info button and find your latest or current IP address on the Main tab of the User Info dialog box. Some telephony applications and Internet games require you to know your IP address or your opponent's IP address, which is why you can view the address in the User Info dialog box. If you happen to be online when someone chooses the Info command, the other person can read your current IP address and know precisely what your address is.

For that reason, we suggest *not* listing your IP address. A knowledgeable computer hacker can uncover an IP address whether or not it is published, but unlisting your address makes finding the number that much harder. And you can always list it again if you want to use a telephony application.

Follow these steps to make sure that your IP address is not listed in the ICQ Global Directory:

1. **Click the ICQ button and choose Security & Privacy on the pop-up menu.**

   You see the Security For dialog box.

2. **Check the Do Not Publish IP Address check box, if it isn't already checked.**

3. **Click the Save button.**

4. **Click the Done button.**

   Next time someone chooses the Info command to find your IP address, it won't be listed in the User Info dialog box. However, we want to draw attention again to the fact that unlisting your address does *not* prevent others from finding it. Knowledgeable computer people know where to look to find an IP address.

Maybe the surest way to keep from getting hacked . . .

This might sound cowardly, but one of the surest ways to keep from getting hacked, nuked, spammed, spoofed, or wormed (all terms for doing damage to a computer) is to be courteous and thoughtful while you're online. In other words, treat other people as you would treat them if you met them in the flesh.

The Internet's anonymity brings out the worst in some people. Some people think the Internet is a rumpus room for name-calling and insults. We respectfully suggest that extending the same courtesies to people online as you extend to them in real life is the surest safeguard against hackers. Don't anger the hackers and you probably won't get hacked.

Ignoring Others so You Don't Receive Communications from Them

Occasionally someone sends you an unwanted message or chat request. Worse yet, sometimes your name lands on the Contact List of somebody you don't care for, and whenever you go online, the pest sends you communications — messages, chat requests, and Web page addresses.

To keep others at bay, you can put their names on the Ignore List, as shown in Figure 14-1. Communications sent to you from people on the list do not arrive. They're swallowed by ICQ. When you go online, the people whose names are on the list do not know it, even if your name is on their Contact List. Put someone on the Ignore List when you want to give him or her the cold shoulder.

Click a message and choose Move To Ignore List.

Or, if the person is on your Contact List,
go to the Security For dialog box.

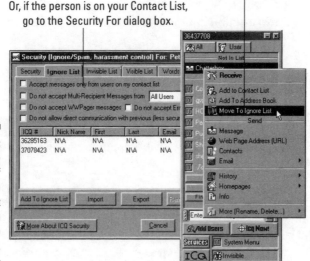

Figure 14-1:
Put the names of people you never want to hear from on the Ignore List.

When you move someone to the Ignore List from the Contact List, the person's name is removed from the Contact List. All records of the messages and chats you exchanged with the person are removed from the Message Archive.

Putting someone's name on the Ignore List

If you get a message out of the blue and you don't care to hear again from the person who sent it, you can put the sender's name on the Ignore List simply by clicking the sender's name under "Not in List" in the ICQ window and choosing Move To Ignore List on the pop-up menu, as shown in Figure 14-1.

But if the name of the person you want to ignore is on your Contact List or is not listed anywhere, you have to enter the name by way of the Security For dialog box (refer to Figure 14-1). What's more, if the person's name is not on your Contact List, you need his or her ICQ number to place the name on the Ignore List. The Security For dialog box offers a way to find someone's ICQ number, but we suggest finding the number before you open the Security For dialog box. Chapter 7 explains how to search for people in the White Pages and obtain their ICQ numbers.

Follow these steps to add a name to the list of people from whom you never want to receive communications:

1. **Click the ICQ button and choose Security & Privacy.**

   You see the Security For dialog box.

2. **Click the Ignore List tab.**

   The tab shows the names of people whom you ignore, if you ignore any-body (refer to Figure 14-1).

   At this point, you can place someone from your Contact List on the Ignore List by dragging the name from the Contact List to the Ignore List. That's right — simply click the name on the Contact List, drag it to the Ignore List, and release the mouse button.

3. **Click the Add to Ignore List button.**

   The Search For Users to Add to Your Ignore List dialog box appears. This dialog box works exactly like the Global Directory ICQ dialog box described in Chapter 7. Enter search conditions and click the Search button if you need to, but if you followed our advice, you already know the ICQ number of the person whose name you want to place on the Ignore List.

4. **Click the ICQ # tab, enter the number in the ICQ # text box, and click the Search button.**

   The bottom of the dialog box opens and you see the name and ICQ number of the person whose name you want to place on the Ignore List.

5. **Right-click the person's name, and choose Move To Ignore List.**

6. **Click the Close button (the *X*) in the Search For Users to Add to Your Ignore List dialog box.**

   Back in the Security For dialog box, you see the name you entered.

7. **Click the Save button and then the Done button.**

   Never again will you be pestered by the person whose name you just put on the Ignore List.

Removing a name from the Ignore List

To remove a name from the Ignore List, open the Security For dialog box (click the ICQ button and choose Security & Privacy), click the Ignore List tab, select the name of the person you want to remove from the list, and click the Remove From Ignore List button. Be sure to click the Save button before closing the dialog box.

After you remove a name from the Ignore List, all traces of the person are lost. Suppose you want to move the name from the Ignore List to the Contact List. Sorry, you can't simply drag the name back to your Contact List. Instead, right-click the name and choose Info on the pop-up menu. In the User Info On dialog box, find out the person's ICQ number. Then click the ICQ button, choose Find/Add Users⇨Find User — Add To List, and find the person in the Global Directory Search Engine by entering his or her ICQ number. When the person turns up, right-click his or her name and choose Add to Contact List.

Making Yourself Invisible to a Specific Someone

Yet another way to safeguard your privacy is to make yourself invisible to the person who has been badgering you. As an invisible man or woman, the person to whom you have made yourself invisible thinks you're offline. Being invisible is different from ignoring someone in that you can still receive communications from the person to whom you're invisible. But you will never be bothered by a chat request. Why? Because the other party is tricked into thinking you're offline at all times. Your name appears permanently under *Offline* on the other party's Contact List.

Declaring yourself invisible is chiefly a way to handle the problem of what to do when your name is on someone else's Contact List and you don't want it to be there. Unless you make yourself invisible to the other person, he or she will know when you're online. And he or she can send you chat requests, files, and other items that require two parties to be online at the same time.

Declaring yourself invisible to people on your Contact List

If the name of the person to whom you want to be invisible is on your Contact List, declaring yourself invisible is easy. Try either of these techniques:

- **One Contact List name at a time:** Click the person's name and choose More (Rename, Delete)⇨Alert/Accept Modes. As shown in Figure 14-2, the Alert/Accept dialog box appears. Click the Status tab, check the Invisible To User check box, and click the OK button. Then click Yes in the confirmation dialog box. The name is placed immediately on the Invisible List, as shown in Figure 14-2.

- **More than one Contact List name at a time:** To enter several names from the Contact List on the Invisible List, start by displaying the Invisible List: Click the ICQ button, choose Security & Privacy, and click the Invisible List tab in the Security For dialog box. Then drag names from the Contact List to the Invisible List. Click the Save button in the Security For dialog box when you're finished.

The names of people on your Contact List to whom you are invisible appear in italics.

Click here to put a name on the Invisible List.

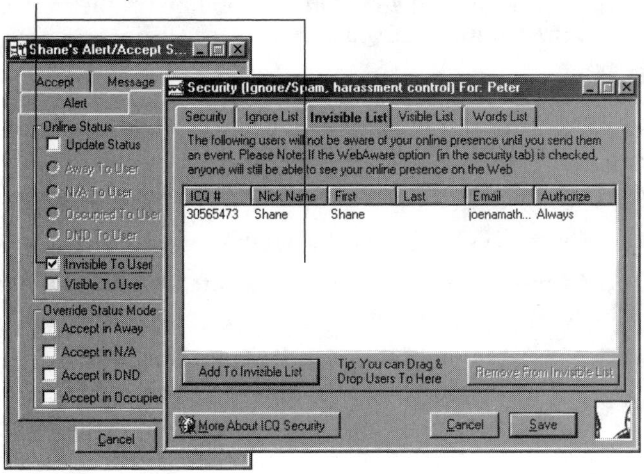

Figure 14-2:
As far as the people whose names are on the Invisible List are concerned, you're always offline and can't be reached.

Declaring yourself invisible to an ICQ member not on your Contact List

If the person who has been badgering you isn't on your Contact List, you need to know his or her ICQ number before you can place his or her name on your Invisible List (refer to Figure 14-2). The best way to track down an ICQ number is to do so by searching the White Pages, as Chapter 7 explains. However, the Invisible List tab in the Security For dialog box also offers a means of tracking down ICQ numbers.

Follow these steps to make yourself invisible to a bothersome person on the ICQ network:

1. **Click the ICQ button and choose Security & Privacy.**

   You see the Security For dialog box.

2. **Click the Invisible List tab.**

   This tab shows the names of people who never know when you're online.

3. **Click the Add To Invisible List button.**

   The Search For Users to Add to Your Invisible List dialog box appears. If you don't know the ICQ number of the person in question, you can get it here by entering search conditions and clicking the Search button.

4. **Click the ICQ # tab and enter the ICQ number of the person you want to add to the list in the ICQ # text box.**

5. **Click the Search button.**

   The ICQ number, nick name, and first and last name of the person appear in the bottom of the dialog box.

6. **Right-click the person's name and choose Add to Invisible List.**

7. **Click OK when ICQ tells you the name has been added to the list.**

8. **Click the Close button (the *X*) to close the Search for Users to Add to Your Invisible List dialog box.**

9. **Click the Save button in the Security For dialog box.**

10. **Click the Done button.**

   How does it feel to be invisible?

Removing a name from the Invisible List

Return to the Invisible List tab of the Security For dialog box (click the ICQ button and choose Security & Privacy) to remove a name from the Invisible

List. Click the name you want to remove and then click the Remove From Invisible List button. Be sure to click Save before closing the dialog box.

You can also click a Contact List name, choose More (Rename, Delete)⇨Alert/Accept Modes, and uncheck the Invisible to User check box on the Status tab of the Alert/Accept dialog box.

Status Indicator: Letting or Not Letting Others Know When You're Online

As you know if you read about declaring your online status to other ICQ members in Chapter 3, you can click the Status button and choose an option to describe your online status. Options on the Status menu include Away, Occupied (Urgent Msgs), DND (Do Not Disturb), and Privacy (Invisible). After you choose an option, the icon that represents the option you chose appears next to your name on others' Contact Lists. Others can see the icon and know whether you care to be disturbed or care to chat.

But declaring your online status by clicking the Status button and choosing an option is only half the story. People who find you by going to your Personal Communication Center or by visiting an interest group where your name is posted (a subject of Chapter 7) can tell whether you're online by glancing at the status indicator in the Action panel, the list of buttons others can click to get in touch with you. They can tell, that is, if your status indicator is enabled.

Figure 14-3 shows three Action panels on three different Personal Communication Center pages. To protect their privacy, some people choose to disable the status indicator so that others can't send them messages or chat requests. Figure 14-3 illustrates the advantages and disadvantages of enabling the online status indicator.

✔ **Indicator enabled; the person is online:** Others can tell that you're online because the Online icon appears above the words *My Status*. Because you're online, the Chat Me button appears on the Action panel. Others can click the button and invite you for a chat. They can also click the ICQ Me button and send you a message.

✔ **Indicator enabled; the person is not online:** Others can be certain that you aren't online because the Offline icon appears above the words *My Status*.

✔ **Indicator disabled; the person may or may not be online:** Others don't know whether you're online or offline because the status indicator has been disabled. In any case, no one can send you chat requests or messages from your Personal Communication Center.

Figure 14-3:
When the status indicator is enabled and you're online, people who visit your Personal Web Communication Center can invite you for a chat or send a message.

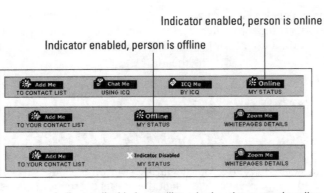

Indicator enabled, person is online

Indicator enabled, person is offline

Indicator disabled, no telling whether the person is online

Enable the status indicator if you want people who reach you at your Personal Communication Center to be able to invite you for a chat or send you a message. Disable the status indicator if you want others not to be able to chat you up or send messages to you.

Follow these steps to enable or disable the status indicator:

1. **Click the ICQ button and choose Security & Privacy.**

   You see the Security For dialog box.

2. **Click the Security tab.**

3. **Under Web Aware, check or uncheck the Allow Others to View My Online Presence on the World Wide Web check box.**

4. **Click the Save button, and then click Done.**

By the way, throughout ICQ, in the Global Directory dialog box and other places, a green flower means that the status indicator is enabled and the person is online, a red flower means that the status indicator is enabled but the person is offline, and a white flower means the status indicator has been disabled.

Making Yourself Visible to the Select Few

Here's another strategy for keeping the riffraff out: Let your ICQ favorites know when you're online while the others see whatever status you chose from the Status pop-up menu. With this strategy, you click the Status button and choose Privacy (Invisible). Most people who have put your name on their Contact Lists see your name under Offline. The select few, however, see your name under Online on their Contact Lists. What's more, the Visible icon, an eyeball, appears beside your name and tells the select few not only that you are online, but that you have made yourself visible to them and to them only.

As shown in Figure 14-4, the names of the select few are kept on the Visible List in the Security For dialog box. The fastest way to put someone on the list is to click his or her name on your Contact List, choose More (Delete, Rename)⇨Alert/Accept Modes, click the Status tab in the Alert/Accept dialog box, and click the Visible To User check box. The names of people on your Contact List to whom you are "visible" are italicized.

Click here to place a name on the Visible List.

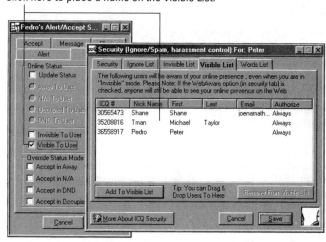

Figure 14-4:
People on your Visible List always know when you're online and willing to receive messages and chat requests.

You can also follow these steps to put a name on the Visible List and always be visible to a certain special someone:

1. Click the ICQ button and choose Security & Privacy.

The Security For dialog box appears.

2. **Click the Visible List tab.**

   As shown in Figure 4-4, this tab lists the people who always know when you're online.

   While the Visible List tab is open, you can place the names of people on the Contact List on the Visible List. To do so, click a Contact List name and drag-and-drop it over the Visible List.

3. **Click the Add To Visible List button.**

   You see the Search For Users to Add to Your Visible List dialog box. Use this dialog box to search for people whose names you want to add to the Visible List.

4. **Enter information in the dialog box and click the Search button.**

   The ICQ number, nickname, and first and last name of the person appear in the bottom of the dialog box.

5. **Right-click the person's name and choose Add to Visible List.**

6. **Click OK in the confirmation dialog box.**

7. **Click the Close button (the *X*) to close the Search for Users to Add to Your Visible List dialog box.**

8. **Click the Save button and then the Done button in the Security For dialog box.**

   There, you did it. You increased your visibility, as advertisers say.

To remove a name from the Visible List, return to the Security For dialog box, click a name, and click the Remove From Visible List button. You can also click a Contact List name, choose More (Rename, Delete)⇨Alert/Accept Modes, and uncheck the Visible to User check box on the Status tab of the Alert/Accept dialog box.

A Visible icon next to someone's name on your Contact List means that the other person has taken a shine to you. The other person has put your name on his or her Visible List. The other person wants you to know when he or she is online. Kind of exciting to see the Visible icon, don't you think?

Passwords for People Who Share Their Computers with Others

When you registered with ICQ, you chose a password for identifying yourself to the ICQ network. Most people don't have to concern themselves with passwords. If you use ICQ at home and don't share your computer with anyone else, you can live happily and never bother with passwords.

But if you use ICQ at work or share your computer with others, you can use your password as a means of protecting your privacy. These pages explain the different ways that passwords can keep others from snooping or tampering with the information that is kept about you in the White Pages. You also find out how to change your password.

Preventing others from tampering with ICQ

As Figure 14-5 shows, the Security tab of the Security For dialog box offers three different security levels for determining how easy or how hard starting ICQ is and whether others can change the information that is kept about you in the White Pages. If you choose the Medium or High option, you have to enter a password in the Password Verification box to complete various tasks. Table 14-1 describes when a password is needed in the Low, Medium, and High security level.

Change your password

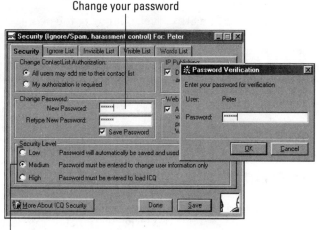

Figure 14-5: Choose a Security Level option — Low, Medium, or High — to make it easier or harder for others to use ICQ.

Choose whether and how others access ICQ

Table 14-1	When Passwords Are Required in the Different Security Levels			
Security Level	*Start ICQ*	*Change Password*	*Change Security Level Settings*	*Change User Info**
Low				
Medium		✔	✔	✔
High	✔	✔	✔	✔

* Click the ICQ button and choose Add/Change Current User⇨View/Change My Details to change the information that is stored about you in the White Pages.

If you share your computer with others and you don't want them to snoop around in your Message Archive or change your personal information, choose the High option. With the High option, no one can open your copy of ICQ without a password, so no one can see your Message Archive, Contact List, or user information.

Follow these steps to reach the Security tab of the Security For dialog box and choose a security level:

1. **Click the ICQ button and Security & Privacy.**

2. **Click the Security tab in the Security For dialog box.**

   Figure 14-5 shows the Security tab.

3. **Choose a new security level: Low, Medium, or High.**

4. **Click the Save button, and then click Done.**

   However, before you can switch from a High or Medium security level, you have to enter your password, as shown in Figure 14-5.

Suppose you opt for a High security level, but one of the people who shares your computer is also a member of ICQ. How can the other person start ICQ if he or she needs your password to do it? The answer: The other person doesn't need your password, nor do you need someone else's if a person who shares your computer and uses ICQ has opted for a High security level. When you start ICQ and the Password Verification dialog box appears, open the User drop-down menu and choose your name. Then enter your password, if it's necessary, and click OK.

Changing your password

To change your password, start by going online and connecting to ICQ. Then click the ICQ button, choose Security & Privacy, and click the Security tab in the Security For dialog box (refer to Figure 14-5). Type your new password in the New Password box and type it again in the Retype New Password box. Then click the Save button.

That's all there is to it, unless you choose the Medium or High security level. In that case, enter your password yet again in the Password Verification dialog box and click OK.

Keeping Profanity from Appearing in Messages and White Pages Entries

We consider the use of profanity a violation of privacy. Not that we're prudes or anything, but everyone should be able to enjoy the pleasure of not being offended by crude language or obscenities.

To keep profanity from offending you, you can make a list of words for ICQ to cross out in messages and the White Pages. In place of the offensive words, you have a choice between seeing asterisks (*) or not seeing the message or White Page entry at all.

Follow these steps to keep from seeing obscenities in messages and White Page entries:

1. **Click the ICQ button and choose Security & Privacy.**

   You see the Security For dialog box.

2. **Click the Words List tab.**

   Figure 14-6 shows the Words List tab.

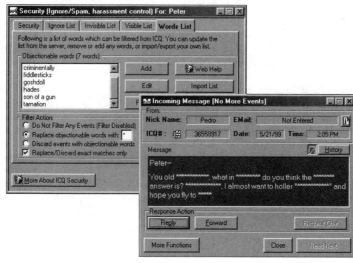

Figure 14-6: Words on the Words List do not appear in messages and White Pages entries — or else the messages and entries are discarded.

3. **Click the Unlock (Enter Protection Password) button, enter your password in the Password Verification dialog box, and click OK.**

   You're ready to start entering the words that offend you.

4. **Click the Add button, and, in the Define New Word dialog box, enter an offensive word and click OK.**

   The word appears in the Objectionable Words list.

5. **Repeat Step 4 as many times as necessary to enter all the words that offend you.**

   To change the spelling of a word, click it and then click the Edit button. To remove a word from the list, click it and then click the Remove button.

6. **Choose an option button to decide how you want ICQ to handle the offensive words.**

   Click one of these option buttons:

   - **Replace objectionable words with a punctuation mark:** As shown in Figure 14-6, words on the list are replaced with asterisks or a punctuation mark of your choice when they appear in messages or White Pages entries. Enter a punctuation mark of your own in the text box, if you want to.

   - **Discard events with objectionable words:** You never see messages or White Pages entries if they contain an objectionable word.

7. **Click the Save button and then the Done button.**

   Never again will the words offend you — at least in ICQ.

Chapter 15

Message Archive: ICQ as a Personal Information Manager

•••

In This Chapter

▶ Locating items in the Message Archive

▶ Re-reading messages you sent to and got from other people

▶ Looking up a name in the Address Book

▶ Writing notes, 2 do notes, and reminder notes

▶ Copying, moving, and deleting items in the Message Archive

▶ Finding items in the Message Archive

•••

A *personal information manager,* in case you didn't know, is one of those programs like Microsoft Outlook or Lotus Notes that schedules meetings, tracks addresses, organizes e-mail messages, and makes toast and coffee. The Message Archive, the ICQ personal information manager, doesn't make toast and coffee, but it does many of the things that personal information managers do.

Like Microsoft Outlook and Lotus Notes, the Message Archive comes with an Address Book. You can also use the program to keep a To Do list, jot down notes, and write reminder notes. Chiefly, however, the Message Archive is for storing and retrieving messages, chats, Web address messages, and other items that were sent to you and that you sent to others.

Read on to discover how to find your way around the Message Archive window, review items that were sent to you or that you sent to others, and open the Address Book to look up someone's address. You also discover how to pass notes — notes, 2 do notes, and reminder notes. At the end of the chapter are instructions for moving, deleting, and finding items in the Message Archive.

About the toast and coffee, ICQ does not want to be outdone by its competitors, and we understand that future editions of ICQ will indeed make breakfast for you.

Finding Your Way Around the Message Archive

Figure 15-1 shows the Message Archive window. In the window is a record of chats you've had, messages you sent and received, and other kinds of communications you sent to or received from the people who are or formerly were on your Contact List. Besides communications, the Message Archive holds items you deleted, notes, reminder notes, "To Do" notes, the Address Book, and the Outbox.

Click plus signs to open folders.   Click to open an item.

Click a folder to see its contents.

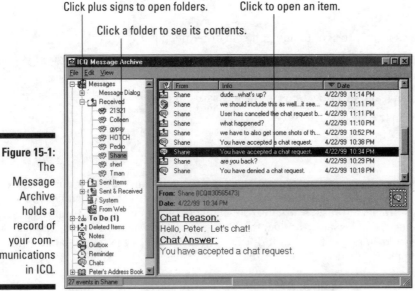

Figure 15-1:
The
Message
Archive
holds a
record of
your com-
munications
in ICQ.

Items in the Message Archive are kept in folders in much the same way that files are kept in folders in Windows 95 and Windows 98. To find an item, click plus signs (+) until you arrive at what you want to see. The items you are looking for — chats, messages, or notes, for example — appear on the right side of the window. Click an item to view it.

Table 15-1 describes all the items that are kept in the Message Archive. To open the Message Archive, do one of the following:

- ✔ Click the ICQ button and choose Message Archive.

- ✔ Click a person's name on the Contact List and choose History➪Open Message Archive. The Message Archive opens to the Messages\Sent & Received folder where messages to and from the person whose name you clicked are stored.

▶ Click the Services button and choose Message Archive➪Open Message Archive.

Table 15-1	The Message Archive
Folder	*What's in It*
Messages	The Message Dialog, Received, Sent Items, Sent & Received, System, and From Web folders, where you will find items you sent to others and others sent to you. See the next section in this chapter for details.
2 do	Notes reminding you to do something. See "Notes, Notes, and More Notes" later in this chapter.
Deleted Items	Items you deleted from the ICQ Archive. Items are kept here in case you want to restore them. See "Deleting items."
Notes	"Sticky notes" you can keep on hand. See "Notes, Notes, and More Notes."
Outbox	Items that have yet to be sent either because you postponed sending them or the other party has to be online to receive them. See Chapter 8.
Reminder	Reminder notes to do something or other. See "Notes, Notes, and More Notes."
Chats	All chats you've had with people who were or are on your Contact List. Chapter 4 explains how to go into the Message Archive, revisit a chat, and play it back.
Address Book	Information from the ICQ White Pages on everyone whose name you've entered in your Address Books. See "Address Book: Keeping Information on ICQ Members."

Follow these instructions to open and close folders in the Message Archive window:

▶ **Viewing the items in a folder:** Click the plus sign (+) beside the folder's name or click the name and choose File➪Open➪Selected Item.

▶ **Viewing all items in all the folders:** Choose File➪Open➪All Items.

▶ **Hiding the items in a folder:** Click the minus sign (-) beside the folder's name.

▶ **Hiding all items in all the folders:** Choose File➪Close All Items.

Keeping items out of the Message Archive

For the sake of privacy or simply because they don't want to waste space on their computers, some people prefer not to keep records of chats, messages, and other communications in the Message Archive. If you are one of those people, follow these steps to keep chats, messages and other stuff from being recorded:

1. **Click the ICQ button and choose Preferences.**

2. **Click the Accept tab.**

3. **Check the Do Not Log Event History check box and click OK.**

You can also keep messages from a person on your Contact List from being recorded in the Message Archive. To do that, click the person's name on the Contact List and choose More (Rename, Delete)⇨Alert/Accept Modes. Then, in the Alert/Accept dialog box, click the Accept tab and check the Do Not Log Event History check box.

The Message Archive window works like other program windows. You can minimize it, maximize it, and change its size. To change the size of the window pane on the left or right side, carefully move the pointer over the border between the two window panes. When you see a double-headed arrow, click and start dragging.

Messages Folder: Reviewing Items Sent to and from Other People

 The Message Archive is very thorough about retaining items you received from others and sent to others. Spend a little time in ICQ and you will be surprised by how many items are in the Messages folder. Big Brother is watching! Messages, chat requests, file requests, Web page addresses, phone number requests, photo requests, and messages sent from outside the ICQ network are all kept in the Messages folder.

Table 15-2 describes the subfolders inside the Messages folder. The Messages folder holds items sent to and received from people whose names were or are on your Contact List. Messages you sent to or received from people whose names never appeared on the Contact List are not logged in the Message Archive.

Table 15-2	Folders in the Messages Folder
Folder	**What's in It**
Message Dialog	Messages you exchanged with others. The folder shows messages you sent and received. Unlike the Sent & Received folder, however, message text is displayed in the window so you can read the exchanges as they occurred.
Received	Messages you received from others.
Sent Items	Messages you sent to others.
Sent & Received	Messages you sent to others and received from others. Messages are marked "To" or "From" in the From/To column.
System	System messages informing you when your name was entered on someone's Contact List, and messages in which you asked to put someone's name on your Contact List.
From Web	Messages sent to your ICQ address from outside the ICQ network.

After you open a folder, people's names appear below the folder. Click someone's name to see his or her communications on the right side of the Message Archive window (refer to Figure 15-1).

To comfortably read an item, double-click it. As shown in Figure 15-2, the History Event window opens. You can enlarge the History Event window and thereby read the item without squinting or resorting to a microscope.

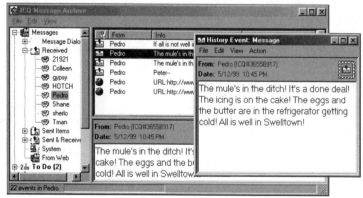

Figure 15-2:
Double-click an item in the Message Archive window to read it comfortably.

Reviewing items from someone on your Contact List

As long as someone's name is on your Contact List, you can bypass the Message Archive window as you search for items in the Message Archive. Try this technique for finding a communication to or from someone on your Contact List:

1. Click the person's name and choose History⇨View Messages History. The History Events Of dialog box appears.

2. Find the item you are looking for on the Incoming, Outgoing, or MessageDialog tab.

3. Double-click the item. The Event Details dialog box appears so you can read the item. And you can click the Forward and Previous button in the Event Details dialog box to search up or down the Incoming, Outgoing, or MessageDialog tab for more items.

Address Book: Keeping Information on ICQ Members

 Address Book is something of a misnomer. It's not as if you can enter people's addresses and phone numbers in the Address Book, although the Address Book does provide a space for jotting down notes about someone. No, the Address Book records what is known about someone in the ICQ White Pages.

Figure 15-3 shows what happens when you click the name of someone in the Address Book — you see the same information and dialog box you get if you find the person in the White Pages. (Chapter 7 explains how to search the White Pages for someone.) You can, however, click the Info/About tab and write a note or two about the person there.

To open the Address Book, click the ICQ button and choose Address Book. The Message Archive window opens with the Address Book folder highlighted and selected.

 Anyone can be in the Address Book, but people whose names are on your Contact List are always there. You can tell who in the Address Book is on the Contact List by glancing at the icons next to the names. A plain face means the person is on the Contact List; a face with a bit of green beside it means that the person is not on the list.

 As Chapter 6 explains, you get the opportunity to keep someone in the Address Book when you remove his or her name from the Contact List. Anyone whose name is in the Address Book can be placed back on the Contact List. To put someone back in the Contact List, right-click his or her name in the Address Book and choose Add to Contact List.

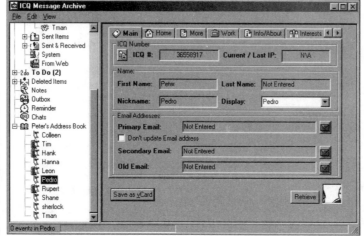

Figure 15-3:
Information
from the ICQ
White
Pages is
kept in the
Address
Book.

Notes, Notes, and More Notes

We think ICQ went a bit overboard with the notes. Not one kind of note, not two kinds of notes, but three kinds of notes? The inventors of ICQ must think we are a forgetful. Or perhaps they know something we don't know. Perhaps they know that staring at a computer screen too long makes you bleary-eyed and scatterbrained.

These pages explain the three kinds of notes that ICQ offers:

- ✔ **Note:** A plain note similar to the stick 'em variety. Go to the Notes folder in the Message Archive to see the notes you've written to yourself.

- ✔ **2 do note:** A more urgent note. After you write a 2 do note, the 2 do icon appears in the lower-right corner of the screen so you know that a 2 do note needs addressing.

- ✔ **Reminder note:** A note that marks a deadline of some kind. When a deadline looms, the ICQ Reminder window pops onscreen and you hear a horrible bleeping sound.

When you get a communication from someone else, you can click the More Functions button to turn the message into a note, a 2 do note, or a reminder note, as shown in Figure 15-4.

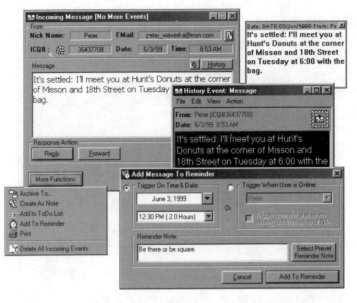

Notes: Writing plain-old notes to yourself

 There's nothing special about notes. ICQ doesn't alert you when notes need your attention. All you can do is write them and, when you need to find out if notes need your attention, go to the Notes folder in the Message Archive.

To write a note to yourself, click the Services button and choose Notes⇨New Note. A Note window similar to the one in the upper-right corner of Figure 15-4 appears onscreen. Type your note. When you're done, either drag the Note window to a corner of the screen where it won't bother you or click the Close button (the *X*) in the Note window and choose Hide from the pop-up menu (or press Ctrl+H) to hide the note.

To read notes you've written, click the Services button, choose Notes, and do one of the following:

- ✔ Choose Open Notes List to open the Notes folder of the Message Archive. From there, you can double-click a note to read it.

- ✔ Choose Open, read the first line of notes on the submenu, and click the note you want to open.

The easiest way to delete notes is to click the Services button and choose Notes⇨Open Notes List to see the notes in the Message Archive window. From there, right-click a note and choose Delete on the pop-up menu.

2 do notes: Reminding yourself that something needs doing

2do The neat thing about 2 do notes is that the 2 do icon appears in the lower-right corner of the screen next to the ICQ flower icon whenever a 2 do note needs your attention. By clicking the 2 do icon, you can open the History Event dialog box and read the note (refer to Figure 15-4).

To write a 2 do note, click the Services button and choose ToDo⇨New. You see the Add To Do Event dialog box. Write the note and click the Add To Do button.

Follow these instructions to open the History Event dialog box and read 2 do notes:

- Double-click the 2 do icon in the lower-right corner of the screen. The first note on your list appears.

- Click the Services button and choose ToDo⇨Open ToDo List. The Message Archive opens to the To Do folder. Double-click a note to read it.

- Click the Services button and choose ToDo⇨Open. The first lines of notes appear on a submenu. Click the Note you want to open and read.

When you're finished reading a 2 do note, click the Close button in the History Event dialog box. Strangely, a message box asks if you want to unmark the note. Click Yes not to unmark the note, but to delete it; click No if you want to keep the note on hand for a later day.

Reminder notes: Staying on top of deadlines

Write a reminder note when you have a serious deadline to meet and you need all the help you can get to meet it. As long as ICQ is running, the ICQ Reminder dialog box, shown on the right side of Figure 15-5, pops onscreen when a reminder note falls due. If you need more time and want to be reminded again, you can choose a period of time from the Remind Again In drop-down menu and see the reminder at a later date.

Choose a deadline.   Choose an option to be reminded again.

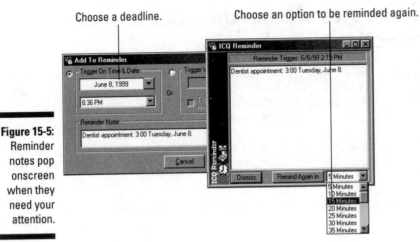

Figure 15-5:
Reminder
notes pop
onscreen
when they
need your
attention.

Follow these steps to write a reminder note:

1. **Click the Services button.**

2. **Choose Reminder⇨New Reminder.**

    You see the Add to Reminder dialog box, shown in Figure 15-5.

3. **Enter the text of the note in the Reminder Note box.**

4. **Choose whether to make the note appear at a certain time or when someone on your Contact List is online.**

    You can also be reminded when someone on your Contact List comes online.

    • **When someone is online:** Click the Trigger When User Is Online option button and choose a name from the drop-down list.

    • **At a certain time:** Click the Trigger On Time & Date button and choose a time and date from the drop-down menus.

5. **Click the Add To Reminder button.**

When the ICQ Reminder dialog box pops onscreen to remind you when a project or appointment is due, either click the Dismiss button to stop being reminded or choose an option from the drop-down menu and click the Remind Again In button to keep being reminded.

To go into the Message Archive and delete reminder notes, click the Services button and choose Reminder⇨Open Reminders List. Then, in the Reminder folder, right-click Reminder notes and choose Delete to get rid of them. If a reminder note needs changing, double-click it and change it in the Update Reminder Details dialog box, which looks and works exactly like the Add To Reminder dialog box (refer to Figure 15-5).

Managing the Message Archive

A Message Archive can grow very large and take on hundreds and hundreds of items. How can you manage so large a beast? The last part of this chapter offers techniques for keeping your Message Archive under control. Grab a whip and a chair, and read on to find out how to create new folders for storing items, move items to different folders, and delete items. You'll also find instructions here for finding items that have strayed, are lost, and cannot be found. One more thing: We'll show you how to play interior decorator with the Message Archive window.

Creating a new folder for storing items

One way to keep items from getting lost is to create a new folder in the Message Archive window. Items that pertain to a project or person can all go in the same folder, where you can find them easily.

Follow these steps to create a new folder:

1. **Click the Messages folder in the Message Archive window if the Messages folder is not already selected.**

2. **Right-click the Messages folder and choose New Folder from the pop-up menu.**

3. **Type a name for the folder and press the Enter key.**

To delete a folder you created, right-click it, choose Delete from the pop-up menu, and click <u>Y</u>es when ICQ asks if you really want to go through with it. Items inside the folder are deleted along with the folder.

As messages, Web pages addresses, and other communications arrive, you can place them in the folder you created by clicking the More Functions button in the Incoming dialog box and choosing Archive To from the pop-up menu (refer to Figure 15-4). Then, in the Move To dialog box, select your personal folder and click OK. The items are stored in your personal folder and nowhere else.

Moving (and copying) items to different folders

To move items from one folder to another, click plus signs if necessary to display both folders in the Message Archive window. Then select the items you want to move and drag the items from one folder to another.

Selecting more than one item at the same time

You can move, copy, or delete more than one item at the same time by selecting more than one item before giving the Move To, Copy To, or Delete command. Ctrl+click or Shift+click to select more than one item:

✔ **Scattered items:** Hold down the Ctrl key and click items to select more than one. Items are highlighted as you select them.

✔ **Items next to each other:** Click the first item and then hold down the Shift key as you click the last item you want to select.

Sorry, you can copy items, but you can only copy them into a personal folder you created. To copy items, select them, right-click, and choose Copy To from the drop-down menu (or choose Edit⇨Copy To). Then click your personal folder in the Move To dialog box and click OK.

Deleting items

 To delete items, start by selecting them. Then either right-click and choose Delete, or choose Edit⇨Delete and click Yes in the dialog box that asks if you really want to delete the items.

But items aren't completely erased from your computer when you give the Delete command. No, items assume a second life in the Deleted Items folder after they are deleted. ICQ puts the items in the Deleted Items folder in case you regret deleting them.

To resuscitate an item you deleted, find it in the Deleted Items folder, right-click, and choose Restore From Deleted on the pop-up menu. The item returns to the folder it was in before you deleted it.

To delete an item once and for all, find it in the Deleted Items folder and choose Edit⇨Delete or right-click and choose Delete from the pop-up menu. Then click Yes in the confirmation dialog box.

Finding a lost item

Finding an item in a Message Archive that is stuffed to the gills with items can be very hard. Not as hard as finding a needle in a haystack, necessarily, but as hard as finding a haystack in a hurricane. After you have scoured the Message Archive, scratched your head a few times, and given up on finding the item by conventional means, see if you can find the item with a Find command.

The Message Archive offers two Find commands. You may as well start with the simple one: Click the folder you want to look in and choose Edit⇨Find. You see the Find dialog box. Enter the text you are looking for in the Find What box and click the Find button. If the item can be found, it is highlighted in the Message Archive window.

Sometimes the Find command can't do the job and you have to resort to the Advanced Find command. Follow these steps to do a thorough search of the Message Archive:

1. **Choose Edit⇨Advanced Find, or, if the Message Archive window is not already open, click the Services button and choose Message Archive⇨Advanced Find.**

   You see the Advanced Find dialog box shown in Figure 15-6.

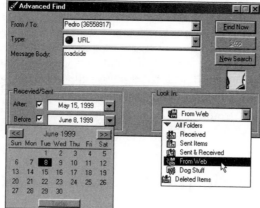

Figure 15-6: Use the Advanced Find command to do a thorough search of the Message Archive.

2. **From the From/To drop-down menu, choose the person you received the item from or sent the item to.**

3. **From the Type menu, choose the type of item you are looking for.**

4. **If you happen to know a word or two in the message, enter the words in the Message Body box.**

5. **If you happen to know roughly when the item was sent or received, click the After and Before check boxes, and then click the down arrow to open the calendar and click dates.**

   Click the arrow buttons to go forward or backward month by month. You can click the Today button to select today's date.

6. **From the Look In drop-down menu, choose the folder you think the item is in or choose All Folders.**

7. **Click the Find Now button.**

Items that match the search conditions are listed below the dialog box.

If the search proves unsuccessful, make new choices in the Advanced Find dialog box and click the Find Now button again. Click the New Search button if you need to start all over from scratch.

Changing the font, text color, and background color

If you think the Message Archive has an ugly face, you can play cosmetic surgeon and change the face of the Message Archive. Follow these instructions to change the font, text color, and background color in the Message Archive window:

- **Changing the font and text color:** Choose View➪Font. You see the Font dialog box, which offers options for changing fonts, font styles, the size of letters, and the color of text. Go to it and click OK when you're done. Be sure to choose a light color for text if you opt for a dark background color, or a dark color for text if you opt for a light background color.

- **Changing the background color:** Choose View➪Background. In the Color dialog box, click the color that makes you happy and then click OK.

Printing items in the Message Archive

Printing an item in the Message Archive is simply a matter of selecting the item and choosing File➪Print. Doing so brings up the Print dialog box, where you can tell ICQ to print more than one copy of the item before clicking OK to start printing.

If you're printing a long message or chat exchange, choose File➪Page Setup before giving the Print command. In the Page Setup dialog box, change the margins if you so desire. You can also opt for printing in the landscape instead of the portrait style. Click OK when you're done. The settings you choose in the Page Setup dialog box determine how all items are printed, so choose options carefully.

Sorting to find items in the Message Archive window

One way to find items in the Message Archive window is to sort them. *Sorting* means to arrange text alphabetically from A to Z (or Z to A), numbers from smallest to largest (or largest to smallest), and dates from past to future (or future to past). By clicking the From/To and Date column buttons at the top of the Message Archive window, you can sort the messages and in doing so perhaps find the one you are looking for.

For example, clicking the From/To button in this illustration sorts messages in alphabetical order from A to Z by name; clicking the button a second time sorts names from Z to A. Similarly, clicking the Date button once sorts messages from earliest in time to latest; clicking a second time sorts messages from latest in time to earliest. You can tell which column messages are sorted in by looking for the arrow. You can tell which direction messages are sorted in by seeing whether the arrow points up or down.

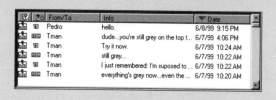

Chapter 16

ICQ as a Launching Pad for Telephony Applications

In This Chapter

▶ Finding out which Internet telephony applications ICQ supports

▶ Configuring ICQ for Internet telephony

▶ Finding and downloading special versions of Internet telephony applications

▶ Exploring ICQ user groups for Internet telephony

▶ Launching an Internet telephony application from ICQ

*Y*ou've loaded ICQ. You've sent a few messages. You've had a few chats and made a few friends. By now you must be wondering what it would be like if to actually *talk* to the new friends you made. Or how about seeing them on your computer screen. Well, ICQ allows you to use numerous Internet Telephony applications, including NetMeeting, VocalTec, VDOPhone, CoolTalk, and CU-SeeMe.

By means of Internet telephony applications, you can use your computer to talk to friends and co-workers. You can use it like a telephone, and, if your computer is equipped with the right components, you can even use it like a videophone!

Of course, you can use telephony applications without ICQ. But you save time when you configure ICQ to work with Internet telephony applications because ICQ saves you the trouble of locating people who have the same application as you. With ICQ, you can see if your friend is online by simply glancing at your Contact List.

When you configure ICQ to work with an Internet telephony application, you also tell ICQ how to find a friend. You don't have to type the information all over again. All you do is insert the ICQ variables. When you click your friend's name on the Contact List and launch the telephony application, ICQ finds your friend's IP through his or her connection to the Internet.

Making Sure You Have the Right Equipment

Time to run an equipment check! You can't do two-way voice and video communications on a computer unless you have the right stuff. These days, voice and video equipment are becoming standard on computers, so you might have the right stuff without knowing it.

Here is a basic list of the stuff you need for two-way voice and video communications:

- **An Internet connection:** That goes without saying.

- **A fast modem:** The faster your modem, the better a telephony application works. A 28.8 or 56K connection is fine for voice transmissions, but you need a faster modem for video. Sure, video works with a 56K selection, but it works much better with an ISDN or better connection.

- **Speakers and a sound card:** If you can listen to a music CD on your computer or play sounds like the ones ICQ makes, you're there. You have speakers and a sound card.

- **A microphone:** You need a microphone to record your voice.

- **The ability to capture video:** Some computers come with a "video in" jack for a video camera. Some are equipped with built-in video cameras.

Internet Telephony Applications that Will Work with ICQ

At present, more than thirty Internet telephony applications will work with ICQ. Table 16-1 lists the applications that ICQ supports as of the writing of this book. In the table are Websites where you find out more about the applications.

Table 16-1	Telephony Applications that ICQ Supports
Application	*Website*
CineVideo/Direct	www.cinecom.com/download.htm
Cu-Seeme	www.cu-seeme.cornell.edu
Intel Iphone	www.intel.com/cpc

Application	Website
IRIS Phone	www.irisphone.com
Microsoft Netmeeting	www.microsoft.com/netmeeting
Netscape CoolTalk	www.netscape.com/eng/mozilla/3.0/ relnotes/windows-3.0b4.html
Netscape CoolTalk	home.netscape.com/navigator/v3.0/ cooltalk.html
Qtalka	www.qtalka.com
QuickCam	www.logitech.com/us/support/ videolist.html
VDOPhone	www.vdolive.com/vdophone
VocalTec Iphone	www.vocaltec.com/iphone4/ip4_dnld.htm
WebPhone	www.webphone.com

Table 16-1 is by no means a comprehensive list of all the Internet telephony applications that will work with ICQ. New ones are introduced all the time. At its Website, ICQ maintains a list of telephony applications that you can use with ICQ. To see the list, go to this Website address: www.icq.com/productsext.html.

ICQ versions of Internet telephony applications

In a sign of the popularity of ICQ, Internet telephony applications are being written especially for ICQ. ICQ keeps a list of these applications on its Website at this address: www.icq.com/download_custom.html. As of the writing of this book, the only custom application listed is ICQ for Netmeeting. This version of ICQ supports various attributes of Microsoft's Netmeeting, Chat, and Vchat applications.

However, rumors abound of telephony applications being written for ICQ. We anticipate seeing many more in the future.

Configuring ICQ for Internet Telephony

Some people are better than others at thinking ahead, so ICQ offers two ways to configure ICQ for an Internet telephony application: You can do it ahead of time or you can do it on the fly as the need arises. In other words, if someone wants to engage you in a chat by means of a telephony application and the thing isn't set up to run on your computer, you can set it up then and there. Meanwhile, if you have the foresight to know you'll need a telephony application, you can configure it in ICQ before the time to use it arises. Better keep reading.

Configuring ahead of time

The faster, more efficient way to configure ICQ for your favorite Internet telephony application is to configure it beforehand. That way, when you are ready to talk with a friend, all you have to do is click and go. Follow these steps to configure ICQ for a telephony application you anticipate using in the future:

1. **Click the ICQ button and choose Preferences.**

   You see the Owner Prefs For dialog box.

2. **Click on the Internet Telephony/Games/Chat tab.**

   As shown in Figure 16-1, this tab lists telephony applications, games, and chat applications that work with ICQ. You can update the list by clicking the Update List button.

Figure 16-1:
Telephony
applications
that work
with ICQ are
listed in the
Internet
Telephony/
Games/Chat
tab.

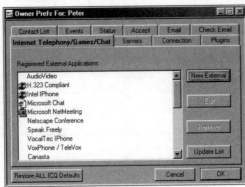

Take a good look at the applications on the list. If the one you want to use is on the list, you've got it made. Keep reading to configure ICQ for an application that isn't on the list.

3. **Click the New External button.**

   You see the Define New External Application dialog box.

4. **In the External Application Name, enter the name of the application.**

   You can use any name you want.

5. **Click the Browse button next to the External Application Executable box, and, in the Open dialog box, locate and select the .exe file of the application; then click the Open button.**

   The path to the application appears in the External Application Executable box.

6. **If any command line-variables apply to the application, enter them in the Command Line box.**

   See the application documentation for information about command-line variables. If the application is a client-to-server application, be sure to click the Client-Server Application button. Then, in the Define New External Application dialog box, enter the path to the program name (or click the Browse button to designate the path in the Open dialog box). Also enter the command-line parameters if there are any and click the Default Application Servers List button to add the servers to which the application will connect. These servers are usually identified by IP address.

7. **Click OK.**

   The name of the application appears on the Internet Telephony/Games/Chat tab.

Once you have registered an application, you may have cause from time to time to edit the parameters that you previously supplied. To do that, select the application in the Internet Telephony/Games/Chat tab, click the Edit button, and update the information.

Configuring ICQ for telephony on the fly

If you're adventurous, you and a friend might decide to try an Internet telephony application. As long as you and your friend both have the application on your computer, you're ready to go. You can start talking.

However, if you ask someone to talk to you, and it turns out that the other person doesn't have the telephony application, you'll receive a notice saying as much. On the other hand, if you are the one without the application, you can download the application as long as it is supported by ICQ.

Follow these steps to configure ICQ so you can run it with a telephony application when you receive an invitation to use the application:

1. **Click your friend's name on the Contact List.**

2. **Choose Internet Telephony/Games⇨View List - Download.**

   A submenu appears with the names of programs supported by ICQ.

3. **Click on a program to download it.**

   You go to the ICQ Website, where you can follow the application's
   instructions to download it properly. ICQ will register the application
   and you'll be ready to go!

Launching an Internet Telephony Application

After you configure a telephony application for use with ICQ, you're ready to
try out the application (the next section in this chapter explains how to find
people who have the same applications as you). Follow these steps to invite
someone to communicate with you by means of a telephony application and
also launch the application:

1. **Click your friend's name on the Contact List.**

2. **On the pop-up menu, choose Internet Telephony/Games and then the
   name of the telephony application that you want to use.**

   As shown in Figure 16-2, the Send Phone/Video/Data Request dialog box
   appears.

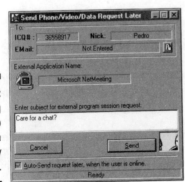

Figure 16-2:
Inviting
someone to
engage in a
telephony
chat.

3. **Type an enticing invitation to chat or play a game in the text box.**

4. **Click the Send button.**

If your friend accepts the invitation, ICQ launches the application from both of your computers and inserts the correct IP address for a connection. You are up and running!

Finding an ICQ Internet Telephony User Group

The purpose of ICQ is to help people with similar interests and ideas find each other, and the same holds true for people who like to use telephony applications. They, too, can find each other without wandering around in the dark and getting lost.

To find people who use the same telephony applications or play the same games as you, go to the PeopleSpace Directory and look in these general areas:

✔ Games

✔ Internet Telephony and Voice Chat

Chapter 12 explains how to find your way around the PeopleSpace Directory.

Part V
The Part of Tens

The 5th Wave   By Rich Tennant

COUNSELORS
OFFICE

"He should be all right now. I made him spend two
and a half hours on a prisoners' chat line."

In this part . . .

Each chapter in Part V offers ten tidbits of good, rock-solid information. With four chapters in this part, that makes 40 — count 'em — 40 tidbits in all.

Here, you will find ten cool things to do in ICQ, ten tips for searching the Internet, ten techniques for maintaining your privacy, and ten common ICQ hoaxes.

Chapter 17

Ten Very Cool Things You Can Do in ICQ

. . . .

In This Chapter

▶ Chatting, chatting, and chatting

▶ Surfing collaboratively on the Web

▶ Bookmarking Web pages — and visiting pages you bookmarked

▶ Participating in Message Board discussions

▶ Being invisible (and other privacy provisions)

▶ Searching the Internet with ICQ iT!

▶ Making the ICQ window disappear automatically

▶ Making ICQ "float" onscreen

▶ Being told when you've got mail

▶ Registering more than once

. . . .

*W*e had a hard time deciding on the ten coolest things you can do in ICQ. We think everything is pretty cool, except of course those "Hi, I'm a Friend and I Just Wanted to Say Hi" messages you sometimes get (see Chapter 20). Herewith is our short list of the ten coolest things, but feel free to disagree with us. ICQ has simply too many cool things to stuff into a ten-item list.

Chatting, Chatting, and Chatting

Chatting, of course, is the best thing going in ICQ. In the course of writing this book, we interviewed about 60 people on six continents. They told us how they use ICQ, tips and tricks for running ICQ, and all kinds of interesting things about themselves (we're saving the juicy stuff for the sequel to this book).

Finding people who share your interests and engaging them in chats is what ICQ is all about. Both the authors of this book come from small towns, and to test how easy or hard it is to look up people in ICQ, we decided to see if anyone in our hometowns had signed on with the network. Amazingly, we not only found ICQ members in our hometowns, but we became friends with them. Things don't change very much in a small town, by the way. Turns out both towns are exactly as we left them.

Chapters 4 and 5 of this book are devoted to chatting.

Surfing Collaboratively on the Web

Thanks to ICQ, you can surf the Web right along with somebody else. We call it "surfing collaboratively." When you find a Web page that you want to bring to someone's attention, perhaps to the attention of someone you're chatting with, all you have to do is click the person's name on the Contact List, choose Web Page Address (URL), and click the Send button in the Send URL Message dialog box.

On the other side, your surfing companion gets a URL message, and all he or she has to do to visit the Website you're visiting is click the Go To URL button in the Incoming URL Message dialog box.

Very civilized, we think. You don't have to type out long Web addresses. Nor does the person who receives the Web page address. And the addresses are passed back and forth almost instantaneously if both parties are online.

Chapter 10 explains how to pass Web page addresses back and forth.

Bookmarking Web Pages — and Visiting Pages You Bookmarked

Bookmarking a Web page whose address you received from someone else is as easy as falling off a log. All you have to do is click the Add To Bookmark button in the Incoming URL Message dialog box, as Chapter 10 explains. We are very impressed with the bookmarking capabilities of ICQ.

Visiting a page you bookmarked is pretty easy, too, as Chapter 10 demonstrates. We wish that bookmarking pages in our Web browsers was as easy as bookmarking pages in ICQ.

Participating in Message Board Discussions

The ICQ Message Board has to be the biggest message board in the world. Certainly every topic under the sun is discussed there. And getting around the Message Board, posting your own messages, and reading replies is very simple. The Message Board even lets you bookmark messages and subscribe to discussions so you can keep abreast of your favorite topics.

Be sure to visit the Message Board on your tour of ICQ Land. Chapter 7 explains how to get there and how to read and post messages.

Being Invisible (and Other Privacy Provisions)

ICQ is very good about helping you maintain your privacy. You can go online, plug into ICQ, and take advantage of all the features ICQ has to offer without anyone knowing you're online. For that matter, you can be visible to some people and invisible to others. If someone offends you, you can arrange never to hear from him or her again.

Chapter 14 explains all the options in ICQ for maintaining your privacy. In Chapter 19, we offer our ten favorite ways to draw the line between your private life and your public life — in ICQ, that is.

Searching the Internet with ICQ iT!

To keep up with the Joneses (we guess), ICQ has its own search engine for searching the Internet called ICQ iT!. ICQ iT! is probably not the best search engine, but it is the easiest to use and get to. As long as you're in Advanced mode, you can start searching the Internet right away by entering a keyword in the Enter Search Keyword box and clicking the GO button.

As Chapter 10 explains, ICQ iT! is very generous about letting you use other search engines. While the ICQ iT! toolbar is displayed, you can open the Select Search Engine menu and search with Excite, AltaVista, or one of 14 other search engines.

Making the ICQ Window Disappear Automatically

The beauty of ICQ is that you can run the program while you do other things. You can trade messages with someone in Madagascar, for example, while you enter data in a spreadsheet. You can do that, we should say, as long as you know how to keep the ICQ window from getting in the way of your work.

Chapter 13 offers a bunch of different techniques for taking charge of the ICQ window. One of our favorite techniques is to make the window disappear automatically when you don't do anything in ICQ for a couple of minutes. Follow these steps to perform the little trick:

1. **Click the ICQ button and choose Preferences.**

   You see the Owner Prefs For dialog box.

2. **Click the Contact List tab.**

3. **Check the Auto Hide Delay check box.**

4. **In the Seconds box, enter the amount of idle time that you want to elapse before the window is minimized automatically.**

5. **Click the OK button.**

   There is no point in letting the ICQ window hog the screen if you can help it, right?

Making ICQ "Float" Onscreen

Another way to keep the ICQ window from getting in your way is to make a Contact List name "float" or the ICQ Status button "float." With this technique, you minimize the ICQ window and you are left with a floating button — either the name of the person on your Contact List with whom you are chatting, or the ICQ button, which you can click to get at most of the commands in ICQ.

For all the details, Chapter 3 and Chapter 6 explain how to make ICQ more buoyant. Here are instructions for making the ICQ Status button and a Contact List name float:

✔ **Floating ICQ Status button:** Click the ICQ button and choose Windows/Alerts⇨Status "Floating" On. Then minimize the ICQ window. When you want to give a command, click the ICQ button.

✔ **Floating Contact List name:** Click the person's name on the Contact List and choose More (Rename, Delete)⇨"Floating" On. Click the Contact List name button and you see the usual set of commands for communicating with the person.

Being Told When You've Got Mail

Without leaving ICQ, you can be alerted when your e-mail account — not your ICQ account, but the private account you keep with an Internet service provider — has received new mail. When mail arrives at your private account, the Outside e-mail icon appears on your Contact List. Double-click the icon and you see the list of e-mail messages that are waiting for your attention.

Chapter 8 describes how to keep on top of incoming mail without leaving the safe confines of ICQ.

Registering More Than Once

As Chapter 2 explains, you can register with ICQ more than once. Not often in life do you get to exercise your alter ego this way. For the fun of it, register once as yourself and once as the Fairy Queen, the Beast, or the Grand Poobah. You will be pleasantly or unpleasantly surprised by who finds you in ICQ and to what extremes your alter ego can go to.

Chapter 18

Ten Tips for Searching the Internet Faster and Better

In This Chapter

▶ Begin with a search service site when you search the Web

▶ Start simple when you enter keywords for a search

▶ Pick a start page you genuinely like visiting

▶ Bookmark your favorite Web pages

▶ Use the Back and Forward buttons

▶ Use the Find command on long pages

▶ Click the Stop button early and often

▶ Open a second window for surfing

▶ Try turning off the images and pictures

▶ Search when traffic is light

*I*n some quarters, the World Wide Web is known as the "World Wide Wait." If you lose patience while you search the Internet, try one of the ten techniques described in this chapter. Even if your browser is a slow one, surfing the Internet doesn't have to be like watching grass grow. It can be more exciting than that.

When You Search the Web, Start from a Search Service Site

The most efficient way to search the Internet is to go to the homepage of an Internet search service and start the search there. That way, you can take advantage of the search options that the service offers. Most services offer special options for searching for phrases, people, and other things.

Experiment with different search services and find one or two that you like. Then bookmark your one or two favorite services. Most search services offer advanced searching options. If you stick with the same service, you learn how to use it well. And you learn how to take advantage of the specialized search commands that it offers.

Table 18-1 lists search services and their addresses.

Table 18-1	Search Services
Service	*Address*
Ask Jeeves	www.askjeeves.com
Excite	www.excite.com
HotBot	www.hotbot.com
InfoSeek	www.infoseek.com
Lycos	www.lycos.com
Snap!	www.snap.com
WebCrawler	www.webcrawler.com
Yahoo!	www.yahoo.com

Start Simple When You Enter Keywords for a Search

A *keyword* is a word that describes what information you hope to obtain in a search of the Internet. To search the Internet, you enter a keyword or several keywords. For the search, the search service finds all Web pages where the keyword or keywords appear.

The Internet is crowded with all kinds of junk. Usually, you have to search several times before you find what you're looking for. We have found that starting simply with one or maybe two keywords is the best way to go. Start the search with one or two keywords, read the results, and see what kind of Web pages your words produce. Once you know that, you can tailor your search by entering more keywords. Next time around, however, you know which keywords to enter to pinpoint the information you're looking for on the Internet.

Choose a Start Page You Genuinely Like Visiting

The *start page* is the page that appears automatically each time you go on the Internet (in Internet Explorer, the term is *homepage*). Strange, but the Microsoft Corporation and other big-stick entities always try to co-op the start page. For example, if you upgrade to Windows 98 and then go on the Internet, you will be surprised to discover that the Microsoft homepage (`http://home.microsoft.com`) has become your start page.

The fact is, companies try to appropriate the start page because they want you to pay them a visit. They want to sell you something. And they know that most people don't know how to choose a start page of their own.

We suggest that you choose a start page that you're genuinely interested in — the local newspaper's homepage, the homepage of a weather bureau, the homepage of an Internet search service. That way, you can get a running start whenever you go on the Internet.

Choosing a new start page in Internet Explorer

In Internet Explorer, go to the page on the Internet that you want to be your start page and follow these steps to make it the page that appears first whenever you go on the Internet:

1. **Click Tools⇨ Internet Options (in Internet Explorer versions previous to version 5, choose View⇨Internet Options).**

   The Internet Properties dialog box appears.

2. **Click the General tab, if necessary.**

   Under Home Page at the top of the dialog box is the address of your start page.

3. **Click the Use Current button to make the page you are currently visiting your start page.**

   The address of the page you are visiting appears in the Address text box.

   If the Use Current button is grayed out and you can't click it, type the address of your favorite page in the Address text box. To find the address, go back to your browser and look for the addresses on the Address bar.

4. Click OK in the Internet Properties dialog box.

You settled it! Next time you go online and connect to the Internet, you go where you want to go, not where a software company wants you to go.

Choosing a new start page in Netscape Navigator

In Netscape Navigator, choose Edit⇨Preferences. In the Preferences dialog box, click the Use Current button or else type the address of your favorite Web page in the Location text box, and then click OK.

Bookmark Your Favorite Web Pages

Bookmarking a Web page means to mark it in such a way that you can visit it again quickly (Chapter 10 explains how to bookmark a Website in ICQ). All browsers offer techniques for bookmarking pages and returning to pages that you have bookmarked. The fastest way to bookmark a Web page is to right-click it and choose Add to Favorites (in Internet Explorer) or Add Bookmark (in Netscape Navigator).

Follow these steps to return to a page you bookmarked:

✔ **In Internet Explorer:** Click the Favorites button (and click the Links sub-folder if you were thoughtful enough to put your bookmarks there), and then click a bookmark name.

✔ **In Netscape Navigator:** Open the Bookmarks menu and choose a bookmark.

Make Use of the Back and Forward Buttons

Everybody knows that you can use the Back button to see the page you last saw and click the Forward button to move to a page from which you retreated. Next to the Back and Forward buttons are down arrows that you can click to open a menu with the last several pages you saw or retreated from. Choose a page on the drop-down menu to leap forward or backward by several pages.

Make Use of the Find Command on Long Pages

On a Web page with lots and lots of text, finding what you are looking for can be difficult. Rather than strain your eyes, use the Find command. All you have to do is enter the text you're looking for and click the Find Next button. The page scrolls to the text you entered. Choose Edit⇨Find to get the Find command.

Click the Stop Button Early and Often

A Web page with many graphic images can take a long time to appear on a computer screen. Often you wait and wait for a Web page to appear, only to discover when you can finally see it that it wasn't worth waiting for.

One way to cut down on wait time is to click the Stop button in your browser after a few seconds have elapsed. After you click Stop, you can see what has downloaded so far. If you like what you see, click the Refresh button (in Internet Explorer) or the Reload button (in Netscape Navigator). Clicking that button tells your browser to start downloading the Web page again. Now you can rest assured that the Web page will be one you want to see when it is finished downloading.

Open a Second Window for Surfing

Opening more than one browser window slows down the computer, but it can make surfing the Internet more fun. To open a second window in Internet Explorer, choose File⇨New⇨Window (or press Ctrl+N). To open a second window in Netscape Navigator, choose File⇨New Web Browser.

With two windows open, you can surf the Internet in one window and leave the other open to a page you want to stick with. Here's another advantage of opening a second window: If you get stuck on a Web page that is taking a long time to download, you can simply click the Close button to close the window without closing your browser altogether.

Try Turning Off the Images and Pictures at Websites

Graphics are nice, but they can take a long time to download, especially if you have a slow connection to the Internet. If reading words on the Internet, not viewing pictures, is your cup of tea, you can tell your browser not to display images or pictures. And you can still see images if you want to. On most Websites, a description of each image appears where normally the image would be when images are turned off. To see the image, right-click it and choose View Image. In Netscape Navigator, you can click the Image button to see all the images on the Web page.

Follow these instructions to turn off images on Web pages:

- ✔ **In Internet Explorer 5:** Choose Tools⇨Internet Options, click the Advanced tab in the Internet Options dialog box, scroll to Multimedia in the Settings list, and uncheck the Show Pictures check box.

- ✔ **In Netscape Navigator:** Choose Options and uncheck the Auto Load Images option.

Search When Traffic Is Light

The Internet is like a highway in that it gets crowded when a lot of people are on it. And when it's crowded, connections take longer. You may have noticed that the Internet slows down during lunch hour, shortly before the workday ends, and shortly after the workday begins. It slows during those times because a lot of people go on the Internet when they arrive at work, at lunch, and shortly before they leave work.

Do your Internet surfing when fewer people are on the Internet and you'll be able to surf faster.

Chapter 19

Ten Techniques for Maintaining Your Privacy

. . . .

In This Chapter

▶ Requiring others to be authorized to put your name on their Contact Lists

▶ Ignoring people who bother you

▶ Appearing offline to other ICQ members

▶ Changing your online status for a particular person

▶ Appearing offline to everybody on the ICQ network

▶ Preventing junk-mail messages from arriving

▶ Preventing e-mail addresses from reaching your ICQ mailbox

▶ Updating your description in the White Pages

▶ Keeping random chatters at bay

▶ Quitting ICQ and registering under a new name

. . . .

*W*hen you register with ICQ, you join a party in progress to which about 30 million other people have been invited. That's a lot of people. A cynic might remark that ICQ members aren't entitled to their privacy, seeing as they've joined a party with 30 million other participants.

The cynics, however, are wrong. You can retain your privacy and still be a very active member of the ICQ community. Chapter 14 is devoted to privacy and security issues. In this chapter, we offer ten techniques for maintaining your privacy with cross-references to the parts of the book where these techniques are discussed in detail.

Require Others to Get Authorization Before Putting Your Name on Their Contact List

People who have put your name on their Contact List know when you're online (well, not necessarily, as "Declare Your Online Status to Others" and "Declare Yourself Invisible to All" explain later in this chapter). To send you a message or ask you to chat, people who have put your name on their Contact List have only to click your name and choose an option from the pop-up menu.

The *Contact List* is a minidirectory of people you want to stay in touch with. If you want to be choosy about who can contact you and who knows when you're online, require others to get approval to put your name on their Contact List. When someone asks for approval, you can click the Info button in the Incoming Request For Authorization dialog box, investigate the person in the ICQ Global Directory dialog box, and yea or nay his request, as shown in Figure 19-1.

Click the Info button... ⌐ ...to find out if you want your name
to be on this person's Contact List.

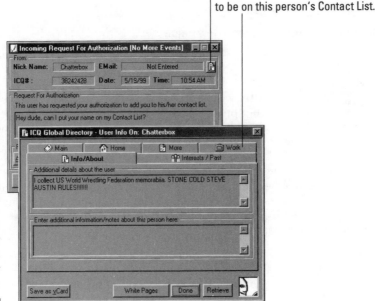

Figure 19-1:
The Incoming Request For Authorization dialog box appears when someone wants to put your name on his or her Contact List.

Go online, connect to ICQ, and follow these steps to require others to get permission before putting your name on their Contact List:

1. **Click the ICQ button and choose Security & Privacy on the pop-up menu.**

   You see the Security For dialog box.

2. **Click the Security tab.**

3. **Click the My Authorization Is Required option button.**

   You will find this button near the top of the dialog box under "Change Contact List Authorization."

4. **Click the Save button.**

5. **Click the Done button.**

Next time someone wants you to be on his Contact List, you will see the Incoming Request For Authorization dialog box (refer to Figure 19-1). Click the Accept button to give approval or the Decline button to keep your name from appearing on the other person's Contact List. Chapter 6 describes the Contact List in detail.

Completely Ignore Someone Who Bothers You

If you get an offensive message from somebody, or if someone pesters you with messages and you don't care to be pestered, you can arrange to never receive any communications from the pest again. The pest may continue to send messages, chat requests, or Web page addresses, but the communications will never arrive. The pest will think they arrived, but really the communications will be swallowed by ICQ and lost forever. You will never see them.

To ignore someone, click the person's name on your Contact List (you will find the name under "Not in List" if you received the communication out of the blue) and choose Move To Ignore List from the pop-up menu. If you want to ignore someone who hasn't sent you a communication or hasn't sent you a communication recently, you have to learn the person's ICQ number and then visit the Security For dialog box to ignore the person. See Chapter 14, which explains how to handle the Ignore List.

Besides ignoring someone, you can make yourself invisible to people you want to avoid. Keep reading.

Make Yourself Invisible to Someone Who Bothers You

Suppose you allow someone to put your name on his or her Contact List, but then you regret it. Whenever you go online, the pest knows it and sends you an invitation to chat or a message. No matter how many times you politely turn down the request to chat or tell the pest you're busy, he or she doesn't take the hint.

Unfortunately, your name is on the other person's Contact List, so he or she knows when you're online and can be bothered. You can't do anything about that — or can you? You can, we are happy to report. You can make yourself invisible to the other person by adding his or her name to the Invisible List, the list of people to whom you always appear to be offline.

As an invisible man or woman, the other party will think you are offline, even when you're online. Your name will permanently appear on the other person's Contact List under the heading "Offline."

To make yourself invisible, click a name on the Contact List and choose More (Rename, Delete)⇨Alert/Accept Modes. The Alert/Accept dialog box, shown in Figure 19-2, appears. Click the Invisible To User check box and then click OK.

Figure 19-2:
From the Alert/ Accept dialog box, you can declare your online status to one person and one person only.

After you're invisible, the other person can still send you communications, and you can answer them if you want. As the previous section in this chapter explained, you can ignore the other party if you want to stop getting messages from someone.

Besides being invisible, you can declare yourself permanently occupied, away, or "undisturbable." Keep reading.

Declare Your Online Status to Others

Besides being invisible to another member of ICQ, you can declare your online status in other ways. With this technique, you tell the other person that you don't care to be bothered and you trust the other person not to bother you. An icon appears next to your name on the other party's Contact List. The icon tells the other party whether you can be bothered or why you can't be bothered. The other party knows you're online, but knows as well that you don't care to be bothered.

Follow these steps to declare your online status to a specific someone whose name appears in the ICQ window:

1. **Click the person's name.**

2. **On the pop-up menu, choose More (Rename, Delete)⇨Alert/Accept Modes.**

   The Alert/Accept dialog box appears.

3. **Click the Status tab (refer to Figure 19-2).**

4. **Click the Update Status check box.**

5. **Click one of the four option buttons: Away To User, N/A To User, Occupied To User, or DND to User.**

   Chapter 3 explains what these options mean in detail. Basically, the options mean the same insofar as whether anyone can send you communications — they can. The options merely describe why you can't be bothered.

6. **Click the OK button.**

So much for how to appear offline to one person. Suppose you want everyone to think you are offline. Keep reading.

Declare Yourself Invisible to All

Sometimes you simply can't be bothered. You're busy and you don't want anybody who has put your name on his or her Contact List to know that you're online. You want to explore ICQ at your leisure without being interrupted by a message or a chat request.

In times like those, you can make yourself invisible to absolutely everybody in ICQ. To do so, click the Status button and choose Privacy (Invisible) on the pop-up menu. Your name will appear under "Offline" on Contact Lists all across the land.

On the subject of invisibility, Chapter 14 explains how you can keep people who visit your Personal Communication Center from knowing when you are online.

Don't Accept Messages That Were Sent to More than One Person

Messages that were sent to more than one person usually fall in the "junk mail" category. As time goes by and more advertisers discover ICQ, you're likely to receive more pesky advertisements from companies and Websites you don't care to hear from.

One way to keep junk-mail messages from intruding on your privacy is to decline all messages that were sent to more than one person. To do so, click the ICQ button and choose Security & Privacy. Then click the Ignore List tab in the Security For dialog box and check the Do Not Accept Multi-Recipient Messages From check box. If you still want to receive messages sent to more than one person from the people whose names are on your Contact List, choose Users Not on My Contact List from the drop-down menu. Be sure to click the Save button before you click Done to close the dialog box.

Don't Accept Messages from People Outside the ICQ Network

Whether you know it or not, you can receive e-mail from people who aren't registered with ICQ. Every ICQ member has an e-mail addresses that consists of an ICQ number followed by @pager.mirabilis.com. For example, if your ICQ number is 11223344, an advertiser can send e-mail to you in ICQ by addressing the messages as follows:

```
11223344@pager.mirabilis.com
```

Unfortunately, many of the messages sent to ICQ members from outside the network come from advertisers. To avoid receiving advertisements sent this way, click the ICQ button, choose Security & Privacy, and click the Ignore List tab in the Security For dialog box. Then click the Do Not Accept Email Express Messages check box and click the Save button.

Tell your friends and enemies who want to reach you in ICQ that they can do so by going to your Personal Communication Center and entering the message in your World-Wide Pager, as shown in Figure 19-3. Everyone who signs on with ICQ gets a Personal Communication Center. Tell your friends to go online and direct their browsers to `http://wwp.icq.com/Your ICQ#` when they want to send you a message (that's *wwp*, not *www*). There, at your Personal Communication Center, others can enter a message in your World-Wide Pager. If you're online and connected to ICQ, you'll get the message immediately.

Figure 19-3: People outside the ICQ network can send you e-mail messages by going to your Personal Communication Center and typing the message into the World-Wide Pager.

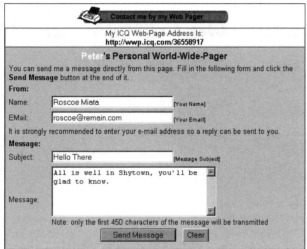

Make Sure the White Pages Only Show What You Want Them to Show

When you registered with ICQ, you submitted a bunch of information to the White Pages, the directory where all that is known about ICQ members is filed away. As Chapter 7 explains, ICQ members can search the White Pages to find people who live in a certain city, are interested in a certain topic, or pursue a certain hobby. In other words, ICQ members can go to the White Pages to find like-minded people.

Because the White Pages are "The Book of Life" as far as ICQ is concerned, you need to make sure that you're described correctly in the White Pages. That way, you won't be bothered by people who don't share your interests. And, more importantly, you will be bothered by people who do share them.

Follow these steps to submit an accurate portrait of yourself to the White Pages:

1. **Click the ICQ button.**

2. **Choose Add/Change Current User➪View/Change My Details.**

   You see the Global Directory dialog box.

3. **Describe yourself in the dialog box and click the Save button.**

   Chapter 9 explains how the dialog box works, in case you need help with it.

Shield Yourself from Random Chatters

ICQ encourages you to find people to chat with at random. Why else would the Find Random Chat Partner button appear in the middle of the ICQ window? Still, some people don't like being bothered by random chat requests.

To keep random chat requests from coming your way, click the Find Random Chat Partner button in the ICQ window. In the Random dialog box, click the Details tab. Then uncheck the I Want to Be Available for Random Chat & Messages check box and click the Save button. Chapter 2 explains random chats in detail.

If Necessary, Quit ICQ and Re-register Under a New Name

Quitting ICQ and re-registering under a new name is a drastic measure. But if you're being bothered by a bunch of different people you don't care to be bothered by, you can simply pull up stakes and leave.

Chapter 2 explains how to unregister a membership in ICQ and how to register a new membership. We suggest registering under a different name before you unregister. That way, you can retrieve the names of people on your Contact List that you want to stay in touch with. To do so, send the names on the list from your old registration number to your new registration number. Chapter 2 explains how to switch from one registered name to another. Chapter 6 explains how to send Contact List names to another ICQ member — in this case to yourself under a different ICQ number.

Chapter 20

Ten ICQ Hoaxes

*I*t happens from time to time: You are chatting away in ICQ when suddenly a message or Web page address arrives from a stranger. You open the message to discover that you might have to pay for ICQ, that a virus is coming your way, or that another dreadful event is about to occur.

The ICQ network is probably the biggest sewing circle in the world. Rumors certainly travel fast. And some of those rumors aren't really rumors. No, they're hoaxes. Following is our list of the ten most prevalent hoaxes in ICQ and advice on how to avoid being the victim of a hoax.

By the way, every hoax message described in the following pages urges you to forward the message after you have read it. You can be sure that if you're supposed to forward a message, the message is likely a hoax.

"Mirabilis Is Going to Start Charging for ICQ"

Variations on this message appear often. Sometimes the message declares that ICQ, Inc., the company that owns ICQ, intends to charge by the month. Sometimes you're told that ICQ, Inc. intends to charge for each message you send. Whatever the charge, you're told to forward the message to all the people on your Contact List — or else!

Here are a few variations on the "forward this or else we will be charged for ICQ" theme:

- ✔ Each time you forward the message, ICQ, Inc. gives you a certain number of brownie points. When ICQ, Inc. starts charging for the service, you will be able to count your brownie points toward paying the monthly fee.

- ✔ Each time you forward the message, a protest message is sent automatically to ICQ, Inc., which is carefully tabulating the number of messages it receives. If we protest loudly enough, the company won't charge for the service.

- ✔ Forward this message to keep ICQ, Inc. from terminating your account. The company is tracking where this message goes. The accounts of people who do not receive this message and forward it will be considered dormant and will be terminated.

- ✔ Go to the Web page address listed here and vote against being charged for ICQ. ICQ, Inc. is tabulating the results of the vote, so be sure to forward this Web page address to all ICQ members you know. Usually, the Website mentioned either doesn't exist or is a private Website not connected to ICQ, Inc., but that doesn't stop people from forwarding the Web page address and promulgating the hoax.

These messages are so prevalent that ICQ occasionally circulates messages of its own to combat them. When you receive a "forward this or else we will be charged for ICQ" message, politely tell the sender that he or she has been hoaxed.

As for plans for charging for ICQ, we think ICQ, Inc. will never charge for the service. But if the company does, you will hear about it at the ICQ Website or in the form of a system message. You won't get the bad news from a panicky, poorly written message that is riddled with spelling errors.

"Be Careful: A Virus Is Being Sent Your Way"

Under no circumstances can a message, chat exchange, Web page address, or e-mail message sent over the ICQ network carry a virus. A virus can travel over the network, but only in the form of an executable file (an .exe, .com, or .bat file). What's more, even if a virus arrives, it can't do any damage unless you launch it. Viruses are mini- (or sometimes not so mini-) computer programs. Before a virus can do its work, you have to start it the same way you start a computer program. In other words, you have to consciously click a Start button or enter a command line to run the file.

The moral of this technical tale is that you don't have to worry about viruses if you never accept files from other ICQ members. And if you accept files, you only have to worry if you accept executable files. And if you accept an executable file, you only have to worry if the file comes from a source you don't know and trust.

Now that you know about viruses and ICQ, you can rest more easily when you get a "virus is being sent your way" message. The message is a hoax. Someone is trying to scare you. And if you forward the message to others, you're helping someone do the dirty work of spreading a hoax on the ICQ network.

If you're interested in viruses and virus hoaxes, check out the Computer Virus Myths site (`www.kumite.com/myths/home.htm`). The site offers a couple of interesting theories as to why hoaxers do it. You'll also find an A-to-Z list of virus hoaxes.

"Don't Connect to ICQ on Such-and-Such Day"

Last time we were told not to connect to ICQ, the day in question was October 31, which we think showed a lack of ingenuity on the hoaxer's part. Were we supposed to think that ghosts would come through the telephone lines and haunt our computer?

"Don't connect on such-and-such day" hoaxes strike the Internet at large as well as ICQ. For example, you aren't supposed to start your computer on March 6, Michelangelo's birthday, or on April 16, the anniversary of the Chernobyl nuclear disaster. A psychologist could probably write an essay about why credence is given to virus threats that fall on birthdays and anniversaries. Anyhow, unless you take pride in being gullible, do not believe the "don't connect on such-and-such day" messages.

"So-and-So Is Evil and Is Sending Viruses"

This message appears from time to time. Usually, the message lists so-and-so's nickname and ICQ number. The message explains that so-and-so is a malicious individual with extraterrestrial powers who can infect your hard disk with a virus even if you so much as communicate over the Internet with him or her.

You can bet that somebody with a grudge against so-and-so wrote the message. The strange part is that others passed it along. Anyway, as we explained earlier in this chapter, you can't get a virus over ICQ unless you accept an executable file (an .exe, .com, or .bat file), so-and-so's evil powers notwithstanding.

"Don't Download ICQ 99 — It Has a Virus!"

Several variations of this theme have arrived in our mailboxes. In one message, ICQ 99 is virus-ridden. In another, you will lose your account with ICQ if you upgrade to ICQ 99.

This type of hoax sort of begs the question, "Why would anyone float a hoax like that?" Someone wants to discourage ICQ members from upgrading to the newest edition of the ICQ software.

For the record and for worrywarts, ICQ 99 does not have a virus and you don't lose your account when you upgrade.

"You Failed to Forward the Last Message and Now You're Toast"

Savvy members of ICQ simply delete hoax messages. Then they get messages like this one, scratch their heads, and think, "Maybe I should have forwarded that message after all."

Variations on this message include the one that says your account will close in 72 hours if you don't forward this, the present message, to everyone on your Contact List, and the one that says your account has already been marked for closure and will stop functioning in 24 hours.

No, you're right to delete all hoax messages and think nothing more about it. Don't worry about this message either. Whoever floated this one is counting on ICQ members to second-guess themselves. Don't do that, but delete this message as swiftly and surely as you delete all hoax messages.

"Get $3 for Every Message You Forward! I've Won $300 So Far!"

The old pyramid scheme transplanted to cyberspace! We can't imagine anyone falling for this one, but the message got passed to us, so at least one person fell for it.

The message didn't say how to collect the money you win from forwarding the message to others. This message reminds us of P.T. Barnum, who said, "There's a sucker born every minute." In one of his circus sideshows, Barnum put out a sign that read, "See a horse whose head is where his tail ought to be and whose tail is where his head ought to be." People who paid the 25 cents to see the freak horse were ushered into a barn, where they saw a horse who had been lead head-first into a stall. Instead of the horse's head peering over the gate, they saw his twitching tail.

"Congratulations! You've Just Won a Free Membership!"

This one is not truly a hoax. For all we know, you really win a free membership when you visit the Web page listed in the message. Whether the membership is worth winning is another matter.

Unfortunately, advertisers have discovered ICQ. In fact, software is available for *spamming* — for sending thousands upon thousands of messages at once — to ICQ members. One of the refreshing aspects of ICQ is that the network is relatively free of advertisements, but the same used to be said of America Online, ICQ's parent company, and now America Online subscribers receive five to ten junk-mail messages a day.

Don't bother protesting an advertisement by replying. Send a protest message to the sender and you send in vain. Your message will not reach the sender. The spamming software makes sure that the sender's address is properly masked and never discovered.

You can, however, stop junk-mail messages from coming. To do so, click the ICQ button and choose Security & Privacy. Then click the Ignore List tab in the Security For dialog box and check the Do Not Accept Multi-Recipient Messages From check box. If you want to receive multiple messages from the people on your Contact List, choose the Users Not on My Contact List option on the drop-down menu.

"Starting Soon, ICQ Will Shut Down for Repairs"

This message claims to be from ICQ itself. It states that the servers need repairing, so the network will shut down for a certain period of time.

ICQ has never shut down in the past, not once. What proves this one a hoax, however, is that the sender asks you to forward the message. ICQ would not do that. ICQ has declared that it will never ask its members to forward messages. Why would ICQ do such a thing? ICQ doesn't need to forward messages — the company knows where everyone is and can simply send everyone a message if that needs doing.

"Hi, I'm a Friend and I Just Wanted to Say Hi"

We saved this one for last. This message isn't really a hoax, at least not like the first nine messages. It doesn't have a malicious intent. The sender just wants to be friendly. Sometimes the message asks you to visit a Website, where you get a warm and fuzzy message of some kind. Sometimes the message merely offers a few sunny words of loving kindness.

Enough already. Are we being curmudgeons if we say that these messages are annoying? We would like the people who send them to stop sending them — at least to us. When we want to feel warm and fuzzy, we go to the greeting card section of supermarket and read the cards. Reading those cards under the fluorescent lights ("the joy you give is a gift to all") makes us feel all warm and fuzzy and sentimental.

Part VI
Appendixes

The 5th Wave   By Rich Tennant

"Mona, this is no way to deal with your chat-line addiction."

In this part . . .

The doctor wanted to remove Part VI, but we insisted on keeping the appendix in this book. And then, to complicate matters further, our book grew three more appendixes, to make a total of four.

The four appendixes in Part VI explain how to get help using ICQ, how to back up important stuff, what chat acronyms and smileys are, and what those strange ICQ terms really mean.

Appendix A

Getting Help with ICQ

• •

"**E**verybody needs a little help, sometime," as the soul singer says. We think the best place to look for help is in this book, but we also want you to know that ICQ offers a Help program as well as numerous Websites where you can seek help. This short appendix explains how to run the ICQ Help program and where you can go on the Web to get help with ICQ.

Running the ICQ Help Program

When you installed ICQ, you also installed a Help program. The ICQ Help program is a standard Windows-style program with three tabs: Contents, Index, and Find, as shown in Figure A-1. You're in familiar territory if you've used a Help program like this before. The ICQ Help program works exactly like other Windows-style Help programs.

Click a tab to try a new way of seeking help.

Click to return to the Help program window.

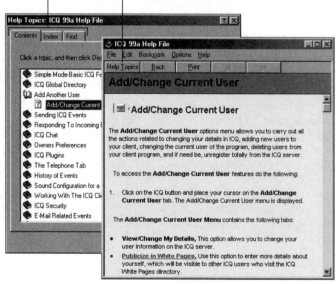

Figure A-1: Starting from the Contents, Index, or Search tab of the Help program window (left), locate a topic that interests you and double-click to read its Help file (right).

To open the Help program, start from the taskbar or the ICQ window:

- ✔ **Taskbar:** Click the Start button and choose Programs➪Icq➪ICQ Help.

- ✔ **ICQ window:** Click the ICQ button and choose Help➪Help Topics (or Help➪Index).

The three tabs in the Help program window present three ways of searching for help:

- ✔ **Contents tab:** Like a table of contents, this tab lists a bunch of general topics. Double-click a book icon and it opens to subtopics, each with a question mark beside its name (refer to Figure A-1). Either double-click a subtopic that interests you or click its name and then click the Display button. You see a Help file like the one in Figure A-1.

- ✔ **Index tab:** Like a book index, this tab lists topics in alphabetical order. Either type a few letters that describe what puzzles you to move down the list or scroll down the list and select a topic. If a topic strikes your fancy, double-click it or click it and click the Display button. A Help file appears so you can read about the topic you chose.

- ✔ **Find tab:** Like a search engine for searching the Internet, this tab allows you to search the Help files by keyword. Either type a word or scroll down the list and click a keyword. The bottom of the Find tab lists the names of Help files in which the word appears. Either double-click the name of a Help file or click a name and then click the Display button.

| Help Topics |

Usually, finding the right set of instructions takes a while. When you need to return from a Help file to the Help program window and search anew, click the Help Topics button.

ICQ Announcements Box: Keeping Up with the Latest from ICQ

As you surely know by now, the ICQ Announcements box appears onscreen whenever you start ICQ. The box usually offers a tip or two and boasts about an exciting new ICQ feature. The box stays onscreen for ten seconds, but if an announcement arouses your interest and you want the box to stay onscreen longer, click the box. Click anywhere — it'll stay onscreen.

At that point, you can click a button or hyperlink or do whatever it is you want to do in the Announcements box. Click the Close button to remove the box. To see it again, click the ICQ button and choose Help➪ICQ Announcements.

Amenities in the Help file window

Searching for instructions can be a frustrating activity, so the Help file window offers a few amenities to take the sting out of searching:

✔ **Bookmark instructions so you can find them later:** Choose Bookmark⇨Define when you come to a set of instructions you likely will need to look up again. In the Bookmark Define dialog box, describe the instruction set and click OK. Next time you want to return to the instructions, choose Bookmark and then the name of the instruction set on the drop-down menu.

✔ **Print instructions to keep them on hand:** Click the Print button to print a set of instructions and always have them on hand. Then click OK in the Print dialog box.

✔ **Jot down notes on the Help files:** Choose Edit⇨Annotate and write notes of your own

in the Annotate dialog box. A paper clip icon appears at the top of the Help file. Click the paper clip icon to see your notes in the Annotate dialog box.

✔ **Click the Back and >> buttons to retrace your steps:** The Help program keeps track of the screens you visit on your journey to the right set of instructions. Click the Back button as many times as necessary to revisit a screen. Click the >> button to return to a screen you retreated from.

✔ **Open the Help History window to retrace your steps:** Choose Options⇨Display History Window to see a list of the Help files you have visited in the course of a search. To return to a Help file, double-click its name in the Help History window.

If you prefer not to see the ICQ Announcements box each time you start ICQ, click the ICQ button and choose Preferences. Then click the Contact List tab in the Owner Prefs For dialog box, check the Don't Show Announcements check box, and click OK.

Going Online to the Technical Support Page

Starting from the ICQ Technical Support page (www.icq.com/support) shown in Figure A-2, you can get advice about many different ICQ topics. To get to the page, click the ICQ button and choose Help⇨Tutorials, Help, Support.

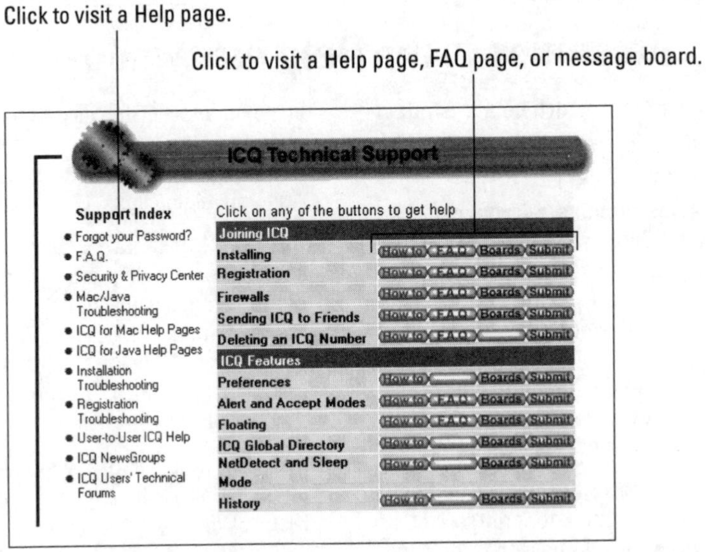

Click to visit a Help page.

Click to visit a Help page, FAQ page, or message board.

Figure A-2:
The ICQ
Technical
Support
page offers
a compre-
hensive list
of all the
ICQ Help
pages on its
Website.

Under "Support Index" is a comprehensive list of all the Help pages and tuto-rials that ICQ offers on its Website. Click a topic on the list to go directly to a Help page and get instructions for completing a task.

In the middle of the ICQ Technical Support page is another list of topics. In the list, you can click a button to get instructions or submit a question of your own:

✔ **How To:** Click to get instructions for completing a task or setting up a feature.

✔ **F.A.Q.:** Click to see a list of frequently asked questions about the topic.

✔ **Boards:** Click to visit a message board with instructions or opinions about the topic (Chapter 7 explains message boards).

✔ **Submit:** Click to submit a question to the ICQ technical support staff. You will receive a reply by e-mail.

Miscellaneous Ways to Seek Help

Besides the ICQ Technical Support page and Help program, ICQ offers these ways to get help with ICQ:

✔ **Reading the NetTips:** A NetTip is not a tip for improving your tennis game, but a little piece of advice for using ICQ. Click the ICQ button and choose Help⇨Net Tip to read the so-called NetTip of the Day. Click the Show Tips on StartUp check box if you want to see a NetTip each time you start ICQ.

✔ **Finding out what's new in ICQ:** Click the ICQ button and choose Help⇨ICQ — What's New to go to the What's New page (www.icq.com/products/news.html) and read a by-date list of innovations that have been made to ICQ.

✔ **Getting the FAQs:** Click the ICQ button and choose Help⇨ICQ F.A.Q. to go to the FAQ page (www.icq.com/support/99afaq), where you can see a list of all the FAQ (frequently asked questions) lists that ICQ maintains.

✔ **Getting tips from other ICQ members:** Click the ICQ button and choose Help⇨User to User Help to visit the User to User Voluntary Help page (www.icq.com/sitecreator/userhelp.html). There, if you scroll to the bottom, you'll find a list of people who maintain Web pages to help others with ICQ.

✔ **Take a tour of ICQ:** Click the Instructions button. You'll find it in the center of the ICQ window. Clicking the button takes you to a Website where you get summary instructions for using ICQ (www.icq.com/icqtour/advanced/).

Appendix B

Backing Up Your ICQ Contact List, Bookmarks, and More

● ●

*I*f something evil this way comes and your computer is lost, stolen, or destroyed, you lose your Contact List as well as the bookmarks, files, and picture files you acquired through ICQ. You also lose all records of the delightful chats you have had.

You lose those items, we should say, if you forgot to back them up. This appendix explains how to back up your Contact List, bookmarks, files, pictures files, and chats.

Backing Up and Restoring Your Contact List

The Contact List holds the names of all the friends you made in ICQ. No doubt it took you a long time to assemble the names on the list. You met your ICQ friends in random chats, chat rooms, and various other places. Finding them all again if you lose the list is well-nigh impossible. If something goes wrong with your computer and you can't recover the list, you're out of luck. You're out of luck, that is, if you didn't back up the Contact List.

Get a floppy disk, label it "ICQ Contact List," put it in the floppy drive of your computer, and follow these steps to back up your Contact List:

1. **Shut down ICQ, if ICQ is running.**

2. **Open Windows Explorer or My Computer.**

   Windows Explorer and My Computer are utility programs for managing folders and files.

3. **Go to the DB folder at this location on your computer: C:\Programs Files\Icq\DB.**

   The DB folder holds your Contact List, or, if you've registered under more than one name, your Contact Lists.

Can't find the DB folder? That's because you upgraded from an earlier version of ICQ. If you're an upgrader, look for the NewDB folder and copy it on the floppy disk.

4. **Copy the DB folder (or NewDB folder) to the floppy disk.**

Put the floppy disk in a safe place where you can find it if you need to restore the Contact List.

And suppose something evil happens to your computer and you lose your Contact List? Follow these steps to transfer the backup copy you made to your computer and thereby restore your Contact List to its original condition:

1. **Shut down ICQ, if the program is running.**

2. **Insert the floppy disk with the backup copy of your Contact List in the A drive of your computer.**

3. **Open Windows Explorer or My Computer.**

4. **Copy the DB folder (or NewDB folder) on the floppy disk into this folder on your computer: C:\Programs Files\Icq.**

When you open ICQ, the names appear again on your Contact List.

Backing Up and Restoring Other Items

As you know if you have spent any time with ICQ, you can receive files and Web Page addresses from other people. You can also chat with others. Files and chats are stored on your computer (chats are stored as long as you tell ICQ to store them when you're done chatting, as Chapter 4 explains).

To keep backup copies of files and chats, copy them from your computer to a floppy disk, zip disk, or other place where files can be stored. Table B.1 lists where on your computer files, picture files bookmarks, and chats are kept. Copy the contents of the folders in Table B.1 to a floppy disk or zip disk if you want to back up this stuff.

Table B.1	Where Bookmarks, Chats, Files, and Picture Files Are Stored
Item	*Stored In*
Bookmarks	C:\Program Files\ICQ\Bookmarks
Chats	C:\Program Files\ICQ\Chats

Item	Stored In
Files	C:\ProgramFiles\ICQ\Received Files *or* C:\ProgramFiles\ICQ\Received Files*Contact Name*
Pictures	C:\Program Files\ICQ\Pictures

Appendix C

Chat Room Acronyms and Smileys

∙ ∙

*N*ot everyone can type quickly. Not everyone is a good typist. For those reasons, a new idiom has developed in chat rooms. Instead of typing out words and phrases, you can rely on acronyms. And to describe your emotional state, you can enter a smiley.

This appendix explains various chat room acronyms and smileys. Next time you feel like a stranger in a chat room because others are entering acronyms and weird punctuation marks that look like chicken scratches, come to this appendix. Here, you can look up those strange acronyms and odd punctuation marks to find out what they mean.

By the way, the ICQ Chat window offers a special command for entering the LOL (laugh out loud) acronym and the smiley face: Choose Other⇨LOL (or press Ctrl+J). Doing so enters the acronym *LOL* followed by a smiley face: LOL:-).

A Minidictionary of Chat Room Acronyms

Thankfully, not all the acronyms listed here are found in every chat room. A chat room is like a tribe in that each has its own language and culture. In some chat rooms, hardly an acronym is seen or heard, but in other chat rooms, the acronyms fly so fast you have to D&C. TTT! IAC, you can always ask the people with whom you are chatting to explain an acronym, and no one will tell you to MYOB. SBT, chatters like explaining acronyms, we have noticed. OC, the more bizarre the subject of the chat, the more likely you are to encounter acronyms. Having trouble understanding an acronym? NP. Look it up in the definitions that follow. EOD.

Acronym	What It Means
AFAIK	As far as I know
AFK	Away from the keyboard
AISI	As I see it

(continued)

Acronym	What It Means
BAK	Back at the keyboard
BBFN	Bye bye for now
BBN	Bye bye now
BBL	Be back later
BFN	Bye for now
BBS	Be back soon
BEG	Big evil grin
BFFL	Best friends for life
BOC	But of course
BRB	Be right back
BTW	By the way
BWK	Big wet kiss
BWL	Bursting with laughter
CMH	Cross my heart
CSS	Can't stop smiling
CUL8R	See you later
CYA	See ya
D&C	Duck and cover
DLN	Don't leave now
DOS	Dozing off soon
E2EG	Ear to ear grin
EOD	End of discussion
F2F	Face to face
FWIW	For what it's worth
GGN	Gotta go now
GIWIST	Gee, I wish I'd said that
GMTA	Great minds think alike
GR8	Great
GRUIT	Get real, you impudent thing!

Acronym	What It Means
GTG	Got to go
H&K	Hug and kiss
HHOJ	Ha ha only joking
HTH	Hope this helps
IAC	In any case
IANAL	I am not a lawyer
IBM	Inadequate, but marketable
IC	I see
IDBI	I don't believe it
IDC	I don't care
IDTS	I don't think so
ILY	I love you
IMHO	In my humble opinion
IMI	I mean it
INPO	In no particular order
IOW	In other words
IYD	In your dreams
JAM	Just a minute
JJ	Just joking
KISS	Keep it simple, stupid
KWIM	Know what I mean?
L8R	Later
LOL	Laugh out loud
LSHMBH	Laughing so hard my belly hurts
LTNS	Long time no see
MORF	Male or female?
MTFBWY...A	May the force be with you...always
MYOB	Mind your own business

(continued)

Acronym	What It Means
NBD	No big deal
NM	Never mind
NP	No problem
NRN	No reply necessary
NTL	Nevertheless
NTTFLS	Not till the fat lady sings
OATUS	On a totally unrelated subject
OC	Of course
OIC	Oh, I see
OMG	Oh, my god!
OTOH	On the other hand
OWTTE	Or words to that effect
PTMM	Please tell me more
ROFL	Rolling on the floor laughing
RSN	Real soon now
S&N	Smile and nod
SBT	Strange but true
SOP	Standard operating procedure
Sup?	What's up (sometimes written as "wassup?")
SYS	See you soon
TANSTAAFL	There ain't no such thing as a free lunch
TCB	Taking care of business
TCS	Take care, sweetheart
TIA	Thanks in advance
TOY	Thinking of you
TTBOMK	To the best of my knowledge
TTFN	Ta ta for now
TTT	That's the truth!
TTYL	Talk to you later

Acronym	What It Means
TY	Thank you
WAB	What a bummer
WAUF	Where are you from?
WB	Welcome back
WHAK	With hugs and kisses
WTG	Way to go
WTTC	Welcome to the club
YHASP	You have a serious problem

The Complete Smiley Lookup Reference

A *smiley*, also known as an *emoticon*, is a bundle of punctuation marks or letters that form a little picture. Smileys are meant to mimic the facial expression that accompany real conversations. To get a better idea what a smiley is, tilt your head to the left and stare at it.

Most of the smileys in the list that follows are there strictly for your entertainment. These days, only two smileys appear with any regularity in chat rooms: the smile, :-), and the frown, :-(. By the way, Chapter 4 explains how you can enter actions and "emotes" in a chat by choosing commands from the Action menu in the Chat window.

Smiley	What It Means
:-)	I just made a joke
:-(	What you said makes me feel sad
;-)	That last remark is accompanied by a wink
;->	That last remark is accompanied by a devilish wink
:-I	I'm completely indifferent
:-/	I'm utterly baffled
:-<	I'm really, really disheartened by what you said
:-C	I'm, like, totally bummed out
:c	I'm pouting

(continued)

Smiley	What It Means
:-7	I just made a wry comment
:'(	I'm in tears
:'-)	I'm so happy I could just cry
:-D	I'm laughing loudly
l=)	I'm tired, but I'm happy
:-#	My lips are sealed, and your secret is safe
:-&	I'm tongue-tied and can't reply
:-J	That last comment was made tongue-in-cheek
%-)	I'm bleary-eyed from staring at the computer screen too long
8-)	I wear glasses
B-)	I'm cool with my sunglasses on
#-(	I'm hungover
:-~)	I'm suffering from a cold
:-P	See me stick out my tongue
:-)~	I'm drooling
:-0	I'm screaming
:-@	I'm yelling
II	I'm fast asleep
:-!	I'm whispering
:-Q	I smoke (now I'm exhaling)
:-?	I smoke a pipe
:-})	I have a moustache
=l:-)	I'm wearing my top hat
*<:-)	I'm Santa Claus
$:-(	Bad hair day
:o)	Big nose
5:-)	Elvis Presley
7:^]	Ronald Reagan
&;^}	Bill Clinton

Smiley	*What It Means*
CI:-=	Charlie Chaplin
d:-)	Baseball player
:-[	Vampire
<:-I	Dunce
0-)	Cyclops
K:-)	Propeller head
:8)	Miss Piggy
@@@@@:-)	Marge Simpson
3:-o	Cow
><(((*>	Fish

Appendix D

Glossary of ICQ Terms

application bar: *See* ICQ window.

Address Book: A folder in the Message Archive where information about ICQ members is kept. Information about members is taken from the White Pages. *See also* Message Archive and White Pages.

Advanced mode: One of two ICQ modes, the other being Simple mode. More options are available to users in Advanced mode, as the ICQ window offers more buttons for opening menus and choosing commands. To switch to Advanced mode, click the To Advanced Mode button in the ICQ window. *See also* Simple mode.

alerts: ICQ offers many ways of being alerted when someone on your Contact List is online and connected to ICQ. Click a Contact List name and choose More (Rename, Delete)⇨Alert/Accept Modes to choose how you want to be alerted in the Alert/Accept dialog box.

availability status: *See* status.

chat master: A person who created and maintains a chat room on the ICQ network.

chat room: A page on the Internet that people can go to and type messages to one another. Any ICQ member can create a chat room.

Communication Center: *See* Personal Communication Center.

connection status: *See* status.

Contact List: The list of friends you have made in ICQ. The Contact List appears on the ICQ window.

discussion: On the Message Board, a handful of messages that concern the same topic.

E-mail Express: Refers to e-mail you send to addresses outside the ICQ net-work and messages that are sent to you from outside ICQ. E-mail Express is faster than the Pony Express, but not nearly as romantic.

emote: A small image, meant to portray your emotional state, that you can send to someone as part of a chat. To send an emote, click the Send Emote button in the Chat window and choose an emote in the Gesture Event dialog box.

event: The catchall word that describes messages, chat invitations, and other stuff that ICQ members can send back and forth.

Global Directory: The means for entering information about yourself in the White Pages. Information you enter in the Global Directory dialog box is recorded in the White Pages. *See also* White Pages.

greeting card: Colorful messages that you can send to other ICQ members. People who receive greeting cards are asked to "Click here to see the card in your Web browser" button. Click the button and you go to a Web page where the card is displayed.

groups: The names of people on the Contact List can be arranged under group names on the Groups tab of the ICQ window. To begin with, ICQ offers four groups — General, Family, Friends, and Co-Workers — but you can create your own.

homepage: Similar to a Web page, an HTML document that others can visit while you are online and connected to ICQ. The homepage is kept on your computer. Using their Web browsers, others can go to your homepage the same way that they can go to Web pages on the Internet.

Homepage Factory: A special program designed to help you create a homepage. Click the Services button and choose My ICQ Page➪Make My ICQ Homepage to start the Homepage Factory program.

ICQ iT!: The name of the ICQ search engine for finding information on the Internet. Type a keyword in the Enter Search Keyword box in the ICQ window and click the GO button to search the Internet with ICQ iT!.

ICQ window: The ICQ "screen" where the Contact List and buttons appear. You can drag the ICQ window wherever you want, or position it on the top, bottom, right side, or left side of the screen. Sometimes called the *application bar*.

Ignore List: The list of ICQ members from whom you refuse to receive communications.

interest group: A group of people who share an interest in a similar topic. ICQ members can find and join interest groups in the ICQ network.

list master: The person who created and maintains a user list.

Message Archive: The place in ICQ where messages, chats, and other communication items are stored. The Message Archive includes an Address Book and folders for storing reminder notes.

Message Board: A place in ICQ for reading and posting messages about various subjects. Click the System Menu button and choose Message Boards on the pop-up menu to reach the Message Board.

NetDetect Agent: A mechanism whereby the ICQ program starts whenever you connect to the Internet. When the NetDetect Agent is turned on, the NetDetect Agent icon appears in the lower-right corner of the screen.

online status indicator: If the indicator is enabled, the online status indicator tells people who visit your Personal Communication Center whether.you are online and connected to the ICQ network. As a privacy measure, you can disable the online status indicator.

Pager address: The Web address of an ICQ member's Personal Communication Center. *See* Personal Communication Center.

PeopleSpace Directory: The directory of general areas, categories, and sub-categories in which user lists, message boards, chat rooms, and interest groups are organized. When you search for a user list, message board, or whatnot, you have to start with the 24 general areas of the PeopleSpace Directory.

PeopleSpace Navigator: A means of searching by topic in the PeopleSpace Directory.

Personal Communication Center: A page on the Web where people can go to contact ICQ members. Each ICQ member has a Personal Communication Center page at this address: `http://wwp.icq.com/ICQ#`. Non-ICQ members can visit Personal Communication Center pages.

plugin: An application such as the Greeting Card application that works in cahoots with ICQ to send messages or make chatting possible.

random chat: Finding someone at random to chat with. Click the Find Random Chat Partner button in the ICQ window to engage in random chatter.

Simple mode: The mode designed for new ICQ members that offers fewer options than Advanced mode. In Simple mode, the ICQ window presents fewer buttons. Simple is the default mode. To switch from Simple to Advanced mode, click the To Advanced Mode button in the ICQ window.

status: Refers to whether you are available for chatting and, just as importantly, whether others know that you are online. To change your status, click the bottommost button on the ICQ window and chose an option from the Status pop-up menu.

Status button: The button in the lower-right corner of the ICQ window. Click the button to see the Status menu and declare your online status to others on the ICQ network.

status indicator: An indicator on the Personal Web Communication Center and other places that tells others whether you are online and connected to ICQ.

Status menu: The menu that you access by clicking the Status button in the lower-right corner of the ICQ window. Choose your online status from the Status menu.

tray area: The area on the Windows taskbar to the left of the clock in the lower-right corner of the screen. You can tell what your online status is by glancing at the flower in the tray area. Icons appear in the tray when some-one has sent you an item.

user list: A list of ICQ members who are interested in the same topic. The lists are not maintained by ICQ, but by members on their Web pages. Members can submit the names of their user lists to ICQ, and ICQ puts the names in the User Created Lists Directory. Also called a *user created list.*

voice message: A recorded message or sound file sent through the ICQ network.

White Pages: Members volunteer information about themselves when they register with ICQ. The information is kept in the White Pages. Any ICQ member can go to the White Pages and learn about another member. You can update your profile in the White Pages by clicking the Services button and choosing ICQ White Pages⇨Publicize in White Pages.

WWPager (World-Wide Pager): A form located in the Personal Communication Center for sending e-mail to an ICQ member. Anyone, signed up with ICQ or not, can go to your Personal Communication Center and write you an e-mail message by filling out the WWPager form. ***See also*** Personal Communication Center.

Index

• *G* •

• *T* •

Notes

Notes

 YOUR ONLINE RESOURCE

WWW.DUMMIES.COM

Discover Dummies Online!

The Dummies Web Site is your fun and friendly online resource for the latest information about ...*For Dummies*® books and your favorite topics. The Web site is the place to communicate with us, exchange ideas with other ...*For Dummies* readers, chat with authors, and have fun!

Ten Fun and Useful Things You Can Do at www.dummies.com

1. Win free ...*For Dummies* books and more!
2. Register your book and be entered in a prize drawing.
3. Meet your favorite authors through the IDG Books Author Chat Series.
4. Exchange helpful information with other ...*For Dummies* readers.
5. Discover other great ...*For Dummies* books you must have!
6. Purchase Dummieswear™ exclusively from our Web site.
7. Buy ...*For Dummies* books online.
8. Talk to us. Make comments, ask questions, get answers!
9. Download free software.
10. Find additional useful resources from authors.

Link directly to these ten fun and useful things at
http://www.dummies.com/10useful

For other technology titles from IDG Books Worldwide, go to
www.idgbooks.com

Not on the Web yet? It's easy to get started with *Dummies 101*®: *The Internet For Windows*®*98* or *The Internet For Dummies*®, 6th Edition, at local retailers everywhere.

IDG BOOKS WORLDWIDE

Find other ...*For Dummies* books on these topics:
Business • Career • Databases • Food & Beverage • Games • Gardening • Graphics • Hardware
Health & Fitness • Internet and the World Wide Web • Networking • Office Suites
Operating Systems • Personal Finance • Pets • Programming • Recreation • Sports
Spreadsheets • Teacher Resources • Test Prep • Word Processing

IDG BOOKS WORLDWIDE BOOK REGISTRATION

We want to hear from you!

Visit **http://my2cents.dummies.com** to register this book and tell us how you liked it!

- ✔ Get entered in our monthly prize giveaway.

- ✔ Give us feedback about this book — tell us what you like best, what you like least, or maybe what you'd like to ask the author and us to change!

- ✔ Let us know any other *...For Dummies*® topics that interest you.

Your feedback helps us determine what books to publish, tells us what coverage to add as we revise our books, and lets us know whether we're meeting your needs as a *...For Dummies* reader. You're our most valuable resource, and what you have to say is important to us!

Not on the Web yet? It's easy to get started with *Dummies 101*®*: The Internet For Windows*® *98* or *The Internet For Dummies*®, 6th Edition, at local retailers everywhere.

Or let us know what you think by sending us a letter at the following address:

...For Dummies Book Registration
Dummies Press
7260 Shadeland Station, Suite 100
Indianapolis, IN 46256-3945
Fax 317-596-5498

**BESTSELLING
BOOK SERIES
FROM IDG**